Google Analytics

Google Analytics

Justin Cutroni

O'REILLY®

Beijing · Cambridge · Farnham · Köln · Sebastopol · Tokyo

Google Analytics
by Justin Cutroni

Published by O'Reilly Media, Inc., 1005 Gravenstein Highway North, Sebastopol, CA 95472.

O'Reilly books may be purchased for educational, business, or sales promotional use. Online editions are also available for most titles (*http://my.safaribooksonline.com*). For more information, contact our corporate/institutional sales department: (800) 998-9938 or *corporate@oreilly.com*.

Editor: Simon St.Laurent
Production Editor: Kristen Borg
Copyeditor: Amy Thomson
Proofreader: Kiel Van Horn

Indexer: Newgen North America, Inc.
Cover Designer: Karen Montgomery
Interior Designer: David Futato
Illustrator: Robert Romano

Printing History:

August 2010:   First Edition.

ISBN: 978-0-596-15800-2

[LSI]   [2011-03-25]

1300466335

Table of Contents

Preface

When Google launched Google Analytics in 2005, it revolutionized web analytics. Heck, it flat out turned the entire industry on its collective head. No longer was web analytics an expensive endeavor that required a substantial investment in software. Measurement tools became irrelevant from a cost perspective, and the focus started to shift to people.

In May 2007, Google gave the analytics industry another shot in the arm when it released version 2 of Analytics. The update included a progressive new interface that simplified the data presentation in hopes that more people, like marketers and PR professionals, would use the data to make business decisions.

By creating a free analytics tool that is easy to understand, Google has helped everyone become a web analyst. Website designers, webmasters, IT teams, C-level executives, and marketers are all using Google Analytics to track and measure website performance and online marketing initiatives.

Let's face it, Google Analytics is sexy as hell right now! Everyone wants a piece of it.

Who This Book Is For

This book is for anyone thinking about using Google Analytics or actively using Google Analytics (GA). You may be an executive who's trying to determine if Google Analytics will work for your organization. You may be a marketing team member trying to figure out how to track different types of marketing initiatives (both online and offline). You may be an IT team member tasked with implementing GA.

I believe that all of you will find something useful in this book. Throughout the book, I try to explain how Google Analytics works so you can understand the impact of various configuration choices. Remember, Google Analytics analyzes business data, which means each business will configure it differently. You need to understand what's important for your business and configure Google Analytics accordingly.

There is no technical prerequisite for reading this book. If you have a basic understanding of the Internet, if you know what a web server is, and if you know what HTML is, you'll understand the subject matter in this book. You may not understand some of the more advanced code samples, but I will make sure you understand the concepts and ideas behind the code.

Who This Book Is Not For

People who are very new to web analytics may have some problems with this book. There is an assumption that you have some basic web analytics knowledge. For example, you should know what a pageview, visit, and visitor are. If you don't have a basic understanding of web analytics, you may want to use this book as a companion to a more thorough web analytics text.

What You'll Learn

My goal in writing this book is to help people understand what Google Analytics can do and show you how to actually do it.

I'll start by talking about your business, not about Google Analytics. Before we even touch on Google Analytics, it's imperative to identify what you want to track on your website. If you don't know what you want to track, you won't know how to configure Google Analytics to track it.

Next I'll describe how Google Analytics actually works. I'll cover how data is collected, processed, and turned into reports. I'll also include some information about the different data-collection mechanisms, like mobile data collection and application (app) tracking.

Understanding how the system works will provide the foundation for our configuration discussion. We'll talk about all of the various settings you can use to control data access, manipulate data, and track goals on a website.

I'll also spend time discussing how to track marketing campaigns. In my opinion, this is one of the most overlooked features and, when done incorrectly, can completely destroy your data. However, when it's done correctly it can lead to a deeper understanding of your marketing initiative and analysis nirvana.

After marketing campaigns, we'll move into advanced topics, like configuring websites that span multiple domains, collecting e-commerce data, event tracking, and custom variables. All of these features allow Google Analytics to adapt and fit the data and analysis needs of your organization. These may not be features you're currently using, but they'll showcase the flexibility of what Google Analytics can do.

By the end of this tour, you should be a Google Analytics guru! It's your job to take your understanding of what Google Analytics can do for your business and implement it on your website.

Other Learning Options

There are lots of different ways to learn about web analytics and Google Analytics. Some people want to learn web analytics in detail before jumping into Google Analytics. That's a perfectly good tactic and if you want to start that way you should explore some of the following publications:

- *Web Analytics, An Hour a Day* by Avinash Kaushik (Sybex)
- *Web Analytics 2.0: The Art of Online Accountability and Science of Customer Centricity* by Avinash Kaushik (Wiley)
- *Complete Web Monitoring* by Alistair Croll and Sean Power (O'Reilly)

You'll definitely want to make sure that whatever books or online documentation you use covers the most recent version of Google Analytics. Google Analytics' perpetual evolution has unfortunately made it dangerous to use a lot of formerly great (but now dated) material—some of it works, some of it doesn't.

If You Like (or Don't Like) This Book

If you like (or don't like) this book, by all means, please let people know. Amazon reviews are one popular way to share your happiness (or lack thereof), or you can leave reviews at the site for the book:

> *http://oreilly.com/catalog/9780596158002*

There's also a link to errata there. This gives readers a way to let us know about typos, errors, and other problems with the book. The errata will be visible on the page immediately, and we'll confirm it after checking it out. O'Reilly can also fix errata in future printings of the book and on Safari, making for a better reader experience pretty quickly.

We hope to keep this book updated for future versions of Google Analytics, and will also incorporate suggestions and complaints into future editions.

Conventions Used in This Book

The following font conventions are used in this book:

Italic
> Indicates pathnames, filenames, and program names; Internet addresses, such as domain names and URLs; and new items where they are defined

Constant width

> Indicates command lines and options that should be typed verbatim; names and keywords in programs, including method names, variable names, and class names; and HTML element tags

Constant width bold

> Indicates emphasis in program code lines

Constant width italic

> Indicates text that should be replaced with user-supplied values

 This icon signifies a tip, suggestion, or general note.

 This icon indicates a warning or caution.

Using Code Examples

This book is here to help you get your job done. In general, you may use the code in this book in your programs and documentation. You do not need to contact us for permission unless you're reproducing a significant portion of the code. For example, writing a program that uses several chunks of code from this book does not require permission. Selling or distributing a CD-ROM of examples from O'Reilly books *does* require permission. Answering a question by citing this book and quoting example code does not require permission. Incorporating a significant amount of example code from this book into your product's documentation *does* require permission.

We appreciate, but do not require, attribution. An attribution usually includes the title, author, publisher, and ISBN. For example: "*Google Analytics* by Justin Cutroni. Copyright 2010 O'Reilly Media, Inc., 978-0-596-15800-2."

If you feel your use of code examples falls outside fair use or the permission given above, feel free to contact us at *permissions@oreilly.com*.

How to Contact Us

We have tested and verified the information in this book to the best of our ability, but you may find that features have changed (or even that we have made a few mistakes!) Please let us know about any errors you find, as well as your suggestions for future editions, by writing to:

O'Reilly Media, Inc.
1005 Gravenstein Highway North
Sebastopol, CA 95472
800-998-9938 (in the U.S. or Canada)
707-829-0515 (international/local)
707-829-0104 (fax)

We have a web page for this book, where we list errata, examples, and any additional information. You can access this page at:

> *http://oreilly.com/catalog/9780596158002*

To comment or ask technical questions about this book, send email to:

> *bookquestions@oreilly.com*

For more information about our books, conferences, Resource Centers, and the O'Reilly Network, see our web site at:

> *http://www.oreilly.com*

Safari® Books Online

Safari Safari Books Online is an on-demand digital library that lets you easily search over 7,500 technology and creative reference books and videos to find the answers you need quickly.

With a subscription, you can read any page and watch any video from our library online. Read books on your cell phone and mobile devices. Access new titles before they are available for print, and get exclusive access to manuscripts in development and post feedback for the authors. Copy and paste code samples, organize your favorites, download chapters, bookmark key sections, create notes, print out pages, and benefit from tons of other time-saving features.

O'Reilly Media has uploaded this book to the Safari Books Online service. To have full digital access to this book and others on similar topics from O'Reilly and other publishers, sign up for free at *http://my.safaribooksonline.com*.

Acknowledgments

First and foremost, this book is dedicated to the three people who sacrificed the most: Heidi, Benton, and Avery. Thanks for giving Daddy the time to explore this amazing opportunity. And Heidi, thanks for keeping life running (as smoothly as possible) during the nights and weekends that I was holed up writing.

A huge thanks to the entire Google Analytics team: Avinash, Brett, Scott, Phil, Amy, Alex, Nick, Jeff, and the countless others, you've become fantastic friends over the last five years. I really appreciate the time you spend helping me learn more about GA so I can spread the word.

Another big thanks to the team at O'Reilly. Simon, Amy, and the entire crew who helped fine-tune my babble into a new version of this book. Your patience borders on insanity! Thanks for sticking by me and helping me get this out the door.

CHAPTER 1

Introducing Web Analytics

This book is about Google Analytics, and at some level that means it is also about web analytics. It's important to note that Google Analytics is not the same as web analytics. Web analytics is a business process used to continuously improve your online business. Google Analytics is a tool to quantitatively measure what happens on your website. Just because you have Google Analytics does not mean you are doing web analytics.

Before we dive into Google Analytics, I believe it's important to establish how Google Analytics should fit into your overall analytics strategy.

Defining Web Analytics

Rather than creating another definition of web analytics (there are a lot of them out there), I prefer to reference Avinash Kaushik's concise yet thorough definition. In his book *Web Analytics: An Hour a Day* (Wiley), Kaushik defines web analytics as:

> The analysis of qualitative and quantitative data from your website and the competition, to drive a continual improvement of the online experience that your customers, and potential customers have, which translates into your desired outcomes (online and offline).

This definition encapsulates three main tasks every business must tackle when doing web analytics:

- Measuring quantitative and qualitative data
- Continuously improving your website
- Aligning your measurement strategy with your business strategy

Let's look at each part of the definition and break it down into more detail.

Quantitative and Qualitative Data

Web analytics is not possible without data. But many organizations fail to realize that they need many different types of data to understand the performance of their website. Tools like Google Analytics, Omniture, WebTrends, and Yahoo! Web Analytics generate quantitative, or clickstream, data. This data identifies where website traffic comes from and what it does on the site. It more or less tells what happened on a website.

While clickstream data is critical, you must collect more than quantitative data—you must also collect qualitative data. While quantitative data describes what happens on your website, qualitative describes *why* it happens. Qualitative data comes from different sources, like user interviews and usability tests. But the easiest way to get qualitative data is through surveys. Asking website visitors simple questions like the ones below can lead to a greater understanding of what visitors want and whether you're making it easy for them:

> Why did you come here today?
> Were you able to do what you wanted to do?
> If not, why?

There are a number of free qualitative data tools, like 4Q and Kampyle, that are easy to implement and provide valuable feedback from your website visitors. In many cases, it's easier to implement these tools than a clickstream data tool like Google Analytics. If you're not collecting qualitative data, start now!

It's not enough, however, to analyze clickstream data from your own website. You must also look at data from your competitors' websites. We live in an amazing age in which competitive data is freely available to everyone.

Competitive data provides valuable context for your own data. It describes your performance as compared to that of your competitors. Compete.com and Google Trends can help you identify simple things like whether your competitors are getting more traffic than you.

The Continuous Improvement Process

The second part of Kaushik's web analytics definition is, "to drive a continual improvement of the online experience that your customers, and potential customers have."

All of the data and analysis must drive a continuous improvement process. This is the most critical part of web analytics. You must take action on the data. That's the whole purpose of web analytics—to improve over time. Figure 1-1 shows a very basic representation of the web analytics process.

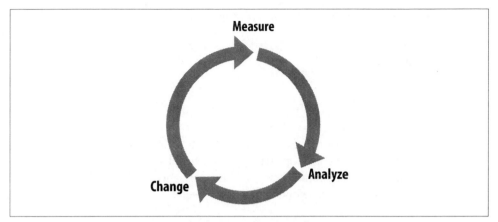

Figure 1-1. The web analytics process: measure, analyze, and change

Knowing how to change as a result of analysis is often difficult, though. Much of our data tells us that there is a problem, but it does not say how to fix it. So how does one go about fixing or optimizing a website based on data? You create different solutions to the problems and test them. Testing is the process of displaying the potential solution to website visitors, in real time, and measuring which one generates the best result. Many people are surprised to learn that testing a website is possible. There are a number of free tools, like Google's Website Optimizer, that provide this service.

Testing has always been part of marketing. Direct-mail marketers have been testing different offers and different ad variations for a long time. And those doing pay-per-click marketing have also been testing for many years, experimenting with different headlines and ad copy to optimize ad expenditures.

However, website testing has failed to gain popularity. I believe the reason testing has been adopted so slowly is because of the many misconceptions about testing. Most people think testing is too hard, too expensive, or takes too much time. But in reality, testing has been changing, just like web analytics. With free tools it's becoming easier and easier to start testing different parts of a website.

Measuring Outcomes

The final part of Kaushik's definition of web analytics is that it "translates into your desired outcomes (online and offline)."

The entire goal of the web analytics process is to increase our desired business outcomes. We are no longer obsessed with just measuring how much traffic our online business generates. We also want to measure how well it performs in business terms.

This means measuring metrics that relate directly to our overall business goals. Every website exists for a reason, and your measurement strategy must align with the business goals of the website.

For the most part, all websites exist for one of the four following reasons:

- To sell a product
- To generate a sales lead
- To generate ad revenue
- To provide support

Some websites do other things as well, but for the most part, this is why websites exist. This is where you should start measuring your website. How does it affect the bottom line of your business? Once you define why you have a website, it becomes much easier to identify the metrics you should focus on. You don't need a lot of metrics—just a handful (3-5) should help you understand if your business is succeeding or failing.

 If you're having trouble identifying key performance indicators (or KPIs) for your site, try *The Big Book of Key Performance Indicators* by Eric Peterson (*http://troni.me/dr08gA*).

What Google Analytics Contributes

Google Analytics provides a core set of tools that supports some of the primary tasks that web analysts perform.

First and foremost, Google Analytics tracks many standard website metrics, like visits, unique visitors, pageviews, bounce rate, and abandonment rate. But, more importantly, it can track business outcomes, called *goals*. Remember, we want to move beyond tracking basic traffic to our websites and begin understanding if our websites are adding to the bottom line of our business.

In addition to tracking goals, Google Analytics does a great job at tracking all different kinds of marketing initiatives. Many people believe that Google Analytics can only track AdWords, but it can track other types of paid searches, email marketing, display advertising, social media, and any other type of ad you can think of.

One of the key activities of any analyst is performing *segmentation*. Segmentation involves diving deeper into the data to understand how smaller buckets, or segments, of traffic perform and ultimately influence the overall performance of the website.

A simple example of segmentation is viewing website traffic based on the physical location of the visitors. Google Analytics does this using the Map Overlay report, shown in Figure 1-2.

This is a very basic segmentation. Each row of data shows all the values for a *dimension*. A dimension is an attribute of a website visitor or the visits that they create. Some common dimensions are country, campaign name, and browser version. There are many, many different types of dimensions, and you can view the complete list at *http://troni.me/9EKc62*.

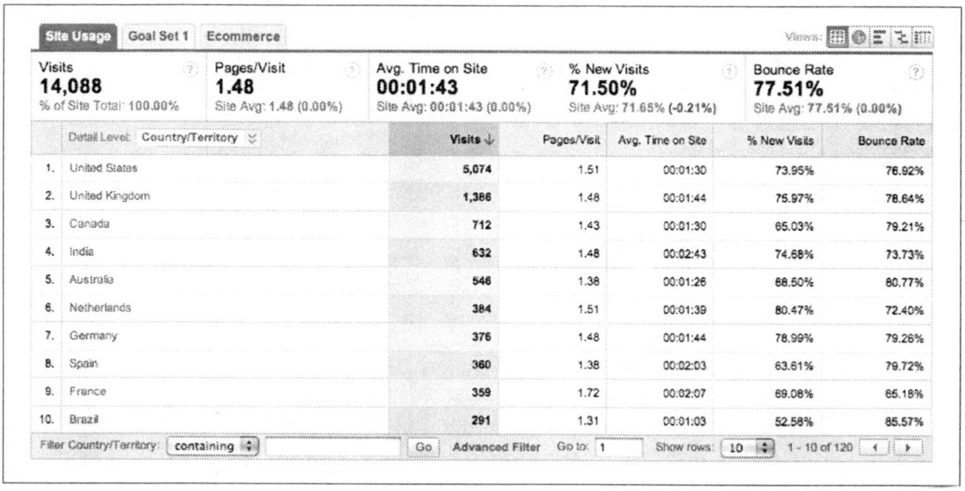

	Detail Level: Country/Territory	Visits ↓	Pages/Visit	Avg. Time on Site	% New Visits	Bounce Rate
1.	United States	5,074	1.51	00:01:30	73.95%	76.92%
2.	United Kingdom	1,386	1.48	00:01:44	75.97%	78.64%
3.	Canada	712	1.43	00:01:30	65.03%	79.21%
4.	India	632	1.48	00:02:43	74.68%	73.73%
5.	Australia	546	1.38	00:01:26	68.50%	80.77%
6.	Netherlands	384	1.51	00:01:39	80.47%	72.40%
7.	Germany	376	1.48	00:01:44	78.99%	79.26%
8.	Spain	360	1.38	00:02:03	63.61%	79.72%
9.	France	359	1.72	00:02:07	69.08%	65.18%
10.	Brazil	291	1.31	00:01:03	52.58%	85.57%

Figure 1-2. The Map Overlay report shows traffic from individual countries

In this case, the dimension is the country. The metrics for that dimension are shown in the columns of the report. Now notice the tabs at the top of the report. The Goal tab displays conversions for the same dimension of traffic. So, if you click the Goal Set 1 tab, Google Analytics will display conversions for each goal for each country.

This is the way all Google Analytics reports work. Every row of data is a different value of the dimension of traffic. For example, in the Traffic Sources report, each row in the table is a different source of traffic (organic search, marketing campaigns, etc.).

But the ability to segment data does not end there. Google Analytics also has a feature called Advanced Segmentation that can segment data on the fly based on attributes that you define. For example, you can build an advanced segment to view all traffic coming from Google AdWords that resulted in transactions greater than $1,000.00. You can do this using a simple drag-and-drop interface, shown in Figure 1-3.

This is a complicated segmentation that you can build and apply in real time! The result is the ability to view the segment we created above, along with other segments of website traffic. Figure 1-4 shows the High Value AdWords traffic along with the total traffic to the website.

This ability to drill down and focus on various segments of traffic is key to all analysis. We want to identify the segments of traffic that are performing well and determine how to promote those segments. We also want to identify the segments of traffic that suck and figure out how to fix them.

Advanced Segmentation is not the only tool that helps facilitate analysis. Google Analytics also contains a custom reporting tool that can greatly simplify your daily reporting and even help simplify common segmentations.

list view
Condition
Value
Matches exactly
google
or
Add "or" statement
and
delete
Greater than
1000
Add "and" statement
Drag and drop dimensions and metrics into the boxes to create a visit segment

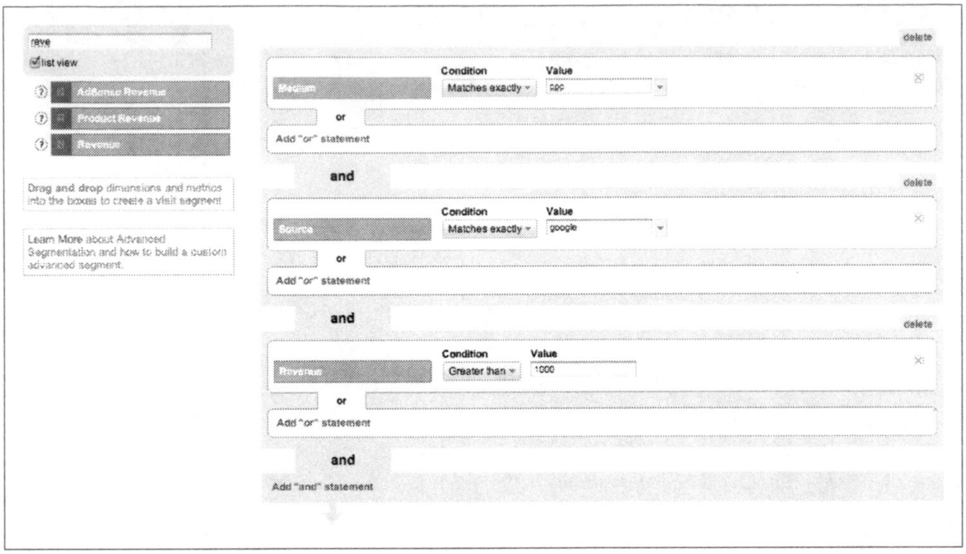

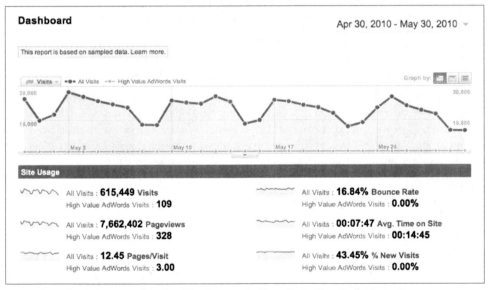

Figure 1-3. The interface to build Advanced Segments

Dashboard
Apr 30, 2010 - May 30, 2010
This report is based on sampled data. Learn more.
Visits
All Visits
High Value AdWords Visits
Graph by:
30,000
15,000
May 3
May 10
May 17
May 24
Site Usage
All Visits : 615,449 Visits
High Value AdWords Visits : 109
All Visits : 7,662,402 Pageviews
High Value AdWords Visits : 328
All Visits : 12.45 Pages/Visit
High Value AdWords Visits : 3.00
All Visits : 16.84% Bounce Rate
High Value AdWords Visits : 0.00%
All Visits : 00:07:47 Avg. Time on Site
High Value AdWords Visits : 00:14:45
All Visits : 43.45% % New Visits
High Value AdWords Visits : 0.00%

Figure 1-4. Viewing a segment of traffic along with all traffic in Google Analytics

The Custom Reporting interface is very similar to the Advanced Segmentation interface. You can drag and drop different pieces of information to create your own reports, as shown in Figure 1-5.

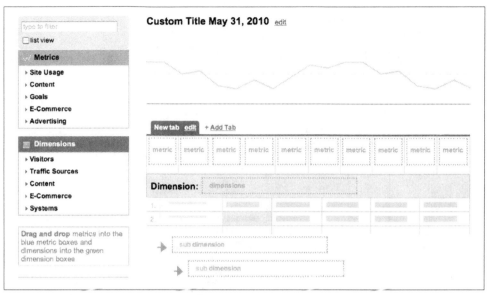

Figure 1-5. The Custom Reporting interface

The rows of data in a custom report represent different dimensions of data. The columns in a custom report are the different metrics in Google Analytics: things like visits, pageviews, conversions, revenue, etc.

For example, to create a report that shows the conversion rate for different marketing campaigns, drag the Campaign dimension to the Dimension section of the screen and drag the Conversion Rate metric to a metric column.

Custom reports also provide the ability to drill down into each dimension and view subdimensions. Notice the subdimension sections of the interface in Figure 1-5. You can add more dimensions under your primary dimension. Using subdimensions, it's easy, for example, to view the different types of visitors (new or returning) in your marketing campaigns and determine what time of day each visitor type converts—just keep dragging dimensions to the interface (Figure 1-6).

These are just a few of the features that are standard in Google Analytics. They don't take any extra configuration. Every user, from day one, can access these features and use them to analyze their own data. I encourage you to experiment with these features: you'll be amazed at how much time they can save you.

How Google Analytics Fits in the Analytics Ecosystem

Obviously, Google Analytics is one of the most popular clickstream data tools that has ever been created. In the five years since its launch, it has been adopted by millions of businesses, both large and small.

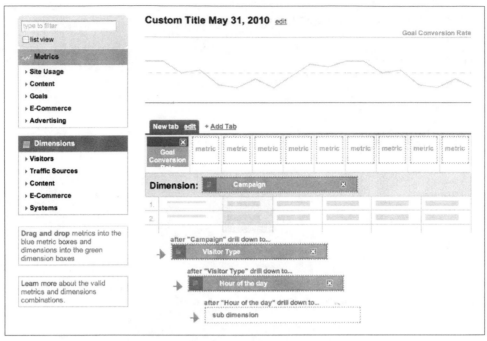

Figure 1-6. A custom report with many subdimensions

Small and mid-sized businesses have access to a world-class analytics tool that can help drive their continuous improvement process. Larger organizations that have traditionally spent six figures on a web analytics tool are migrating to Google Analytics because it provides 90% of all the reporting and analysis functionality that their organizations need. They can save tremendous amounts of money and reallocate those funds to skilled analysts who can help make the data actionable.

As we discuss Google Analytics throughout this book, though, remember that it's just a small piece of your web analytics strategy. It's a tool (and a very good one in my opinion) that provides clickstream data. Google Analytics will help you identify what is working and what is not working with your online business, but remember, the world of web analytics is much bigger than Google Analytics!

CHAPTER 2

Creating an Implementation Plan

Google Analytics is a business intelligence tool and, because every business has different data needs, your implementation may be very different from someone else's. Do not believe that you can simply slap some tags on the site and collect valid data. It is very rare that an implementation involves only page tagging. There are many configuration steps required to generate accurate, actionable data.

With that said, there are some standard things that everyone should do to get reliable data for analysis. Implementing Google Analytics does take some planning and foresight. The Google Analytics support documentation does contain a rough implementation guide that includes the various steps to get Google Analytics installed and running. I have modified that process as follows:

1. Gather and document business requirements.
2. Analyze and document website architecture.
3. Create a Google Analytics account and configure profiles.
4. Configure the Google Analytics tracking code and tag website pages.
5. Tag marketing campaigns.
6. Create additional user accounts and configure the following reporting features:
   - Report access
   - Automated email report delivery
   - Reporting customizations (Custom Reports, Advanced Segments)
7. Perform the following optional configuration steps:
   - Enable e-commerce transaction tracking
   - Implement event tracking
   - Implement custom variables

Gather Business Requirements

You probably noticed that step 1 has very little to do with Google Analytics. As I mentioned before, Google Analytics is just a tool that you can use to measure the performance of your business. How you define and measure success for your business will be different than for other organizations. Take the time at the start of this process to understand your organization's data needs.

Sit down with the different stakeholders and interview them. Ask them what data they need to make better decisions and document the answers. The information you collect should be the driving force for your implementation. What you measure needs to align with your business objectives. Remember, you need to collect and define the KPIs for your organization.

It's also important to ask if there are any existing reports distributed internally. If so, you can use these as a template for your Google Analytics reports.

Analyze and Document Website Architecture

Once you have an understanding of what's important to the business, it's time to analyze your website. During this step, you should identify any aspect of the website architecture that may interfere with measuring your business objectives defined in the previous step. During this step you should ask questions like the following:

- Does the website span multiple domains?
- Does the website have multiple subdomains?
- Is the website dynamic (does it have query-string parameters)?
- Does the website use Frames or iFrames?
- Does the website use any redirect?
- Does the website contain any Ajax, Flash, or other elements you want to track?

All of the items listed here can cause issues with Google Analytics. While they complicate the implementation process, they will not keep you from using Google Analytics, but it's critical to identify them before starting the implementation.

The amount of work it takes to complete this step depends on how large your organization is and how many websites you have. Regardless of how big your company is, take the time to answer these questions through experimentation and interviews. Browse your own website or websites to determine if it uses any of the above configurations. Meet with IT people and ask them to explain as much as they can about how the website works.

And document everything you learn. Having written documentation about the website architecture will make the entire process easier.

Create an Account and Configure Your Profile

Once you've got all of your business requirements, it's time to start working in Google Analytics. Begin by creating an account. If you've already got a Google Analytics account, there is no need to create another one. Once you have an account, configure your profile settings, such as Site Search, Filters, and Goals.

Configure the Tracking Code and Tag Pages

We'll discuss how to configure the tracking code later, but, briefly, based on your website architecture, you may need to alter the tracking code to compensate for things like subdomains or multiple domains. Luckily, there is a code configuration tool that makes changing the JavaScript rather simple.

Once you have created and configured the profiles and the tracking code, it's time to tag the pages. Because most sites use some type of template system, like WordPress, Drupal, or some custom content management system, this makes tagging pages fairly easy. In most cases, you can place the page tag in your footer template, and in about three hours you should start to see data. If your website does not use a templating system, you will need to manually add the tag at the bottom of all the pages on your site.

Tag Marketing Campaigns

Tagging marketing campaigns is one of the most critical parts of configuring Google Analytics. This is the process of identifying your different marketing activities (like paid search, display advertising, and email marketing) to Google Analytics. You do this using a process called *link tagging*. If you do not tag your marketing campaigns, it will be impossible to measure the success of your online marketing initiatives. I will thoroughly describe how to tag your marketing campaigns in Chapter 9.

Create Additional User Accounts and Configure Reporting Features

Once analytics is up and running and you've started to collect data, it's time to configure various features that provide access to data. This is the time to create user accounts so coworkers and others can access analytics.

This is also the time to configure some of the reporting tools that Google Analytics provides. Features like automated report email messages and custom reports can greatly reduce the time it takes to generate any standard reports that an organization may need.

Perform Optional Configuration Steps

There are many Google Analytics features that generate additional data. E-commerce tracking, custom variables, and event tracking are optional features that all collect other types of data. While it is not necessary to implement these features, they often provide additional information that can provide you with more insight.

For example, custom variables can collect demographic information about your site visitors, event tracking can measure how people interact with different types of content, and e-commerce tracking can collect revenue and transactional data in real time.

Some organizations may make these features a high priority based on the metrics they provide. If you're one of them, these implementation steps may not be optional for you. Schedule the implementation of these features based on your priority and implementation resources.

To some extent, the implementation process is iterative. Don't expect to get it right the first time. Once you have installed the tracking code and you have some data in the reports, check the data. Does it make sense? Should you modify the data to manipulate how it looks? It may be that you need to add an additional filter or change a profile setting to improve the quality. Can you reconcile the data with a different tool? Granted, the data is unlikely to be exactly the same between tools, but is it fairly consistent? Do you see the same trends in the data?

The key to a successful implementation is to take a structured approach, take your time, and document everything you do.

CHAPTER 3

Under the Covers: How Google Analytics Works

Understanding the Google Analytics architecture—how it collects data, processes data, and creates reports—is the key to understanding many of the advanced topics that we will discuss later in this book. Google Analytics can collect data from a number of different platforms using different tracking technologies, which makes things complicated.

Google Analytics is no longer a simple "hit collector" for websites, but rather an information aggregation system that collects data from standard websites, mobile websites, Adobe Air applications, and iPhone and Android apps. Google has progressively added more data collection methods as technology has driven new and different ways of distributing content to people.

In this book, we will primarily focus on tracking websites, but I will briefly discuss the other tracking methods as well. Let's start with the simplest configuration: tracking a website.

Data Collection and Processing

Figure 3-1 shows how Google Analytics collects, processes, and displays data.

Google Analytics uses a common data collection technique called *page tags*. A page tag is a small piece of JavaScript that you must place on all the website pages you want to track. We affectionately call this code the Google Analytics Tracking Code, or GATC for short. If you do not place the code on a page, Google Analytics will not track that page.

The data collection process begins when a visitor requests a page from the web server. The server responds by sending the requested page back to the visitor's browser (step 1 in Figure 3-1). As the browser processes the data, it contacts other servers that may host parts of the requested page, like images, videos, or script files. This is the case with the GATC.

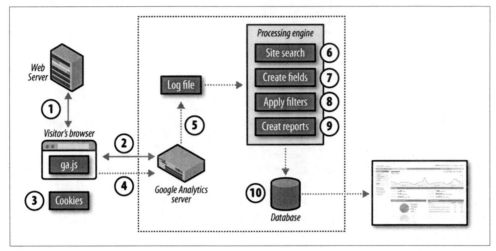

Figure 3-1. Google Analytics processing flow

When the visitor's browser reaches the GATC, the code begins to execute. During execution, the GATC identifies attributes of the visitor and her browsing environment, such as how many times she's been to the site, where she came from, her operating system, her web browser, etc.

After collecting the appropriate data, the GATC sets (or updates, depending on the situation) a number of first-party cookies (step 2), which are discussed later in this section. The cookies store information about the visitor. After creating the cookies on the visitor's machine, the tracking code waits to send the visitor data back to the Google Analytics server.

While the data is collected and the cookies are set, the browser is actively downloading a file named *ga.js* from a Google Analytics server (also step 2). All of the code that Google Analytics needs to function is contained within *ga.js*.

Once the *ga.js* file is loaded in the browser, the data that was collected is sent to Google in the form of a *pageview*. A pageview indicates that a visitor has viewed a certain page on the website. There are other types of data, like events and e-commerce data, that can be sent to Google Analytics (we will discuss these later).

The pageview is transmitted to the Google Analytics server via a request for an invisible GIF file (step 4) named *__utm.gif*. Each piece of information the GATC has collected is sent as a query-string parameter in the *__utm.gif* request, as shown below:

```
http://www.google-analytics.com/__utm.gif?utmwv=4.6.5&utmn=1881501226&utmhn
    =cutroni.com&utmcs=UTF-8&utmsr=1152x720&utmsc=24-bit&utmul=en- s
    &utmje=1&utmfl
    =10.0%20r42&utmdt=Analytics%20Talk%20by%20Justin%20Cutroni&utmhid
    =465405990&utmr=-&utmp=%2Fblog%2F&utmac=UA-XXXX-1&utmcc=
    __utma%3D32856364.1914824586.1269919681.1269919681.1269919681.1%3B%2B
    __utmz%3D32856364.1269919681.1.1.utmcsr%3D(direct)
    %7Cutmccn%3D(direct)%7Cutmcmd%3D(none)%3B&gaq=1
```

When the Google Analytics server receives this pageview, it stores the data in some type of temporary data storage. Google has not indicated exactly how the data is stored, but we know that there is some type of storage for the raw data. Think of this data storage as a large text file or a logfile (step 5).

Each line in the logfile contains numerous attributes of the pageview sent to Google. This includes:

- When the data was collected (date and time)
- Where the visitor came from (referring website, search engine, etc.)
- How many times the visitor has been to the site (number of visits)
- Where the visitor is located (geographic location)
- Who the visitor is (IP address)

After the pageview is stored in the logfile, the data collection process is complete. The data collection and data processing components of Google Analytics are separate. This ensures Google Analytics will always collect data, even if the data processing engine is undergoing maintenance.

The next step is data processing. At some regular interval, approximately every 3 hours, Google Analytics processes the data in the logfile. Data processing time does fluctuate. Google Analytics does not process data in real time. While data is normally processed about every 3 hours, it's not normally complete until 24 hours after collection. The reason the data is not complete until 24 hours after processing is that the entire day's data is reprocessed after it has been collected.

 Be aware that this processing behavior can lead to inaccurate intraday metrics. It is best to avoid using Google Analytics for real-time or intra-day reporting.

During processing, each line in the logfile is split into pieces, one piece for each attribute of the pageview. Here's a sample logfile; this is not an actual data storage line from Google Analytics, but a representation:

```
65.57.245.11 www.cutroni.com - [21/Jan/2010:19:05:06 -0600]
"GET __utm.gif?utmwv=4.6.5&utmn=1881501226&utmhn=cutroni.com&utmcs=UTF-8&utmsr
    =1152x720&utmsc=24-bit&utmul=en-us&utmje=1&utmfl=10.0%20r42&utmdt
    =Analytics%20Talk%20by%20Justin%20Cutroni&utmhid=465405990&utmr
    =-&utmp=%2Fblog%2F&utmac=UA-XXXX-11&utmcc
    =__utma%3D32856364.1914824586.1269919681.1269919681.1269919681.1%3B%2B
```

```
__utmz%3D32856364.1269919681.1.1.utmcsr%3D(direct)%7Cutmccn%3D(direct)
%7Cutmcmd%3D(none)%3B&gaq=1"__utma
=32856364.1914824586.1269919681.1269919681.1269919681.1; __utmb
=100957269; __utmc=100957269; __utmz=100957269.1164157501.1.1.utmccn
=(direct)|utmcsr=(direct)|utmcmd=(none)"
```

While most of this data is difficult to understand, a few things stand out. The date and time (Jan 21, 2010 at 19:05:06) and the IP address of the visitor (65.57.245.11) are easily identifiable.

Google Analytics turns each piece of data in the logfile record into a data element called a *field*. Later, the fields will be transformed into dimensions. For example, the IP address becomes the Visitor IP field. The city that the visitor is visiting from becomes the Visitor City field and the City dimension.

It's important to understand that each pageview has many, many attributes and that each one is stored in a different field or dimension. Later, Google Analytics will use fields to manipulate the data and dimensions to build the reports.

After each line has been broken into fields and dimensions (steps 6-9), the configuration settings are applied to the data. This includes features like:

- Site search
- Goals and funnels
- Filters

This is shown in step 7.

Finally, after all of the settings have been applied, the data is stored in the database (step 10).

Once the data is in the database, the process is complete. When you (or any other user) request a report, the appropriate data is retrieved from the database and sent to the browser.

Once Google Analytics has processed the data and stored it in the database, it can never be changed. This means historical data can never be altered or reprocessed. Any mistakes made during setup or configuration can permanently affect the quality of the data. It is critical to avoid configuration mistakes, as there is no way to undo data issues.

This also means that any configuration changes made to Google Analytics will not alter historical data. Changes will only affect future data, not past data.

Reports

When you log in to Google Analytics to view a report, Google Analytics creates that report in real time. Reports are created by comparing a dimension, like the Visitor City, to a numerical piece of information called a *metric*. Metrics include common web analytics numbers like visits, pageviews, bounce rate, conversion rate, revenue, etc. When viewed alone, a metric provides a site-wide total for that metric. But when viewed compared to a dimension, the metric represents the total for that specific dimension.

For example, a website may have a conversion rate of 2.87%. The metric in this case is conversion rate and the value is 2.87%. However, if you view conversion rate based on the City dimension, Google Analytics will display the conversion rate for each country in the database (see Figure 3-2).

Site Usage	Goal Set 1	Ecommerce			Views 🔲 ◉ ☰ ⇄ ᦙᨗ
Visits ⑦	**Goal1: All Purchases** ⑦	**Goal2: PWS Purchases** ⑦	**Goal Conversion Rate** ⑦	**Per Visit Goal Value** ⑦	
700,323	**1.76%**	**0.67%**	**2.43%**	**$0.00**	
% of Site Total: 100.00%	Site Avg: 1.76% (0.00%)	Site Avg: 0.67% (0.00%)	Site Avg: 2.43% (0.00%)	Site Avg: $0.00 (0.00%)	

	Detail Level: City ⌄	Visits ↓	All Purchases	PWS Purchases	Goal Conversion Rate	Per Visit Goal Value
1.	Calgary	17,293	0.74%	0.23%	0.97%	$0.00
2.	New York	16,410	1.65%	0.74%	2.39%	$0.00
3.	Houston	14,936	2.00%	0.94%	2.93%	$0.00
4.	San Francisco	12,830	2.01%	0.83%	2.84%	$0.00
5.	Edmonton	11,725	0.72%	0.14%	0.85%	$0.00
6.	Atlanta	9,623	2.38%	1.06%	3.44%	$0.00
7.	Los Angeles	9,352	1.30%	0.45%	1.75%	$0.00
8.	Dallas	8,836	2.25%	1.06%	3.32%	$0.00
9.	Chicago	8,362	1.89%	0.68%	2.77%	$0.00
10.	Denver	6,227	1.81%	0.82%	2.63%	$0.00

Filter City: [containing ⌄] [_____] [Go] Advanced Filter   Go to: 1   Show rows: [10 ⌄] 1 - 10 of 9,004 ◀ ▶

Figure 3-2. This report shows the conversion rate (a metric) for the City dimension

Each row in Figure 3-2 is a different value for the City dimension. Notice that there are many columns, or metrics, in the report. Google Analytics can associate many different metrics for a single dimension.

Almost every report is created in the same manner. Google Analytics displays various metrics for a given dimension. If you are interested in a certain metric that Google Analytics does not include in a report, you can create a custom report to display that metric for the dimension.

About the Tracking Code

As mentioned earlier, Google Analytics uses a very common web analytics technology called page tags to identify visitors, track their actions, and collect the data. Each page on your website that you want to track must be "tagged" with a small snippet of Java-Script. If the tracking code is not on a page, that page will not be tracked.

No tracking code, no data. It's as simple as that.

The following is the GATC JavaScript snippet:

```
<script type="text/javascript">
  var _gaq = _gaq || [];❶
  _gaq.push(['_setAccount', 'UA-XXXXXX-YY']);
  _gaq.push(['_trackPageview']);

  (function() {❷
    var ga = document.createElement('script'); ga.type = 'text/javascript';
    ga.async = true; ga.src = ('https:' == document.location.protocol ?
        'https://ssl' : 'http://www') + '.google-analytics.com/ga.js';
    var s = document.getElementsByTagName('script')[0];
    s.parentNode.insertBefore(ga, s);
  })();

</script>
```

❶ This part of the tracking code does all of the work. It starts by creating a queue (named _gaq), or list of Google Analytics commands. These commands are also called *methods*. When you want Google Analytics to do something, you add, or push, a command into the queue.

The standard page tag adds the first two methods to the queue for you. The first method is _setAccount(). This method links the data collected from your site to your Google Analytics account using a unique number. The number is found directly after the "UA-". Once the _setAccount() method has been added, the tracking code knows where to send all of the data.

The second method, _trackPageview() is the part of the code that collects information about the visitor, stores it in cookies, and sends the data back to Google. This is the true workhorse of Google Analytics.

Remember, this part of the tracking code is a queue of methods. Up to this point, the only thing that has happened is two methods have been added to the queue. The queue has not been processed and no data has been sent to Google Analytics.

❷ Before any code can execute the *ga.js* file, which contains all of the Google Analytics logic, this code loads that logic into the browser and requests *ga.js* from a Google server. This file is geo-load-balanced across all of Google's global data centers. This means the visitor's browser will connect with the closest data center to reduce the time it takes to retrieve the file. The visitor's browser caches this file, so it's possible that it doesn't even need to load from a Google data center. Once the browser has retrieved the file, the queue of commands begins to execute. Notice the ga.async=true part of the code. This part of the code tells the browser to load the *ga.js* file asynchronously. This means that the browser can load *ga.js* while it continues to render the page for the visitor. Even if there is a communication issue between the browser and Google's Analytics servers and Google's servers stop transmitting *ga.js* to the browser, the browser will continue to render the page for the visitor.

Not all browsers can load files asynchronously. At the time of this writing, Firefox 3.6 and later are the only browsers that support true asynchronous loading. For browsers that do not support asynchronous loading, the code is optimized to dynamically add the script directly to the document object model (DOM). This more or less creates the asynchronous behavior for browsers that do not support true asynchronous loading.

When it comes time to place the code on your pages, Google suggests that you place the tracking code immediately before the </HEAD> tag of each page. If your website uses a content management system or some type of template engine, you can add the tracking code to template files or another mechanism that automatically generates common HTML elements. This is a fast, effective way to tag all website pages.

The Evolution of the Tracking Code

Some of you may be wondering why the tracking code on your site looks dramatically different than the tracking code in this book. In May 2010, Google changed the tracking code format to the version you see in this book. Google replaced the previous version, commonly referred to as the "standard" tracking code, with this new version, called the "asynchronous" or "async" tracking code.

Google changed to an asynchronous version of the tracking code to reduce the amount of time it takes for the tracking code to load and execute. This, in turn, should speed up your website. Google has indicated the page load time is a factor in its ranking algorithm, and it would be embarrassing if one of its products increased load times.

The async version of the tracking code is, from a functional perspective, the same as the "standard" version of the tracking code. Other than loading asynchronously, the only difference is the syntax.

Switching from the "standard" Google Analytics tracking to the async tracking code can be time-consuming and complicated. It all depends on the complexity of your implementation. If you've got a simple site that does not use events, custom variables, virtual pageviews, or e-commerce tracking, you can probably migrate without too much pain. You'll probably just need to change the tags on your site. But if you use any of the earlier Google Analytics features, you'll need to do additional coding to reformat all of your code to the new asynchronous format.

It is possible to host the *ga.js* file on your own server, regardless of whether you use the standard GATC or the async GATC. Why would you do this? Some large enterprise organizations have policies that restrict where some or parts of their sites can be hosted. Other organizations want more controls and choose to host the file locally.

To host the *ga.js* locally, copy the contents of *ga.js* by viewing the file in your browser. Just enter *http://www.google-analytics.com/ga.js* in your browser, copy the resulting code, and place it in a file on your server. Next, update the GATC to reference the new file location on your server and not the *ga.js* located on the Google Analytics server:

```
<script type="text/javascript">
  var _gaq = _gaq || [];
  _gaq.push(['_setAccount', 'UA-XXXXXX-YY']);
  _gaq.push(['_trackPageview']);

  (function() {
    var ga = document.createElement('script'); ga.type = 'text/javascript';
    ga.async = true; ga.src = ('https:' == document.location.protocol ?
      'https://ssl' : 'http://www') + '.YOUR-WEBSITE-DOMAIN/THE-PATH/YOUR-FILE-NAME.js';
    var s = document.getElementsByTagName('script')[0];
    s.parentNode.insertBefore(ga, s);
  })();
</script>
```

Google updates *ga.js* without notifying users. If you decide to host *ga.js* on your own servers, make sure you periodically check for updates. Google publishes a *ga.js* change log at *http://troni.me/cUNRvq*.

The Mobile Tracking Code

The Google Analytics tracking code relies on JavaScript and cookies to collect visitor data. While some mobile devices support these technologies, like iPhones and Android-powered phones, there is a huge ecosystem of mobile devices that do not support either of these technologies. Google Analytics therefore needs a different way to collect data for visitors using a device that does not support cookies and JavaScript. Thus was born the mobile tracking code.

The mobile tracking code collects data at the server level rather than at the browser, or device, level. Because the mobile tracking code collects data at the server level, you must implement it in the language that you used to build your web application. Google provides four mobile tracking libraries to make the process easier: PHP, Java, ASP, and Perl. All of the libraries work in the same basic way. You can download the mobile tracking libraries from the Google Analytics code site at *http://troni.me/bULXyd*.

Regardless of the language you use to implement mobile tracking, the data collection process is the same. Let's walk through the mobile tracking process using a PHP example, shown in Figure 3-3.

To track a mobile site built in PHP, you must add a block of PHP code before the <HTML> tag on all your mobile pages. You must also add a small block of PHP code immediately before the closing </BODY> tag.

When the server processes the first block of PHP (step 1 in Figure 3-3), it creates a URL containing information about the visitor. Then it places the URL that was generated in the first block of code in an HTML IMG tag (step 2 in Figure 3-3).

The image request is actually a request for the *ga.php* file. This file takes the requested URL, extracts the data, and sends the data back to the Google Analytics server (step 3 in Figure 3-3). This image passes data back to your server, where a request for the *__utm.gif* image is made. This *__utm.gif* request is nearly identical to the *__utm.gif* request that the JavaScript makes.

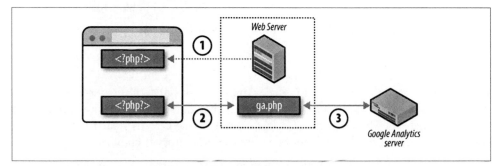

Figure 3-3. How the Google Analytics mobile tracking code collects data

Examining the first block of PHP code, you'll notice that you need to add your account number to the top of the block. You'll also need to change the path to the *ga.php* file to match your website architecture:

```php
<?php
// Copyright 2009 Google Inc. All Rights Reserved.
$GA_ACCOUNT = "MO-XXXXXX-YY";
$GA_PIXEL = "/ga.php";

function googleAnalyticsGetImageUrl() {
    global $GA_ACCOUNT, $GA_PIXEL;
    $url = "";
    $url .= $GA_PIXEL . "?";
    $url .= "utmac=" . $GA_ACCOUNT;
    $url .= "&utmn=" . rand(0, 0x7fffffff);
    $referer = $_SERVER["HTTP_REFERER"];
    $query = $_SERVER["QUERY_STRING"];
    $path = $_SERVER["REQUEST_URI"];
    if (empty($referer)) {
        $referer = "-";
    }
    $url .= "&utmr=" . urlencode($referer);
    if (!empty($path)) {
        $url .= "&utmp=" . urlencode($path);
    }
    $url .= "&guid=ON";
    return str_replace("&", "&amp;", $url);
}
?>
```

The second block of PHP code is much simpler. It is simply two lines of PHP code that reference a function in the first block of code:

```php
<?php
  $googleAnalyticsImageUrl = googleAnalyticsGetImageUrl();
  echo '<img src="' . $googleAnalyticsImageUrl . '" />';?>
```

When both blocks of PHP work, the result is an image tag at the bottom of every page on your mobile website. The resulting HTML looks something like this:

```html
<img src="/ga.php?utmac=MO-XXXXXX-YY&;utmn=669391585&;utmr=-&;
utmp=%2Ftesting%2Fmobile%2Findex.php&;guid=ON" />
</body>
</html>
```

It's important to understand that Google Analytics not only collects mobile data in a different manner, but also processes it differently than data it collects using the standard tracking code. The reason is that Google cannot define certain visitor metrics when tracking a mobile site is because mobile phones don't support cookies.

Another thing to notice is the account number. It's in the utmac query-string parameter above. It starts with MO, not UA, as the standard tracking code. This helps Google Analytics identify data coming from a mobile device and send it to a different processing engine. Google Analytics uses a separate processing engine for mobile to deal with session definition. Once it processes the data from a mobile device, Google Analytics places it in the same profile as data it collects using the standard tracking code.

At this time, the mobile GATC can only track pageview and event data. It cannot track any specialized data, like custom variables or e-commerce data. The methods to collect these other data types simply do not exist in the mobile tracking code.

If you have a mobile version of your website, it is worth the time to invest in tracking.

App Tracking

In addition to tracking mobile and standard websites, Google Analytics can also track mobile apps. Tracking apps is fundamentally different than tracking websites, because apps function differently than websites. The user experience (how people interact with the app) is completely different, because the device offers different ways to interact. There is no mouse and (potentially) no keyboard. With many devices, people use their finger to interact with the app. This change in how people interact with content leads to new and different types of data.

While Google Analytics has the capability to track apps, it uses the standard web measurement data model. This means it uses pageviews and visits to measure apps. Both software developer kits (SDKs) also support tracking events in apps. While it's useful to useful to have app tracking, it can be confusing to force the data into a web metrics paradigm.

App tracking is currently available for iPhone and Android applications. Those interested in tracking apps can download the SDK from the Google code site at *http://troni .me/aOnRye*.

App tracking has many unique features that are specific to apps and mobile devices. For example, the SDK includes a feature called *dispatch*. This feature allows the developer to cache, or hold, requests for the *__utm.gif* image and send multiple requests at the same time. This can help reduce the bandwidth the device uses.

The (Very) Old Tracking Code: urchin.js

For those of you who have been using Google Analytics for a long, long time, you may have noticed that the GATC has changed dramatically. The original version of the Google Analytics tracking code was named *urchin.js*. While *urchin.js* is still supported, it is recommended that all users migrate to the current version of the tracking code. The current version of the tracking code will load faster in the visitor's browser, contains new functionality, and is continuously updated by Google.

When planning a conversion from *urchin.js*, consider your implementation. Do you use e-commerce tracking? Does your website span multiple domains? Are you tracking Flash or Ajax? All of these things complicate the migration from *urchin.js*, because they are customizations of the tracking code. While I do recommend migrating from *urchin.js*, I recommend that you take the time to plan your migration carefully.

Understanding Pageviews

The most important part of the GATC is `_trackPageview()`. This method collects visitor data, stores that data in cookies, and sends the data to the Google Analytics server. The `_trackPageview()` portion of the GATC is shown in bold in the following code:

```
<script type="text/javascript">

  var _gaq = _gaq || [];
  _gaq.push(['_setAccount', 'UA-XXXXXX-YY']);
  _gaq.push(['_trackPageview']);

  (function() {
    var ga = document.createElement('script'); ga.type = 'text/javascript';
    ga.async = true; ga.src = ('https:' == document.location.protocol ?
    'https://ssl' : 'http://www') + '.google-analytics.com/ga.js';
    var s = document.getElementsByTagName('script')[0];
    s.parentNode.insertBefore(ga, s);
  })();

</script>
```

Every time `_trackPageview()` executes, a pageview is created by sending the data to Google Analytics (step 4 in Figure 3-1). Remember, each pageview includes many, many dimensions, like the visitor's IP address, city, country, region, etc. The actual page the visitor was looking at is captured in a dimension called *page*. You can use the page dimension to create many of the reports in the Content section of Google Analytics. Figure 3-4 shows some sample data from the Top Content report.

Content Performance		
Pageviews (?)	Unique Pageviews (?)	Time on Page (?)
7,500	**5,564**	**00:02:23**
% of Site Total: **100.00%**	% of Site Total: **100.00%**	Site Avg: **00:02:23 (0.00%)**

URL	Pageviews ↓
/blog/index.php	1,060
/blog/2006/08/04/getting-more-out-of-google-analytics-goals/index.	574
/blog/2007/05/08/welcome-to-the-new-google-analytics/index.php	376
/blog/2007/03/19/tracking-clicks-with-ga-pt-1-about-urchintracker/i	363
/blog/2006/11/10/google-analytics-campaign-tracking-pt-1-link-tagg	312
/blog/2006/11/10/how-does-google-analytics-track-conversion-refe	294

Figure 3-4. Top Content report showing pageview "names"

During the data collection process, _trackPageview() copies the information from the location bar of the visitor's browser. It modifies the value by removing the domain name and domain extension. The only things left are the directories, filename, and query-string parameters. This becomes the Request URI field or page dimension, and it is created during data processing.

For example, the URL *http://www.cutroni.com/pages/index.php?id=110* will appear in the Top Content report as /pages/index.php?id=110. So, in this example, the request URI is the part of the URL that comes after *http://www.cutroni.com*.

That's the default behavior of _trackPageview(). You can override this behavior and specify how _trackPageview() names a pageview by passing a value to _trackPage view(). For example, to change the way the pageview for */index.php* appears in Google Analytics, modify _trackPageview() on the */index.php* page as follows:

```
_gaq.push(['_trackPageview', '/index page']);
```

This modification forces _trackPageview() to name the pageview */index page* rather than */index.php*. The deeper effect of this change is that the value for the Request URI field and the page dimension is not */index.php*, but index page. This will have an impact on other configuration settings, like goals and funnels, which we'll discuss in Chapter 7.

You can execute _trackPageview() anywhere you can execute JavaScript. So, if you place _trackPageview() to the onclick attribute of an image, a pageview will be created in Google Analytics when a visitor clicks on the image. How will the pageview appear in Google Analytics? By default, it will use the request URI value. However, if you pass it a value, you can name the click anything you want.

You can use this technique to track visitor clicks, actions, and other browser events. For example, to track clicks on links to other websites (called *outbound links*), simply add the _trackPageview() method to the onclick attribute of the appropriate anchor tags. Don't forget to pass _trackPageview() a value so the visitor click is identifiable. There are more tricks on using _trackPageiew() to track clicks, Flash, Ajax, and non-HTML files in Chapter 4.

Every time _trackPageview() executes, a new pageview is created in Google Analytics. By using this technique, you can greatly distort the actual number of pageviews for a website, which is bad! You can use a feature in Google Analytics called Event Tracking to track visitor actions and, in fact, this feature is more appropriate for tracking clicks and actions. Event tracking is discussed in Chapter 10.

CHAPTER 4

Tracking Visitor Clicks, Outbound Links, and Non-HTML Files

The simple implementation for tracking visitor actions, or clicks, involves adding the _trackPageview() function to an HTML tag. For example, to track a visitor click on an image, just add _trackPageview() to the onclick event of that element:

```
<img src="/image.jpg" onclick="_gaq.push(['_trackPageview', '/image.jpg']);" />
```

When a visitor clicks on the above image, a pageview will be created for *image.jpg*. You can also use this method to track non-HTML files:

```
<a href="/schedule.pdf" onclick="_gaq.push(['_trackPageview',
    '/vpv/downloads/pdf/schedule.pdf']);" />PDF</a>
```

When creating pageviews for non-HTML files, try to use a consistent naming convention. This will make it easier to identify them in the reporting interface. For example, you may want to create a virtual directory structure using _trackPageview().

In the previous code example, I added **/vpv/downloads/pdf/** to the value passed to _trackPageview() (vpv stands for "virtual pageview"). This makes it easy to identify the non-HTML files in the reports.

Outbound links are tracked in the same manner:

```
<a href="http://www.cutroni.com" onclick="_gaq.push(['_trackPageview',
    '/vpv/outbound/'+this.href]);" />www.cutroni.com</a>
```

This outbound link will appear as **/vpv/outbound/http://www.cutroni.com** in the reports. Again, be logical in your naming convention. By placing all outbound links in the */vpv/outbound/* directory, you can easily filter the data in the Top Content report or the Content Drilldown report.

Clicks on outbound links are not "real" pageviews. If you need an accurate count of the number of pageviews your website generates, make sure you filter out any clicks on outbound links. An exclude filter, using the request URI and a filter pattern that matches your outbound link structure, will do the job.

An alternate method for tracking clicks is to use event tracking rather than virtual pageviews. See Chapter 9 for more information about event tracking.

There is an easier way to track outbound links and non-HTML files. Create a simple DOM script to automatically apply the `_trackPageview()` method to links the moment a visitor clicks them.

The problem with DOM scripts is the browser compatibility. If a browser changes the way it interprets the DOM, the script can break. This actually happens more often than you might think. Another challenge with DOM scripts is keeping them up to date. At the time of this publication, there are no DOM scripts that support the new async version of the tracking code.

 In October 2007, Google announced that automatic file download tracking and automatic outbound link tracking would be included in Google Analytics. It has been almost three years and this feature has still not appeared. Google assures us that it is coming, but we still have not seen it.

If you are tracking file downloads or outbound links, it is critical to your business that you do *not* wait for Google to launch this functionality.

One modification that I do recommend adding is a timer, especially when tracking outbound links or file downloads. In some instances, the browser can redirect the visitor to the file or requested website before the Google Analytics code can generate the virtual pageview or event. By adding a short timer, you can increase the chances that Google Analytics will record your data.

Adding a timer means you must create a small function that intercepts the visitor's click, creates the pageview, and lets the browser execute the visitor's actions. You modify an outbound link like this:

```
<a onclick='trackClick(this);return false;' href="http://www.redsox.com/" >
Red Sox
</a>
```

Next, create a JavaScript function as follows and place it in the HEAD tag on all pages where you need to track outbound links:

```
<script type="text/javascript">
function trackClick(this) {
  _gaq.push(['_trackPageview', '/vpv/outbound/'+this.href]]);
  setTimeout('document.location = "' + this.href + '"', 100);
}
</script>
```

About the Tracking Cookies

Google Analytics uses up to five first-party cookies to track and store information about a visitor. These cookies, set by the _trackPageview() method, track attributes of the visitor, such as how many times she has been to the site and where she came from. The cookies do not store any personally identifiable information about the visitor. Here is a list of all the tracking cookies, their format, and other information:

__utma

> Expiration: 24 months from the last session
>
> Format: domain-hash.unique-id.ftime.ltime.stime.session-counter
>
> The __utma cookie is the visitor identifier. The unique-id value is a number that identifies this specific visitor. ftime (first time), ltime (last time), and stime (start time) are all used to compute visit length (along with the __utmb and __utmc cookies). The final value in the cookie is the session or visit counter. It tracks how many times the visitor has visited the site and is incremented every time a new visit begins.

__utmb

> Expiration: 30 minutes from the last action (pageview, event, transaction)
>
> Format: domain-hash.session-pageview-count.session-event-count.stime
>
> The __utmb cookie, in conjunction with the __utmc cookie, computes the session length.

__utmc

> Expiration: End of the browser session
>
> Format: domain-hash
>
> The __utmc cookie, in conjunction with the __utmb cookie, computes visit length.

__utmz

> Expiration: By default, 6 months, but you can customize this value
>
> Format: domain-hash.ctime.nsessions.nresponses.utmcsr=X(|utmccn=X|utmctr=X|utmcmd=X|utmcid=X|utmcct=X|utmgclid=X)
>
> The __utmz cookie is the referrer-tracking cookie. It tracks all referrer information regardless of the referrer medium or source. This means all organic, cost-per-click (also known as CPC), campaign, or plain referral information is stored in the __utmz cookie. Data about the referrer is stored in a number of name-value pairs, one for each attribute of the referral:

utmcsr

>Identifies a search engine, newsletter name, or other source specified in the `utm_source` query parameter.

utmccn

>Stores the campaign name or value in the `utm_campaign` query parameter.

utmctr

>Identifies the keywords used in an organic search or the value in the `utm_term` query parameter.

utmcmd

>A campaign medium or value of the `utm_medium` query parameter.

utmcct

>Campaign content or the content of a particular ad (used for ad testing). The value from `utm_content` query parameter.

utmgclid

>A unique identifier used when AdWords autotagging is enabled. This value is reconciled during data processing with information from AdWords.

__*utmv*

>Expiration: 6 months

>Format: domain-hash.value

>This is a custom variable cookie. This cookie is not present unless you have implemented a visitor-level custom variable. The cookie is created using the `_setCustomVar()` method, which we will discuss in Chapter 10.

 Google can change the number and format of the cookies at any time. Before using any of this information, you should check the format of the cookies to ensure they have not changed.

Google Analytics uses first-party cookies. A first-party cookie belongs to your website. Some web analytics tools use a third-party cookie. A third-party cookie is not owned by your website, but rather a different website. By default, many browsers block third-party cookies, which can cause issues for any tool that tracks visitors with a third-party cookie. It is always preferable to use an analytics tool that tracks visitors with first-party cookies.

There are numerous studies, white papers, and blog posts estimating the rate at which user cookies are blocked by browsers and deleted by users. Eric Petersen first wrote about the pitfalls of cookies in a 2005 study for Jupiter Research. The latest formal cookie study was done by comScore, an online measurement company: *http://troni.me/ca7sDU*.

In my opinion, the best course of action to mitigate cookie deletion and its effects on your data is to look for trends and patterns in your data and to avoid absolute numbers.

Issues with JavaScript and Cookie Tracking

Google Analytics does not track visitors who have configured their browsers to block first-party cookies or disabled JavaScript.

Also, if a visitor deletes his cookies, he will appear as a new visitor the next time he visits the website. If a visitor visits the site from multiple browsers or multiple computers, he will appear as multiple visitors. These are issues faced by every analytics package that uses JavaScript and cookies. The best course of action is to avoid looking at absolute metrics in Google Analytics and focus on trends.

It is also possible to use the mobile version of the tracking code to track visitors who have cookies or JavaScript disabled. However, the mobile tracking code has difficulty calculating certain metrics (like visits) or certain dimensions (like the visitor's location). This can lead to inconsistencies in your data. Be aware of this if you try to use mobile tracking for a standard website.

CHAPTER 5

Google Analytics Accounts and Profiles

Google Analytics is divided into a simple hierarchy of accounts and profiles. Many people confuse a Google Analytics account with a Google account. A Google account is a way for Google to identify you, as a person. A Google Analytics account is your instance of Google Analytics used to track websites.

Google uses an email address to identify your Google account. Some people believe that you must have a Gmail address, like *analytics-fan@gmail.com*, to have a Google account. This is not true. You can turn any email address into a Google account. This means that your work email address, like *jim-rice@redsox.com*, can be a Google account.

Once you have a Google account, Google attaches various services to your account. These services can include Gmail, Google Docs, AdWords, etc. Google Analytics is just one service that you can associate with your Google account. If you've ever signed up for a Google service, you have a Google account. Figure 5-1 represents the hierarchy of Google accounts and the Google Analytics account.

Figure 5-1. A Google account can contain many Google services, including Analytics

Google Analytics Accounts

For the most part, Google Analytics accounts organize the different web properties that you track. Google Analytics makes it easy for you to identify everything you are tracking by placing everything in one account. Google ties the data coming from your website to your Google Analytics account using a unique account number. You can find your account number in the tracking code you place on your site. The location of the account number is shown in bold in the code below.

```
<script type="text/javascript">

  var _gaq = _gaq || [];
  _gaq.push(['_setAccount', 'UA-XXXXXX-YY']);
  _gaq.push(['_trackPageview']);

  (function() {
    var ga = document.createElement('script'); ga.type = 'text/javascript';
    ga.async = true; ga.src = ('https:' == document.location.protocol ?
    'https://ssl' : 'http://www') + '.google-analytics.com/ga.js';
    var s = document.getElementsByTagName('script')[0];
    s.parentNode.insertBefore(ga, s);
  })();

</script>
```

The XXXXXX is your account number. The YY part is the profile number, which we'll discuss shortly. When combined in the format UA-XXXXXX-YY, it is called the profile ID.

There is a one-to-many relationship of a Google account to Google Analytics accounts. This means you can access multiple Google Analytics accounts simply by adding your Google account to an existing Google Analytics account (Figure 5-2).

A Google Analytics account is used primarily to hold all of your profiles and organize everything you're tracking. There are a few settings that are specific to a Google Analytics account. These features pertain to data sharing and will be discussed in the section "Creating a Google Analytics Account" on page 35.

Within a Google Analytics account is a structure called a profile. Most people think of a profile as the data from a website. But in fact a profile is a collection of data *and* configuration settings. It is possible, and actually recommended, to have multiple profiles for each of your websites. I'll explain more about how to create multiple profiles and why you would want to later. You are allowed to create up to 50 profiles in your Google Analytics account.

Google identifies your analytics account and the profiles within the account using a unique ID. This number appears in the GATC. When the JavaScript executes, Google uses the ID to route the data to your Analytics account. If you look at the tracking code for your site, you can see the unique ID. It's preceded by a UA-, as shown in the code above.

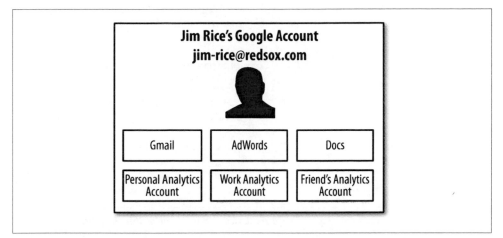

Figure 5-2. A single Google account can access multiple Google Analytics accounts

Also, notice the -YY in the tracking code. This is the profile number within your account. Together the account number and the profile number are called a web property ID. When the JavaScript executes, it sends the data to the specified web property ID.

Also, remember that you can use Google Analytics to track different types of things, like mobile apps. It is possible to track an app in its own dedicated profile rather than in a profile that contains traffic from a website.

Creating a Google Analytics Account

If you're new to Google Analytics, you'll need to create a Google Analytics account. The recommended way to create a Google Analytics account is through AdWords, because it's easier to link your AdWords account to your Analytics account if you create the Analytics account from within AdWords. Log in to your AdWords account and choose Google Analytics in the Reporting menu. Next, enable the Create my Free Google Analytics Account option and click Continue, as shown in Figure 5-3.

If you don't have a Google AdWords account, you can create a Google Analytics account at *http://www.google.com/analytics*.

Google will walk you through a number of steps to create your Analytics account. First, you'll need to specify some basic information about your website, like the domain name (Figure 5-4). You can also choose to give your Google Analytics account a name to make it easier to identify in a list. If you do not give it a name, Google will use the website domain as the name of the account.

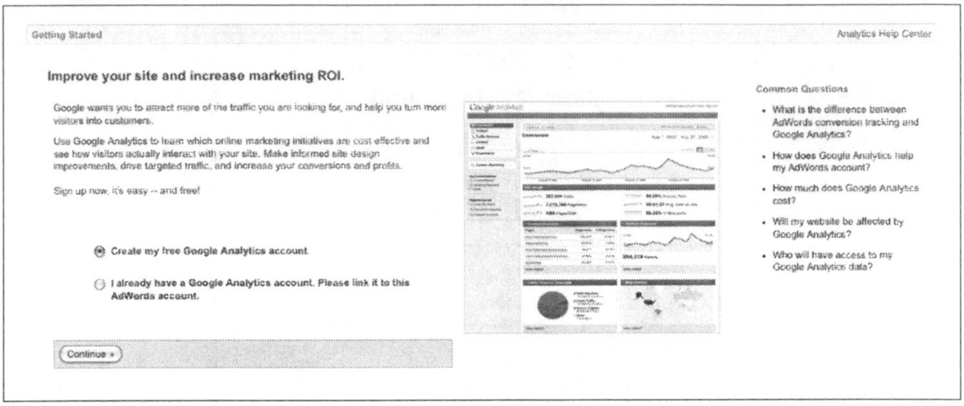

Figure 5-3. The first step in creating a Google Analytics account from within AdWords

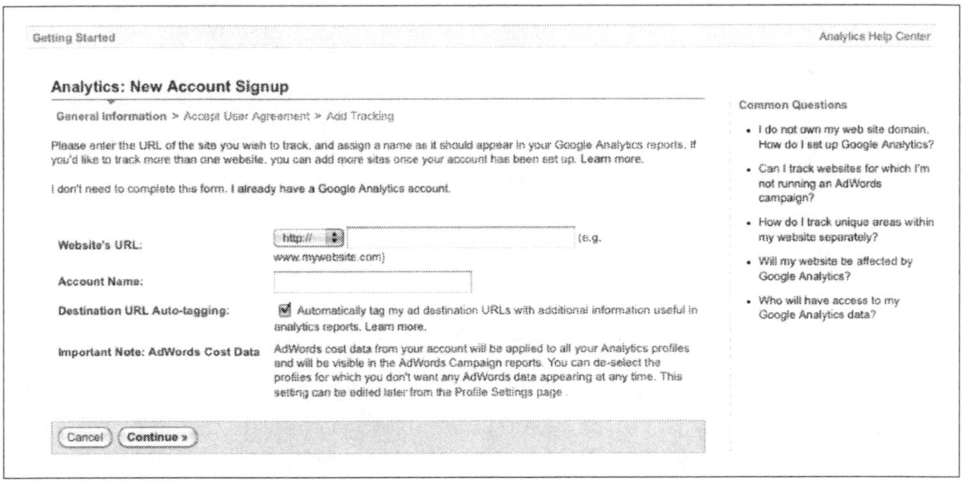

Figure 5-4. You must specify a website URL when creating your Google Analytics account

When creating your account, you can enable destination URL tagging and configure AdWords cost data. These features make it easier to identify and analyze traffic from Google AdWords in your Google Analytics data. Google also warns you that the cost data from Google AdWords, meaning how much money you spend on Google AdWords, will be imported into your Google Analytics reports. I will discuss these features in more detail in Chapter 9. However, it is recommended that you accept the default settings at this step.

After submitting the form, you will need to agree to the Google Analytics terms of service, shown in Figure 5-5. You should take the time to read the terms of service. It identifies how you can and cannot use Google Analytics. It also stipulates how Google will protect your data and how long Google will store your data. While there are no big surprises in the terms of service, it's a good idea to read it at some point.

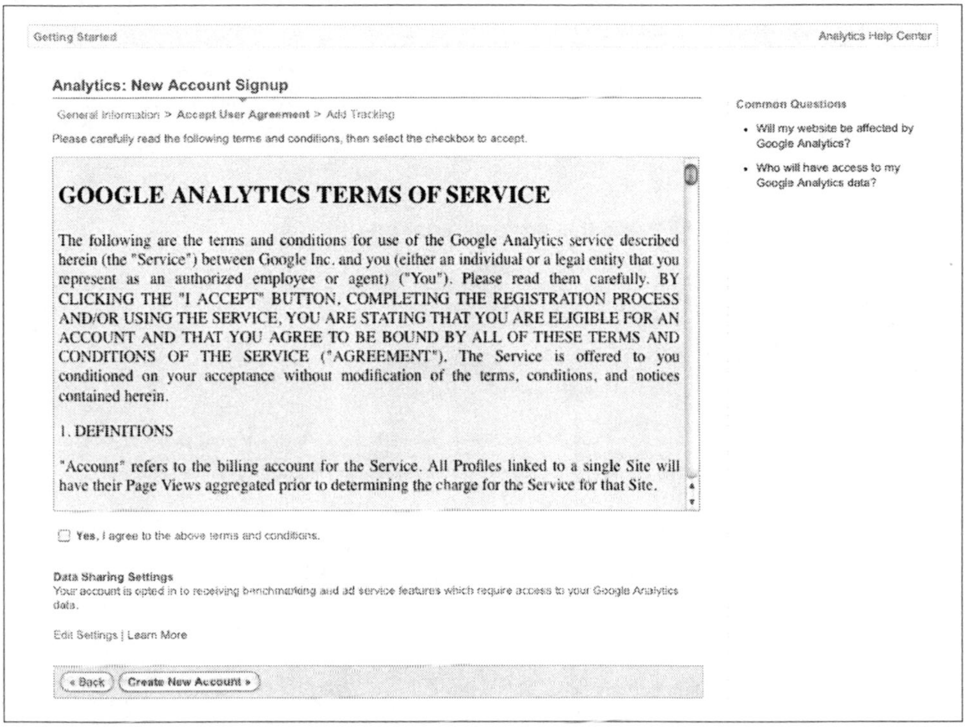

Figure 5-5. The Google Analytics terms of service

Also notice on this page that Google has specified some data-sharing options that are enabled automatically unless you opt out. Both of these options expand the functionality of Google Analytics and Google AdWords. Specifically, according to Google, you can share your data with:

Other Google Products: If you choose this option Google will share your Google analytics data with Google AdWords, Google AdPlanner and other Google products. Google uses the data to enable certain features. For example, when you share your Google Analytics data with AdWords, you can use the Conversion Optimizer feature. You can also import your Google Analytics goals into Google AdWords to measure conversions. In general this is a useful setting.

Other Google Analytics Users: If you choose this option, Google will anonymize your data and merge it with data from other Google Analytics users. This data will be used for a feature called Benchmark, which allows you to compare your website data to aggregate data from all other websites in your industry.

I recommend that you accept the default settings for data sharing, as they provide some helpful functionality and useful data in Google Analytics.

Finally, after you click Create New Account, Google will display the GATC configuration wizard, shown in Figure 5-6.

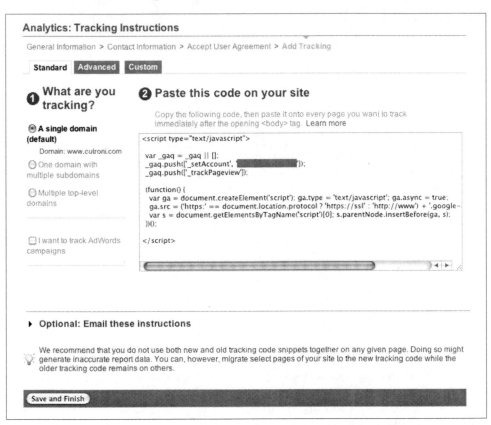

Figure 5-6. After you create a Google Analytics account, the tracking code will appear

That's it: you're done creating the account. Google has created a profile in your new account. Simply copy the code in the text area, add it to your site, and you'll have data in a few hours. The code configuration tool lets you modify the tracking code to meet your business needs and work within the architecture of your website. Very rarely do you just slap the code on your site; you will usually have to modify it in some way. This tool makes it easy to modify the tracking code without writing any JavaScript. We'll discuss the various ways to alter the tracking code throughout this book.

How to Manage Client Profiles

If you are a marketing consultant or agent, or work for any company that manages multiple Google Analytics accounts, you should *not* add your clients as profiles in your Google Analytics account. You should create a separate Google Analytics account specifically for each of your clients. Then add yourself as an administrator to the client's Google Analytics account. This will provide you with access to the account, but your client will "own" the account.

If you add a client as a profile in your Google Analytics account, there will be no way to separate the profile from your account if the client ever chooses to leave. You cannot move profiles from one Google Analytics account to another.

Creating Additional Profiles

It is a best practice to create multiple profiles in Google Analytics for every website you would like to track. Creating multiple profiles helps protect against configuration mistakes, normalizes the data to make it more useful, and can help you control who accesses your data.

To create an additional profile, simply click the "Add new profile" link on the main administrative screen (Figure 5-7).

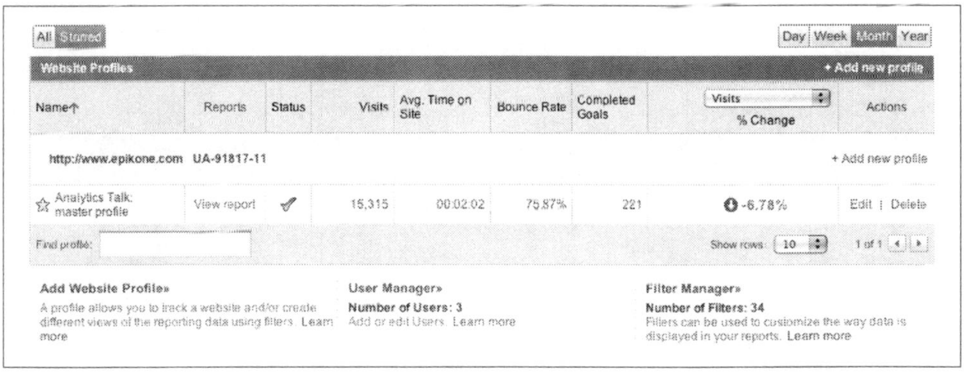

Figure 5-7. Click "Add new profile" to create a duplicate profile for an existing website

The next screen, shown in Figure 5-8, has two sections. The first section gives you the choice to create a new profile for either an existing or a new domain.

When creating a new profile for an existing domain, Google Analytics literally copies the data it collected from the tracking code that is already installed on the website. Google Analytics detects that there is already a piece of tracking code deployed for that website and copies the data into each profile.

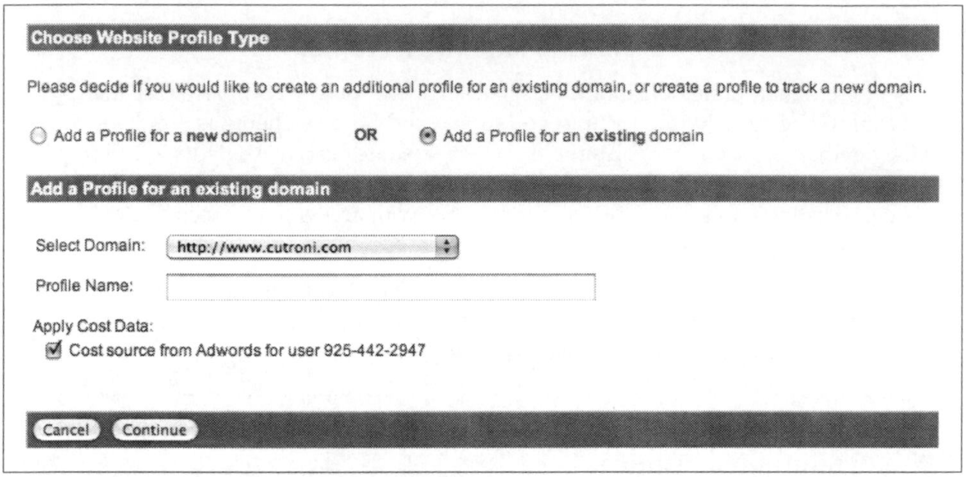

Choose Website Profile Type

Please decide if you would like to create an additional profile for an existing domain, or create a profile to track a new domain.

○ Add a Profile for a **new** domain   **OR**   ◉ Add a Profile for an **existing** domain

Add a Profile for an existing domain

Select Domain: [http://www.cutroni.com ▾]

Profile Name: [   ]

Apply Cost Data:
☑ Cost source from Adwords for user 925-442-2947

(Cancel)   (Continue)

Figure 5-8. Creating an additional profile

There aren't too many options when creating a duplicate profile for an existing domain. You need to give the profile a name and specify whether you want to apply AdWords cost data. If you choose not to apply the cost data, there will be no AdWords reports or ROI (return on investment) calculations in the e-commerce reports.

When you are finished creating the new profile, you'll see all of the profiles (including the new one) for that domain, as shown in Figure 5-9. Notice that the profiles are all nested under the same web property ID.

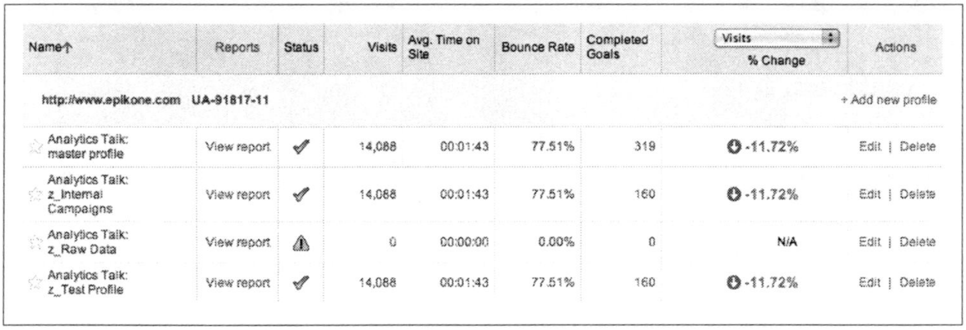

Name↑	Reports	Status	Visits	Avg. Time on Site	Bounce Rate	Completed Goals	Visits ▾ % Change	Actions
http://www.epikone.com UA-91817-11								+ Add new profile
Analytics Talk: master profile	View report	✓	14,088	00:01:43	77.51%	319	⬇ -11.72%	Edit	Delete
Analytics Talk: z_Internal Campaigns	View report	✓	14,088	00:01:43	77.51%	160	⬇ -11.72%	Edit	Delete
Analytics Talk: z_Raw Data	View report	⚠	0	00:00:00	0.00%	0	N/A	Edit	Delete
Analytics Talk: z_Test Profile	View report	✓	14,088	00:01:43	77.51%	160	⬇ -11.72%	Edit	Delete

Figure 5-9. All of the profiles for a single web property

We will discuss the kinds of profiles you should create and the settings that go along with each of them in Chapter 8.

In addition to creating duplicate profiles, you can also create new profiles for other websites. Click the "Add new profile" link at the top of your profile list, shown in Figure 5-10.

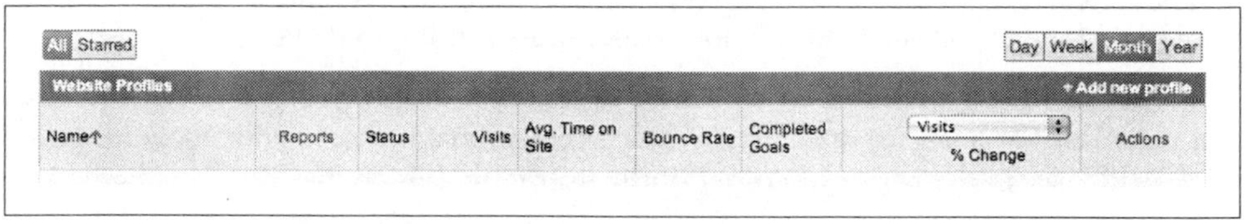

Figure 5-10. Click "Add new profile" to create a new profile for a new website

Google Analytics will prompt you for the domain of the new website, as shown in Figure 5-11, and will prompt you to specify whether you would like to apply cost data to this profile.

Once you supply this information, you must get the tracking code from the Profile Settings section for the newly created profile and add it to the site.

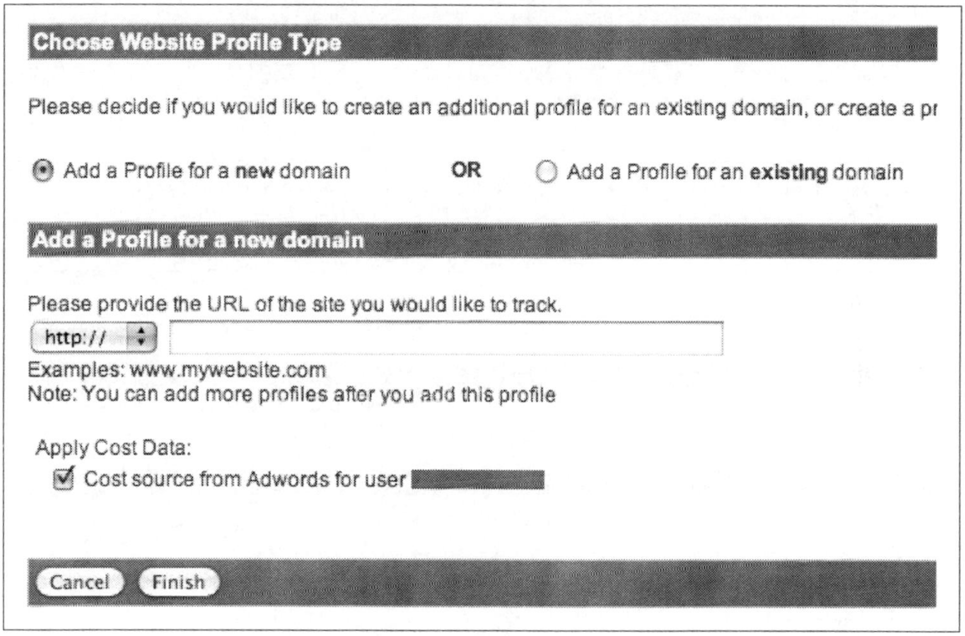

Figure 5-11. Creating a profile for a new domain

Access Levels

There are two types of users in Google Analytics: users and administrators. The difference between the two is very simple. Administrators have complete access to everything in a Google Analytics account. They can view all of the data and they can change any setting. Because administrators have such wide-reaching permissions, it's best to keep the number of administrators in your account to a minimum. Users can only access data in profiles that they have been given access to. They cannot change any settings.

There are two ways to add users to your Google Analytics account. First, you can use the User Manager on the main account page, shown in Figure 5-12.

The User Manager provides an easy way to access multiple profiles. Click the User Manager link to view a list of all users who currently have access to your account. Next, click Add User in the top right corner of the user table (Figure 5-13).

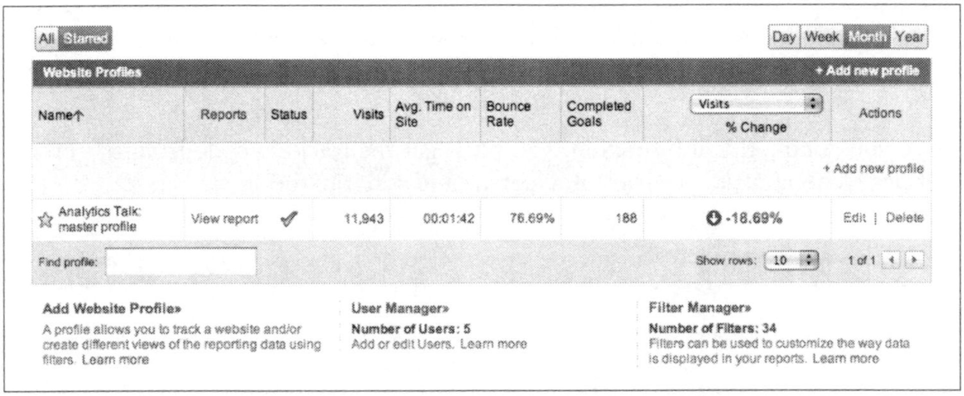

Figure 5-12. You can access the User Manager at the bottom of the main account page

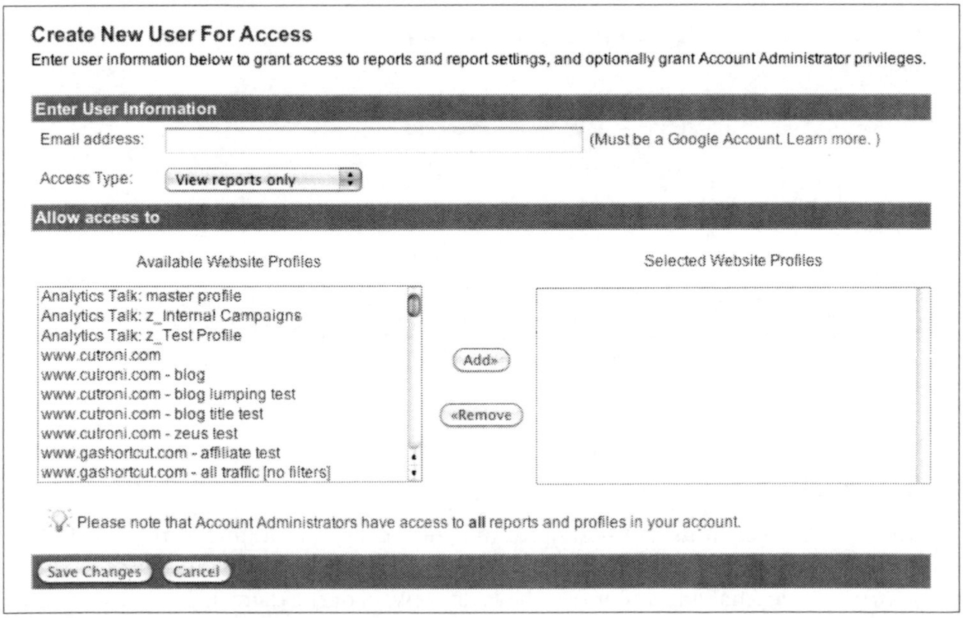

Figure 5-13. The new user form

To add a user, simply enter the Google Account email address in the Email address field. Remember, this must be a Google Account, not a Gmail account. Next, choose the access type. If you choose Administrator, the user will have access to all profiles in the account, and if you choose User, you must specify which profiles the user can access.

All About Profiles

As mentioned earlier, Google Analytics is divided into a structure of accounts and profiles. When data is sent to Google Analytics, it is stored in a profile. Most documentation describes a profile as data for a website. But a profile is more than just data: each profile has a number of settings that can affect the data within the profile.

A more accurate way to describe a profile is a collection of data and business rules. The business rules modify the data in the profile. In Google Analytics, the business rules are profile settings and filters (I'll discuss filters more in Chapter 6).

Each profile can have different settings and filters, thus changing the data in each additional profile created for a website. So, even though you may have two profiles for *http://www.cutroni.com*, the data in the reports could be dramatically different because of the different settings and filters applied to each profile.

Why would you create multiple profiles for a single website? To create different sets of data for different types of analysis or to control data access for different users. Understanding how each setting alters the data in the profile is important when you're setting things up.

Basic Profile Settings

You can access all the settings for a profile by clicking the Edit link next to each profile name (Figure 5-14).

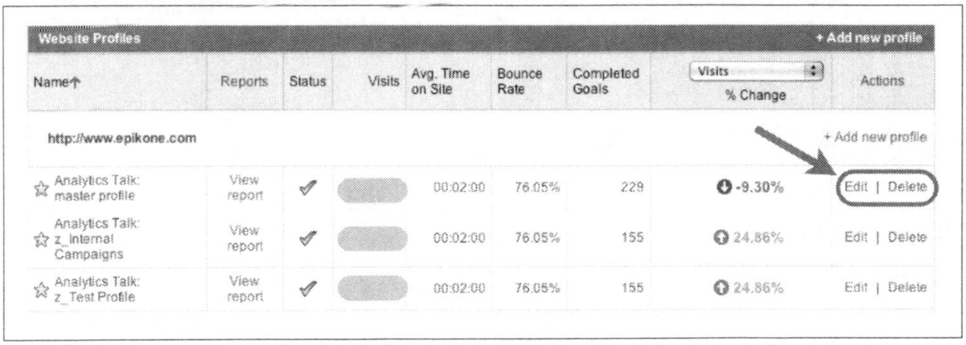

Figure 5-14. Click Edit to access the settings for each profile

There are multiple types of settings associated with a profile, as shown in Figure 5-15. There is the basic profile information, filters, goals, and access to the profile. Let's begin by walking through all of the Main Website Profile Information. Click the Edit link in the top right corner of the Main Profile Information table.

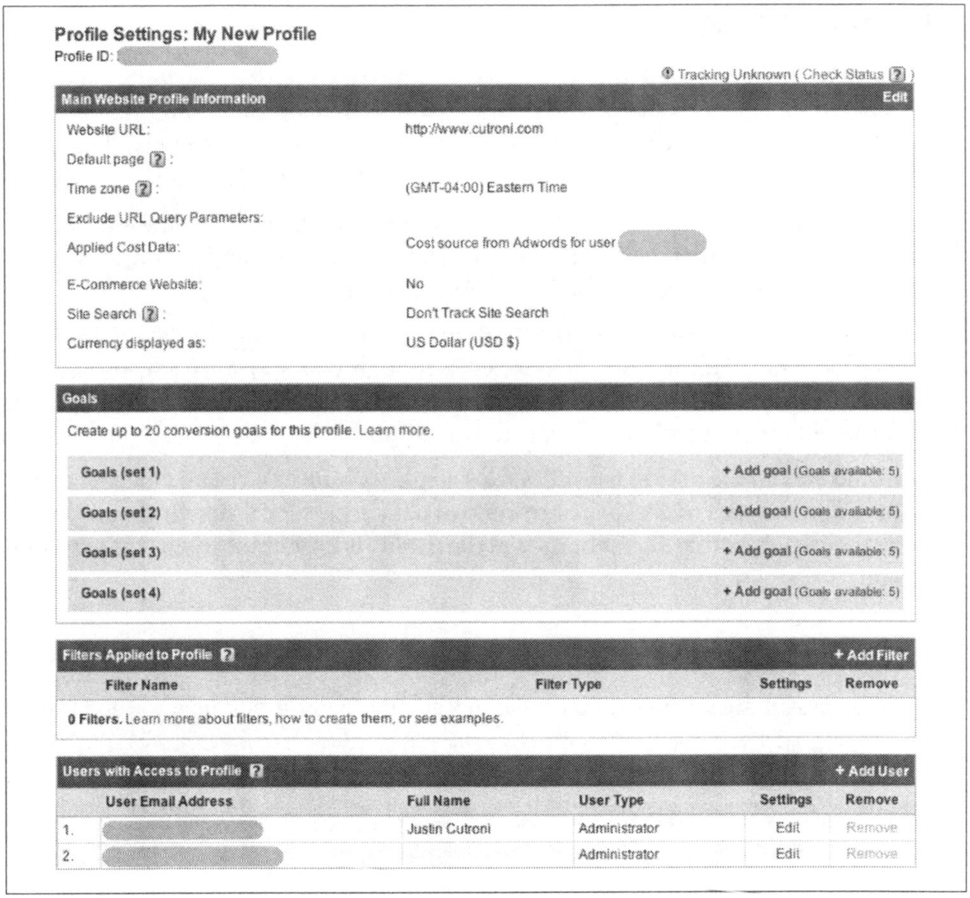

Figure 5-15. Each profile can have different settings

Profile Name

The Profile Name (shown in Figure 5-16) identifies each profile in a list. There are no restrictions on how to name a profile. You can even create two profiles with the same name, but I don't recommend this. How would you differentiate them in a list?

When thinking about profile names, remember how Google Analytics displays the profiles in your account. The interface displays the URL associated with the profile at the top of the table (Figure 5-17).

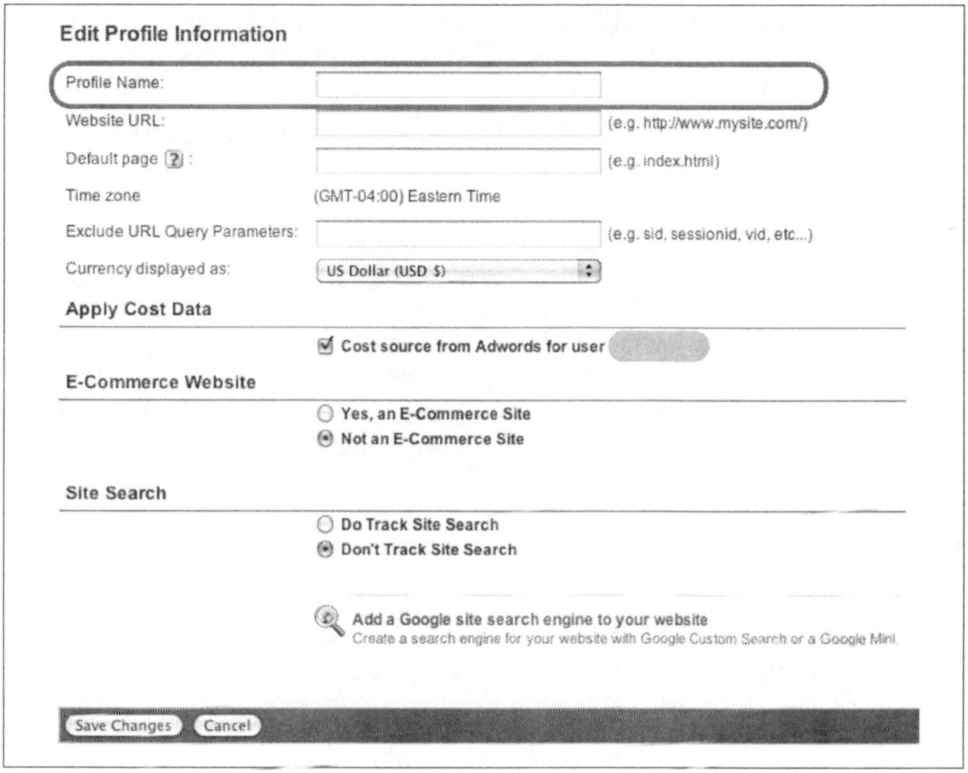

Edit Profile Information

Profile Name: _____

Website URL: _____ (e.g. http://www.mysite.com/)

Default page [?] : _____ (e.g. index.html)

Time zone   (GMT-04:00) Eastern Time

Exclude URL Query Parameters: _____ (e.g. sid, sessionid, vid, etc...)

Currency displayed as: US Dollar (USD $)

Apply Cost Data

☑ Cost source from Adwords for user ▭

E-Commerce Website

○ Yes, an E-Commerce Site
◉ Not an E-Commerce Site

Site Search

○ Do Track Site Search
◉ Don't Track Site Search

🔍 Add a Google site search engine to your website
Create a search engine for your website with Google Custom Search or a Google Mini.

[Save Changes] [Cancel]

Figure 5-16. Editing profile settings

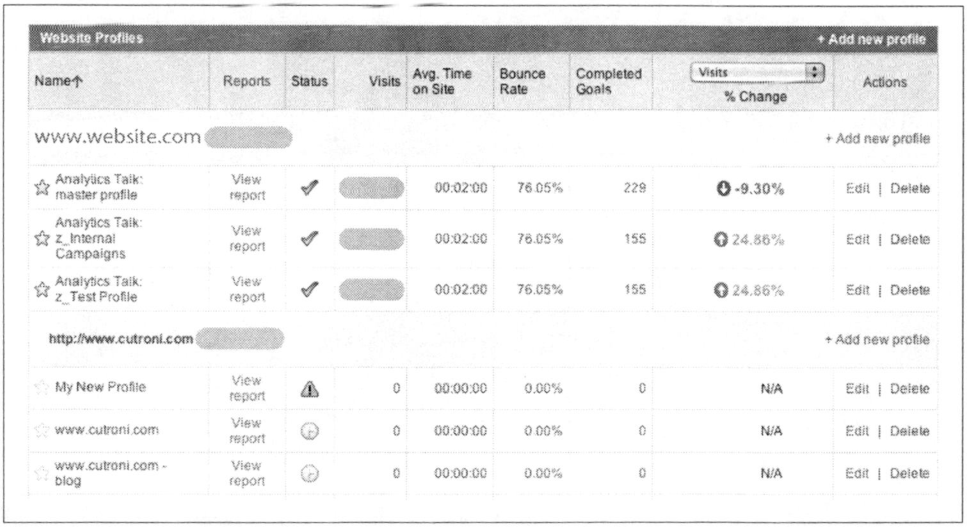

Name↑	Reports	Status	Visits	Avg. Time on Site	Bounce Rate	Completed Goals	Visits % Change	Actions
www.website.com ▭								+ Add new profile
☆ Analytics Talk: master profile	View report	✓	▭	00:02:00	76.05%	229	⬇ -9.30%	Edit | Delete
☆ Analytics Talk: z_Internal Campaigns	View report	✓	▭	00:02:00	76.05%	155	⬆ 24.86%	Edit | Delete
☆ Analytics Talk: z_Test Profile	View report	✓	▭	00:02:00	76.05%	155	⬆ 24.86%	Edit | Delete
http://www.cutroni.com ▭								+ Add new profile
☆ My New Profile	View report	⚠	0	00:00:00	0.00%	0	N/A	Edit | Delete
☆ www.cutroni.com	View report	⊙	0	00:00:00	0.00%	0	N/A	Edit | Delete
☆ www.cutroni.com - blog	View report	⊙	0	00:00:00	0.00%	0	N/A	Edit | Delete

Website Profiles   + Add new profile

Figure 5-17. Profiles for various domains

I suggest naming profiles something descriptive that all users will understand. If there are filters applied to a profile, include a short description explaining how the filter changes the data in the profile.

For example, Figure 5-17 includes a profile named Analytics Talk: z_Test Profile. By the name, we can easily identify that this profile contains test data.

Ideas for Profile Names

Wondering when a profile was created? You can add the creation date to the profile name; that way, you'll always know how much data exists in the profile. If you don't know when the profile was created, look at the reports. Go back in time and identify when the profile started to collect data. That's probably when the profile was created.

Additionally, Google Analytics sorts profiles alphanumerically. You can order profiles by adding a number or letter to the beginning of a profile name.

Website URL

Google Analytics uses your website URL for several tasks. First, Google Analytics uses it to check the installation of the tracking code. After you create a profile, Google Analytics will ping the website URL and search for the tracking code to ensure that it exists on the page. Google Analytics will not scan the entire site, just the page located at the website URL you provide. This is normally the homepage of the site.

Second, Google Analytics uses the website URL in the reporting interface. Certain content reports provide a link to the website URL in the Top Content reports. Figure 5-18 shows the links you can click to open a URL in a new window or tab.

	Page	None ⌄
1.	⎘ /blog/index.php	
2.	⎘ /blog/2008/11/04/email-tracking-with-google-...	
3.	⎘ /blog/2006/11/10/google-analytics-campaign-...	
4.	⎘ /blog/2010/04/19/faster-better-stronger-the-g...	
5.	⎘ /blog/2008/01/22/google-analytics-e-commer...	
6.	⎘ /blog/2008/01/13/google-analytics-e-commer...	
7.	⎘ /blog/2007/07/07/google-analytics-goals/inde...	
8.	⎘ /blog/2008/09/02/tracking-twitter/index.php	
9.	⎘ /blog/2007/11/19/tracking-sub-domains-with-...	
10.	⎘ /blog/2010/05/04/google-analytics-launches-...	

Figure 5-18. Click the small icon at the beginning of each data row in a content report to view that page in the browser

---

Google Analytics also uses the website URL in the creation of the Site Overlay report. When the Site Overlay report is generated, Google Analytics retrieves the website URL value and displays the page in a new window. It then adds various pieces of data to each link on the page. This includes the number of pageviews, conversions resulting from the page, and, if the site is an e-commerce site, the amount of revenue the page helped generate.

The website URL value is set when you create your Google Analytics account. (Figure 5-19). If you need to change the value, you can edit it in the Profile Information section. But be aware that if you change the value, it can have a negative effect on the reports mentioned above. If the website URL value does not exactly match the URL of your site, the links to the live page in the content report and the site overlay may not work.

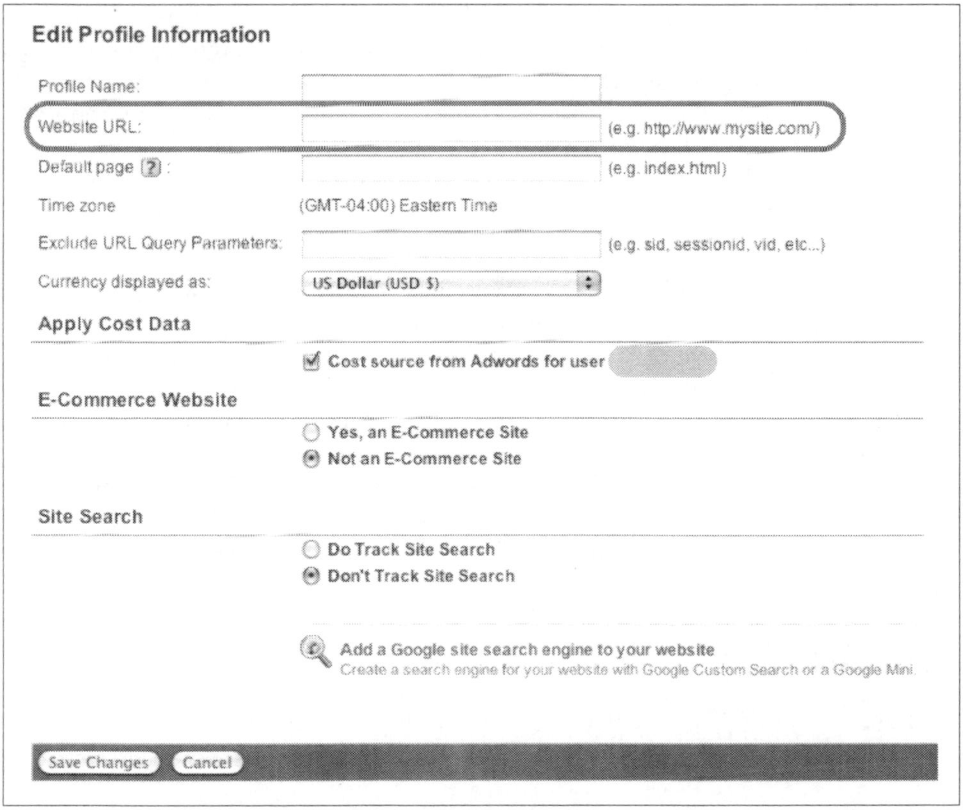

Edit Profile Information

Profile Name:	
Website URL:	(e.g. http://www.mysite.com/)
Default page [?] :	(e.g. index.html)
Time zone	(GMT-04:00) Eastern Time
Exclude URL Query Parameters:	(e.g. sid, sessionid, vid, etc...)
Currency displayed as:	US Dollar (USD $)

Apply Cost Data

☑ Cost source from Adwords for user

E-Commerce Website

◯ Yes, an E-Commerce Site
◉ Not an E-Commerce Site

Site Search

◯ Do Track Site Search
◉ Don't Track Site Search

🔍 Add a Google site search engine to your website
Create a search engine for your website with Google Custom Search or a Google Mini.

Save Changes   Cancel

Figure 5-19. The website URL setting is in the Profile Information section

Time Zone

You can change the time zone setting of your Google Analytics account only if it is *not* linked to an AdWords account. If you've linked your Analytics account to an AdWords account (which is the default setting), the time zone setting will be the time zone you defined in your Google AdWords account. Applying the AdWords time zone to the Analytics data ensures the Google AdWords reporting in Google Analytics is accurate.

If your Analytics account is not linked to an AdWords account, you can change the time zone to match the time zone where your business is located. This makes it easier to understand when people use your site in relation to your operating hours.

Default Page

Setting the default page for a website is a simple configuration step that ensures the quality of your Google Analytics report data. The default page for a website is the page shown to a visitor when they enter the website domain in the browser's location bar. For example, if you type *http://www.cutroni.com* in your browser, the web server returns the *index.php* file located at that domain. You won't see *index.php* in the browser's location bar, but that's the page the server returns. This is the same for directories within your website.

Why does this matter? When the GATC executes, it creates pageviews using the page URL the visitor requested. What if there is no page URL, as is the case with *http://www.cutroni.com*? Google Analytics creates a pageview and names it /. However, when the user types *http://www.cutroni.com/index.php*, Google Analytics creates a pageview for */index.php*. Although the visitor sees the same content, Google Analytics creates a pageview for / and a pageview for */index.php*: two different pageviews for the same page. Pageviews for a page should be summarized as a single line item in Google Analytics, not two. Remember, Google Analytics will collect pageviews for / and */index.php* separately. Figure 5-20 illustrates how two pageviews can exist for a single page.

Content Performance					Views:
Pageviews ? **1,252** % of Site Total: 18.88%	Unique Pageviews ? **1,117** % of Site Total: 26.52%	Time on Page ? **00:00:53** Site Avg: 00:01:10 (-24.29%)	Bounce Rate ? **58.91%** Site Avg: 20.20% (191.56%)	% Exit ? **56.63%** Site Avg: 22.76% (148.81%)	$ Index ? **$0.00** Site Avg: $0.00 (0.00%)
URL	Pageviews ↓	Unique Pageviews	Time on Page	Bounce Rate	% Exit	$ Index
/	1,231	1,105	00:00:51	59.37%	57.03%	$0.00
/index.html	21	12	00:02:28	16.67%	33.33%	$0.00
Find URL: containing ▼ index|/$ Go				Show rows: 10 ▼ 1 - 2 of 2 ◄ ►

Figure 5-20. Though they are the same page, /index.html and / appear as separate line items

To remedy this problem, enter the default page for your website in the Default page field in the main website Profile Information configuration section. Be sure to enter only the page name. Do not include a slash before the page name and do not use regular expressions (Figure 5-21).

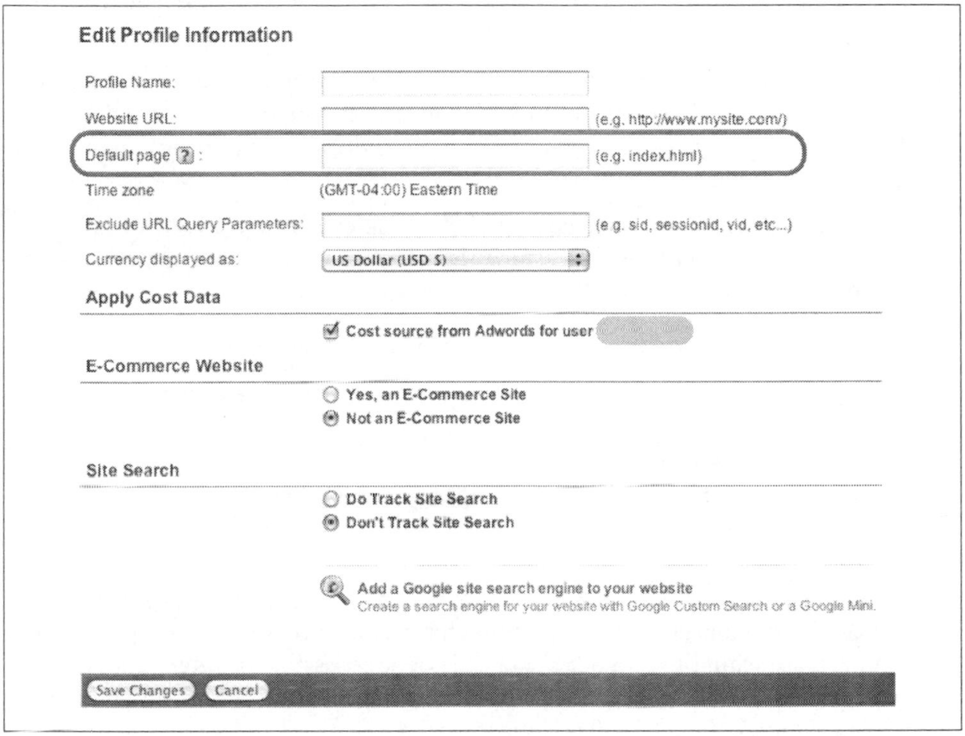

Figure 5-21. Setting the default page

Exclude URL Query Parameters

A dynamic website uses query-string parameters to determine what content visitors are consuming. Google Analytics automatically includes query-string parameters when it creates the Page Path Dimension. Table 5-1 illustrates how a URL in the browser's location bar becomes the Page Path Dimension in the Google Analytics report.

Table 5-1. How Google Analytics creates page names

URL in browser	Resulting page path in Google Analytics
www.mysite.com/dir/index.php? sess=1234&cat=3&prod=foo&var2=bar	/dir/index.php?sess=1234&cat=3&prod=foo&var2=bar
www.mysite.com/dir/index.php? sess=4567&cat=6&prod=bar&var2=foo	/dir/index.php?sess=4567&cat=6&prod=bar&var2=foo

The content reports can become cluttered due to the number of query-string parameters. Some query-string parameters indicate the content that a visitor is viewing, and these parameters are useful for analysis. However, many of the query-string parameters are just useless data. For example, some query-string parameters exist only for your web server or web application and provide no insight into the visitor's actions or the content she views. You do not need these variables and you should eliminate them from Google Analytics.

To configure Google Analytics to remove query-string parameters during processing, simply list the unwanted parameters in the Exclude URL Query Parameters field in the Edit Profile Information section (Figure 5-22). List multiple query-string parameters as a comma-separated list.

For example, we can remove the query-string variables *sess* and *var2* from the page names given in Table 5-1. Table 5-2 shows how the same URLs will appear after excluding these parameters.

Table 5-2. How a URL looks after removing unnecessary query-string parameters

URL in Google Analytics	Page paths after excluding unnecessary parameters
www.mysite.com/dir/index.php?sess=1234&cat=3&prod=foo&var2=bar	/dir/index.php?cat=3&prod=foo
www.mysite.com/dir/index.php?sess=4567&cat=6&prod=bar&var2=foo	/dir/index.php?cat=6&prod=bar

Excluding query-string parameters from Google Analytics will affect other parts of the application. Removing a query-string parameter here also removes it completely from the system. This means the parameter data will not be accessible via filters, goal settings, or funnel settings, so if a goal utilizes a particular query-string parameter and the parameter is excluded, the goal will no longer work.

Which parameters should you eliminate? In general, you should remove any parameter that does not provide insight into what visitors are doing and what content they are viewing. I've found the easiest way is to let Google Analytics collect some data and use the Top Content report to identify all query-string parameters. Sort the pageview metrics in ascending order. This will help you quickly identify which URLs get only one or two pageviews. These URLs usually contain a unique query-string parameter that may or may not be useful. Use the Top Content report as a master list of parameters and check with your IT staff to learn what each one means. Once you've identified which parameters add no value to your analysis, exclude them. This process is not easy, but it is important.

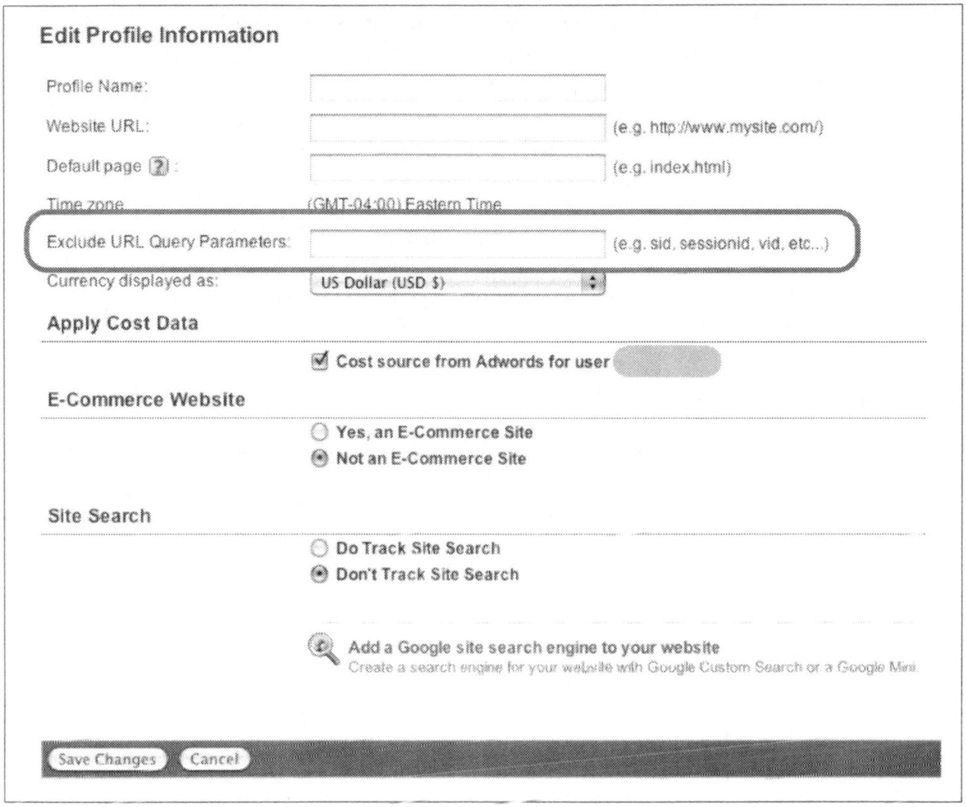

Edit Profile Information

Profile Name:

Website URL: (e.g. http://www.mysite.com/)

Default page ② :   (e.g. index.html)

Time zone   (GMT-04:00) Eastern Time

Exclude URL Query Parameters: (e.g. sid, sessionid, vid, etc...)

Currency displayed as: US Dollar (USD $)

Apply Cost Data

☑ Cost source from Adwords for user

E-Commerce Website

○ Yes, an E-Commerce Site
◉ Not an E-Commerce Site

Site Search

○ Do Track Site Search
◉ Don't Track Site Search

🔍 Add a Google site search engine to your website
Create a search engine for your website with Google Custom Search or a Google Mini.

[Save Changes] [Cancel]

Figure 5-22. Use the Exclude URL Query Parameters text box to remove unwanted query-string parameters

The Trouble with Query-String Parameters

It is very common for websites to use a query-string variable called a session ID to identify each individual visitor. Session IDs are unique strings that may appear in the query string of every page. A session ID will make every pageview unique because each session ID is unique. You should eliminate session IDs from Google Analytics using the method described above.

Other common query-string parameters that can create unique URLs are order ID values and timestamps.

If every page comes through as unique because of the unique query-string parameter, every page will have only one pageview. Only when you aggregate the data by removing the query-string parameter will you fix the problem. Some websites add the session ID as a directory in the file path. In this case, use an advanced filter to restructure the Request URI field. See "Advanced Profile Filters" on page 66 for more information.

As usual, changing the Exclude URL Query Parameters setting will not affect data that has already been processed by Google Analytics. Only data processed in the future will reflect this change.

 It is against the Google Analytics privacy policy to store any personally identifiable information in Google Analytics. If your website uses query-string parameters to pass personal information about your visitors (like email address, name, or address), that information will be stored in Google Analytics, thus violating the privacy policy. *You must exclude all query-string variables that may contain personally identifiable information.*

E-Commerce Settings

There are two settings relevant to e-commerce in the profile information section, shown in Figure 5-23. To include e-commerce reports on the reporting interface, set the E-Commerce Website feature to Yes. Use the "Currency displayed as" setting to specify the currency format for your Google Analytics reports.

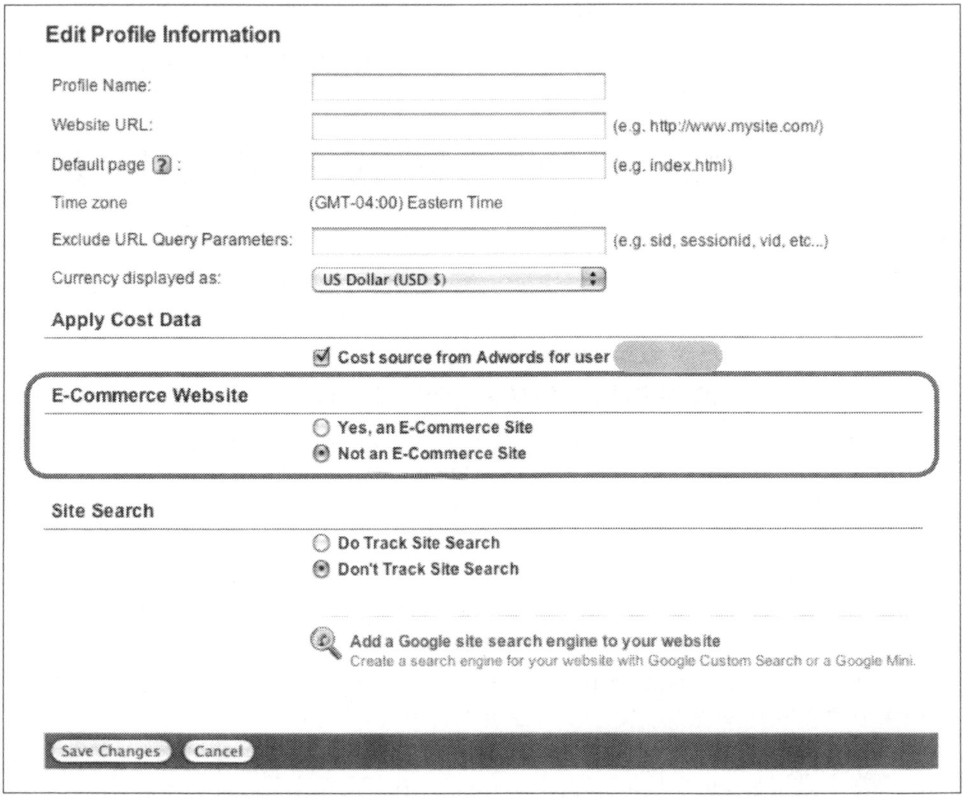

Edit Profile Information

Profile Name:

Website URL: (e.g. http://www.mysite.com/)

Default page ② :   (e.g. index.html)

Time zone   (GMT-04:00) Eastern Time

Exclude URL Query Parameters: (e.g. sid, sessionid, vid, etc...)

Currency displayed as: US Dollar (USD $)

Apply Cost Data

☑ Cost source from Adwords for user

E-Commerce Website

○ Yes, an E-Commerce Site
◉ Not an E-Commerce Site

Site Search

○ Do Track Site Search
◉ Don't Track Site Search

🔍 Add a Google site search engine to your website
     Create a search engine for your website with Google Custom Search or a Google Mini.

(Save Changes) (Cancel)

Figure 5-23. E-Commerce settings

If you create multiple profiles for a website, you will need to enable e-commerce tracking for each profile. By default, this setting is set to off.

Tracking On-Site Search

On-site search data lets you measure what people search for on your website. These are the words and phrases people enter into your site's search engine (Figure 5-24). This can be powerful data, because it represents how people think of your products or services.

For example, I once worked with a client that offered a large selection of sunglasses on its site, but there was very little traffic to the sunglasses section. A quick examination of the on-site search terms showed that visitors were looking for "sunglasses," "sun glasses," and other variations of the term. When we looked at the site navigation, we noticed that the website navigation listed "eyewear," not "sunglasses." The website designers had not anticipated how visitors would think of their products.

On-site search data also provides remarkable insight into how people navigate your website and can help you identify business opportunities. Are visitors searching for a product or service you do not offer? If so, what would it take to add that product or service?

To access the Search Terms report, select Content→Site Search→Search Terms.

There were 790 unique searches via 578 search terms

Site Search Usage | Goal Set 1 | Ecommerce

Views:

Total Unique Searches	Results Pageviews/Search	% Search Exits	% Search Refinements	Time after Search	Search Depth
790	**1.24**	**24.81%**	**17.84%**	**00:03:14**	**1.60**
% of Site Total: 100.00%	Site Avg: 1.24 (0.00%)	Site Avg: 24.81% (0.00%)	Site Avg: 17.84% (0.00%)	Site Avg: 00:03:14 (0.00%)	Site Avg: 1.60 (0.00%)

	Search Term	None	Total Unique Searches	Results Pageviews/Search	% Search Exits	% Search Refinements	Time after Search	Search Depth
1.	custom variables		26	1.08	34.62%	3.57%	00:04:22	1.50
2.	event tracking		23	1.70	26.09%	2.56%	00:04:56	2.26
3.	ecommerce		10	1.00	20.00%	40.00%	00:05:35	1.40
4.	goals		9	1.00	11.11%	0.00%	00:02:55	1.22
5.	crm		8	1.38	12.50%	9.09%	00:05:39	3.12
6.	funnel		8	1.00	0.00%	12.50%	00:00:19	1.25
7.	e-commerce		7	1.00	0.00%	0.00%	00:05:52	3.00
8.	omniture		7	1.14	28.57%	12.50%	00:04:20	1.14
9.	Google Analytics Campaign Tracking Pt. 2		6	1.00	16.67%	33.33%	00:00:27	1.50
10.	campaign tracking		6	1.67	16.67%	0.00%	00:05:34	3.00

Filter Search Term: containing ___ [Go] Advanced Filter

Go to: 1 | Show rows: 10 | 1 - 10 of 578 | ◄ ►

Figure 5-24. The Search Terms report shows the key phrases visitors search for on your website

Basic implementation

Configuring site search is fairly simple. Begin by performing a search on your site, then look at the URL for the search results page and attempt to find the term you searched for.

For example, if I perform a search for "jackets" on a website, I would try to find the term "jackets" in the search results page URL. Here's a sample URL that contains the search term in a parameter named "query."

http://store.com/category.asp?searchtype=keyword&query=jackets

Once you have identified the parameter that contains the search term, copy that parameter from the URL. Navigate to the profile settings for a profile in Google Analytics and activate the Site Search reports by choosing Do Track Site Search, shown in Figure 5-25.

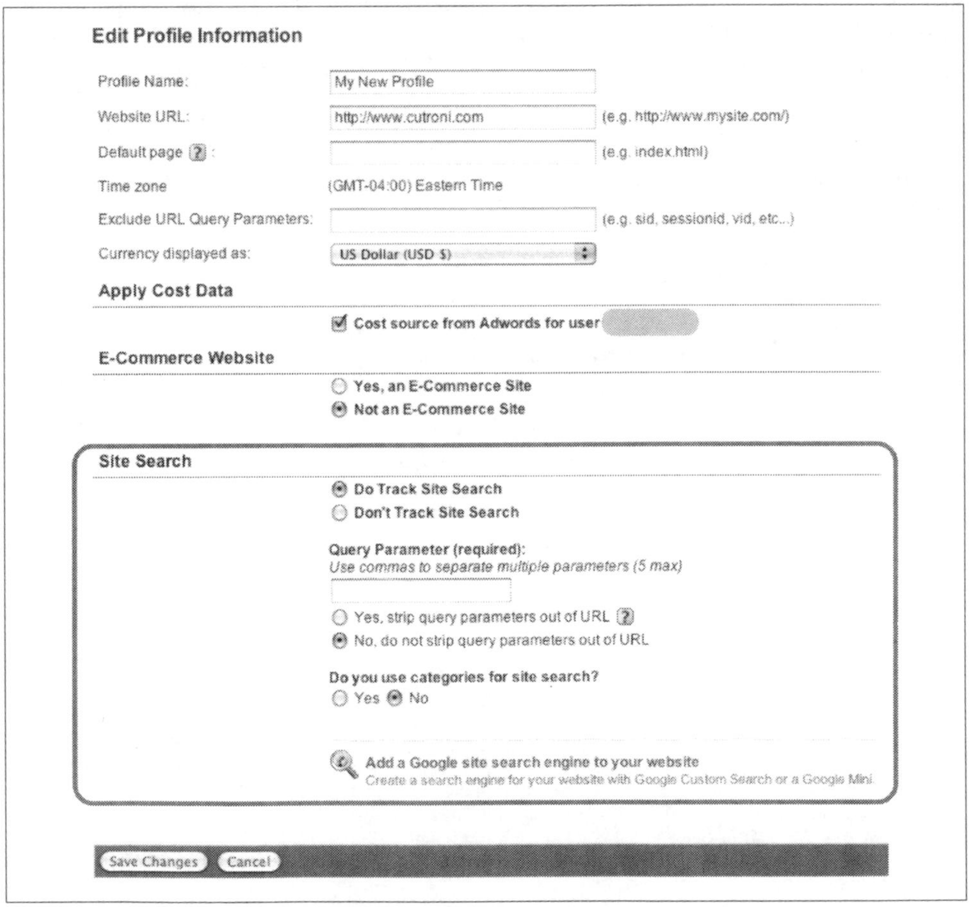

Figure 5-25. Activating Site Search reports in the Profile Settings section

This will reveal a number of configuration options that you can set for your specific site's search engine.

Begin by pasting the parameter that holds the search term in the Query Parameter field. Google Analytics will extract the search term as it processes site data.

Below the Query Parameter field is an important setting called Strip Query Parameter. This feature will remove the search term and search term parameter from the request URI after the site search has been processed. This will help normalize the Top Content report by reducing the number of instances for the search results page from thousands to one.

For example, if there are 1,000 searches for 1,000 different terms, there will be 1,000 different versions of the search results page in the Top Content report. By removing the search term from the URI, Google Analytics will only show one version of the search results page in the Top Content report, which is a good thing.

You can specify up to five parameters in the Query Parameter field. In all likelihood, your website will only use one parameter to store the site search term. However, large sites that use multiple on-site search solutions may have multiple parameters. Simply list all of the parameters your site uses and Google Analytics will extract the search terms.

Below the Query Parameter field is the option to enable Search Category Reporting. Many websites include this option to search within a specific category. For example, on the Amazon website (Figure 5-26) you can narrow your search by category.

Figure 5-26. Amazon.com allows visitors to search within certain categories; Google Analytics can track which search terms appear in each category

Understanding the search terms used in specific categories can help you understand how visitors think about products or services. For example, if you know which product is the most popular in a particular category, based on search, you can place that product in a more visible location, thus making it easier to find.

Configuring Google Analytics to track search categories is identical to the search term configuration. Simply perform a search on the site and examine the search results page. The URL below is the search results page when a visitor searches for "web analytics" in the "books" category:

> *http://www.amazon.com/s/ref=nb_sb_noss?url=search-alias%3Dstripbooks&field-keywords=web+analytics&x=0&y=0*

The search term parameter is fairly easy to identify, as it's literally named "field-keywords." But the category parameter is a bit harder. It looks like the parameter named "url" is the category, as it contains something resembling the chosen category, books. Once you identify the parameter that holds the category, paste it into the Category Parameter field (Figure 5-27).

You also have the option to strip the category query-string parameter after Google Analytics processes the site search data. It is recommended that you choose Yes, as you did with the search term parameter.

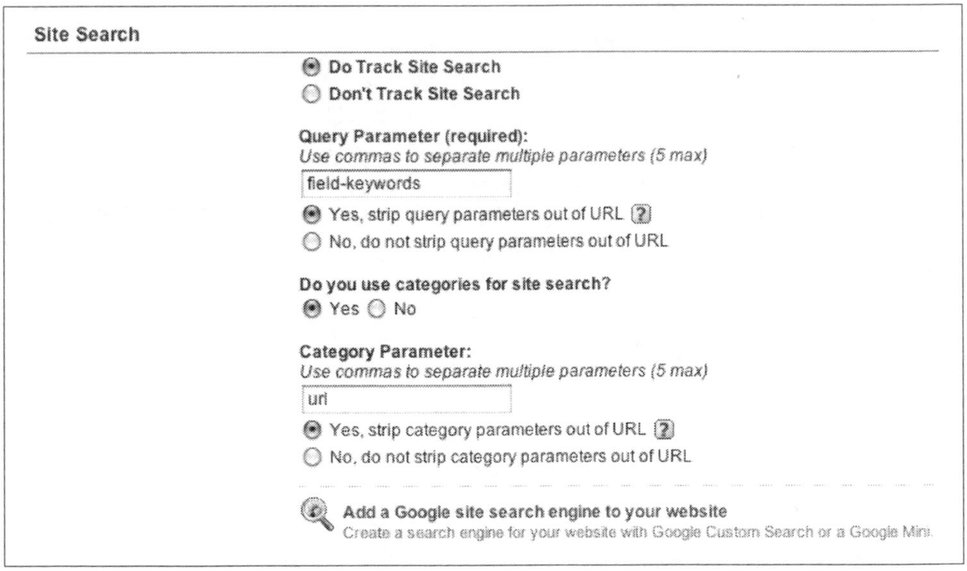

Figure 5-27. The Site Search settings

Google Analytics processes site search data before it applies profile filters. This means it is not possible to normalize site search data using the standard profile settings or filters. Google Analytics search terms are case-sensitive, so subtle differences in case will create separate searches and increase the overall number of searches.

Variations of the same term can also increase the number of searches. For example, consider all of the variations that users can enter for "perfume":

- PERFUME
- Perfume
- Parfum
- PErfume
- Fragrance
- Cologne

As an analyst, you will need to review the search terms and identify which data can be consolidated.

The only way to modify site search data is by changing the data when it is collected via JavaScript. While you cannot use filters to modify site search data, you can apply them to a profile to segment site search data. If you create multiple profiles based on different traffic sources (direct, organic, etc.), Google Analytics will correctly filter the site search data.

One awesome feature of Site Search reports is that they display which internal searches lead to conversions and transactions. Transactions or goals are attributed to the search term immediately preceding the goal or transaction. So, if a visitor performs two searches on the site before converting, the last search receives credit for the conversion.

Another helpful report is the Search Term Refinement report. This report identifies *adjacent* search terms, or search terms that were used sequentially. Most people start searching by using a general phrase and then refine it. Knowing how people search can help you better tailor the search results. In reality, this report simply shows sequential searches; Google Analytics does not verify that the terms are related, just that they occurred one after the other.

Advanced implementation

Some websites do not pass site search terms via a query-string parameter. In this case, it is still possible to configure Google Analytics to track site searches, but the implementation requires a programmatic change—you must create a virtual pageview that inserts the search term as a query-string parameter. If you don't know what a virtual pageview is, please refer to Chapter 2.

You can create the virtual pageview by changing the Google Analytics page tag on the search results page, or by creating a virtual pageview when the site search is submitted. The key is that the search term *must* be a query-string parameter. Here's how the code might look:

```
onclick="_gaq.push(['_trackPageview', '/site-search?term=web-analytics']);"
```

This code will create a virtual pageview in Google Analytics named */site-search? term=web-analytics*. Obviously, the real code must insert the actual search term dynamically—"web analytics" is just an example.

Once you have made the necessary code changes, add the query-string parameter to the search term to the Site Search settings. In the code example above, the query-string parameter is a term. This would be added to the Query Parameter field in the Site Search settings (Figure 5-27).

 You can also add site search categories to your virtual pageviews if the category is not passed as a query-string parameter. Just remember to use the category query-string parameter that you create with your virtual pageview in the Site Search settings.

Applying Cost Data

The Cost Data feature automatically imports cost data from AdWords into Google Analytics. You *must* enable the Apply Cost Data option to correctly track Google AdWords traffic, otherwise AdWords data could appear as (direct) traffic.

Remember, making changes to any profile setting will not alter the data that has already been processed by Google Analytics. It will affect the data processed after the settings have been changed. There is no way to alter this behavior.

CHAPTER 6

Filters

There is no Google Analytics concept that is more important but less understood than filters. Functionally, filters are business rules. You add them to a profile when you have a business need to modify the data in a profile. For example, it is very common to exclude website traffic generated by internal employees. This data can skew the data generated by actual customers, thus causing incorrect analysis.

You can apply multiple filters to a profile to create data that meets your needs and the needs of your organization.

The key to understanding filters is understanding how Google Analytics structures website data. I discussed this earlier in Chapter 3; if you have not read that chapter, please do so.

There are two types of filters in Google Analytics: predefined filters and custom filters. *Predefined filters* are common filters that most people use. Google has bundled these common filters together and simplified their implementation.

Custom filters are different. You need to do all the configuration work when creating a custom filter. While it can be challenging, custom filters truly offer you advanced control over the data in your profiles.

In general, custom filters and predefined filters work on the same premise. Filters involve three components:

- Filter field
- Filter pattern
- Filter type

As Google Analytics processes site data, it executes the filters that have been applied to the profile. When a filter executes, Google Analytics compares the filter pattern against the filter field and, if the pattern matches any part of the field, the filter performs an action. When the action occurs, the data in the profile is changed. Figure 6-1 shows the representation of the three parts of a filter in the Custom Filter interface.

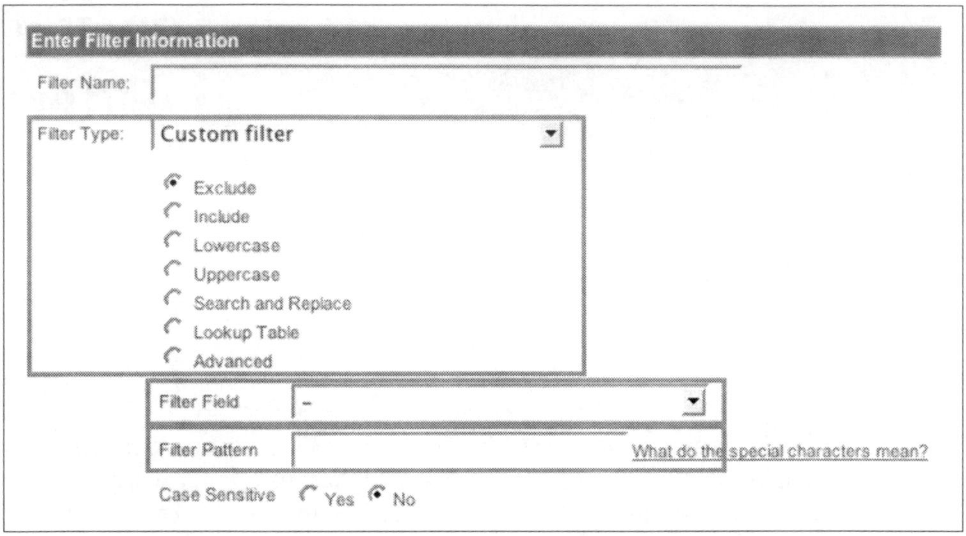

Figure 6-1. The three primary parts of a filter

Let's look at each part of a filter in more detail.

Filter Fields

The first part of a filter is the filter field. These data elements are created when Google Analytics processes the data in the logfile (Figure 3-1). Each filter field is an attribute of a pageview in Google Analytics. There are many different filter fields in Google Analytics, each of which you can use to create a filter. You can find a complete list of filter fields and what they represent in the Google Analytics support documents at *http: //troni.me/aNak8f*.

Table 6-1 lists some of the most common filter fields.

Table 6-1. The most commonly used filter fields

Filter field	Description
Request URI	The Request URI is created using the information in the location bar of the browser. Google Analytics removes the subdomain, the hostname, and the domain extension. Everything remaining becomes the request URI.
Hostname	This is the primary domain and subdomain (if present) listed in the location bar of the visitor's browser.
Visitor IP address	The IP address of the person visiting your website. While this field is available for use in filters, it is not visible. The value of the IP address, which is protected by the Google Analytics privacy policy, cannot be displayed in reports.

Each field represents a piece of data that can have many values. For example, the Visitor City field can contain Boston, San Francisco, Seattle, etc. To find the different values stored in a field, use the Google Analytics reports. As mentioned previously, each report is constructed using a field, so all the values in a field are displayed in the report built from that field.

Filter Patterns

The second part of a filter is the filter pattern. The pattern is applied to the filter field and if the pattern matches *any part* of the field, the pattern returns a positive result, thus causing an action to occur. The patterns used in Google Analytics are called regular expressions.

A *regular expression* is a set of characters that represents a larger set of data. These characters may be standard alphanumeric characters (like letters or numbers) or special characters (like the * or +). You can find more information about regular expressions in Appendix B.

Filter Type

The final part of a filter is the filter type. The filter type is the action applied to the data if the filter pattern matches the filter field. There are seven different types of filters, each with a distinct function.

Include/Exclude Filters

Include/exclude filters are the most common custom filters in Google Analytics. They're also the easiest to understand. The action for an include filter is *inclusion*. This means that if the regular expression matches the filter field, the data is included in the profile.

Exclude filters operate in the opposite manner. If the filter pattern matches the filter field, the data will be excluded from the profile.

Include/exclude filters are extremely powerful because you can use them to segment your data in different ways. For example, to analyze the visitation habits of visitors from California, create an include filter like the one shown in Figure 6-2.

The result of this filter is that all data stored in the profile and displayed in the reports is for visitors from California (the Visitor Region field stores the U.S. state name).

Figure 6-3 shows a similar example that uses an include filter for visitors from New York.

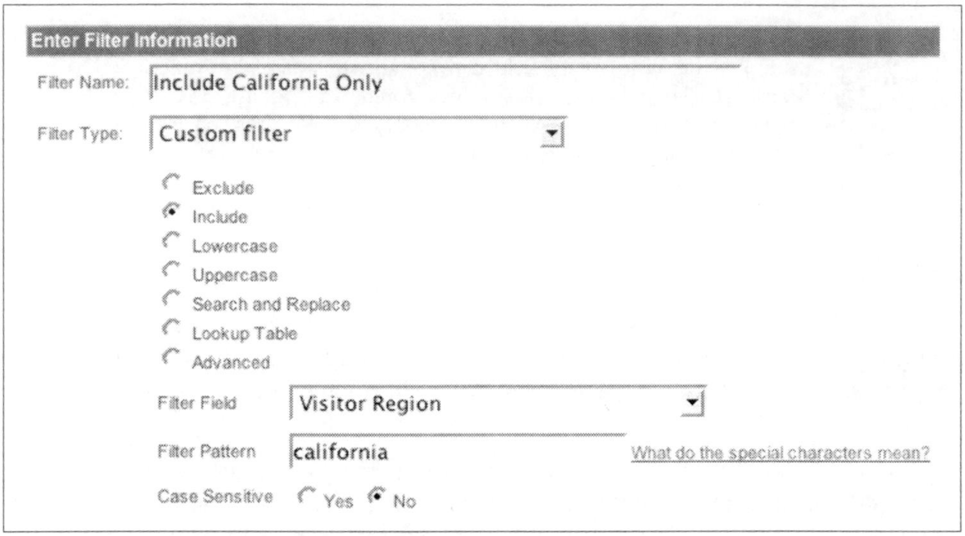

Figure 6-2. An include filter that lets in data from California

Figure 6-3. A filter to include visitors from New York

Now, how would you include visitors from either of two places, New York and California? The answer is not as easy as applying two filters to the profile.

When more than one filter is applied to a profile, they are executed sequentially, in the order they are listed. The output from one filter is used as the input to the next filter.

Applying two filters to a profile, one to include visitors from New York and one to include visitors from California, would not work because the first filter (e.g., New York) would naturally exclude all results from the filter pattern of the second filter (e.g., California). To combine the functionality of these two filters, use a single filter like the one shown in Figure 6-4.

Enter Filter Information

Filter Name: Include New York

Filter Type: Custom filter

- Exclude
- Include
- Lowercase
- Uppercase
- Search and Replace
- Lookup Table
- Advanced

Filter Field Visitor Region

Filter Pattern New York|California

Case Sensitive Yes No

Figure 6-4. A filter to include visitors from either New York or California

This filter uses a regular expression to indicate that the Visitor Region must be New York *or* California.

Search and Replace Filters

The search and replace filter is a simple tool for replacing one piece of data with a different piece of data. This is most often used to replace long, unreadable URLs with more human-readable information.

Search and replace filters are slightly different than other filters, because they do not have a filter pattern. Instead, they have a search string, which is the same as a filter pattern.

When you apply a search and replace filter to a profile, the filter searches the filter field for the search string. If the search string is found in the filter field, the filter replaces the *first occurrence* of the search string with the replace string. Figure 6-5 illustrates a basic search and replace filter.

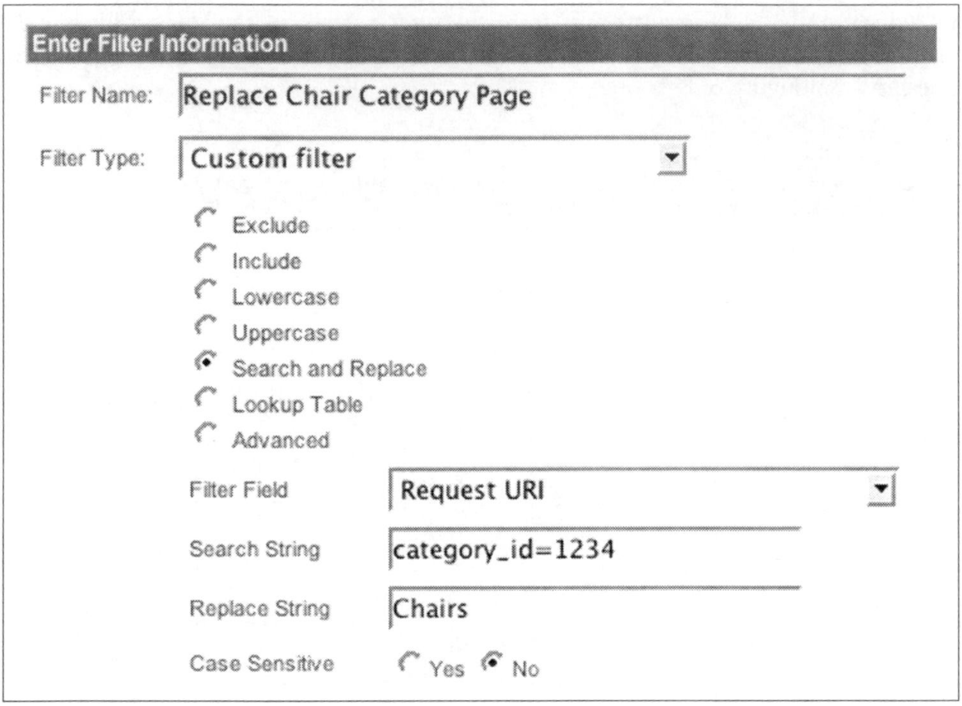

Enter Filter Information	
Filter Name:	Replace Chair Category Page
Filter Type:	Custom filter ▼

    ○ Exclude
    ○ Include
    ○ Lowercase
    ○ Uppercase
    ◉ Search and Replace
    ○ Lookup Table
    ○ Advanced

Filter Field	Request URI ▼
Search String	category_id=1234
Replace String	Chairs
Case Sensitive	○ Yes ◉ No

Figure 6-5. A basic search and replace filter

This filter searches the Request URI field for the pattern *category_id=1234.* If the search string is found in the request URI, 1234 will be replaced with the string "Chairs."

 The Replace String field is standard text. It is not a regular expression.

While the search and replace filter may seem like a savior, capable of transforming obscure, unreadable URLs into easily accessible data, it is difficult to scale it. For example, suppose you would like to replace all category ID numbers with the name of the category. You would need a search and replace filter for each category ID and you would need to remember to add a new filter every time you create a new category.

Search and replace filters are best used when you need to simply tweak one or two pieces of data.

 The first match in the Filter Field is replaced with the Replace String. So if there are any other filters attached to a profile, and those filters use the same filter field as the search and replace filter, those filters may not work if the search and replace filter first modifies the value in the filter field.

Lowercase/Uppercase Filters

Lowercase/uppercase filters (Figure 6-6) are different from other filters in that they do not require a filter pattern, only a filter field. Simply put, a lowercase or uppercase filter changes the selected filter field to all lowercase characters or all uppercase characters, respectively.

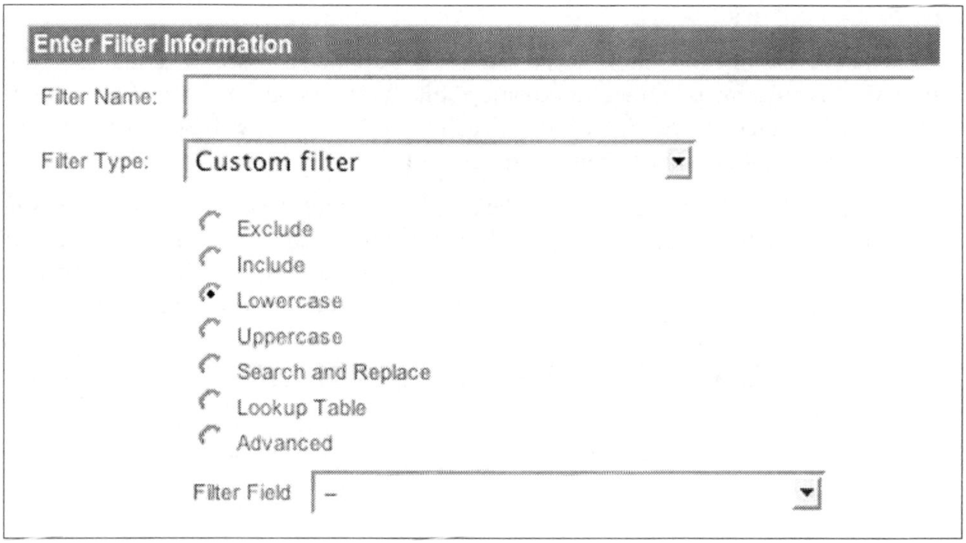

Enter Filter Information

Filter Name:

Filter Type: Custom filter

- Exclude
- Include
- ● Lowercase
- Uppercase
- Search and Replace
- Lookup Table
- Advanced

Filter Field: –

Figure 6-6. Lowercase filter setup form; uppercase filters have the same settings

So, when might you use this filter? Some web servers, particularly Microsoft IIS servers, create pageviews with mixed-case URLs. Being case-sensitive, Google Analytics will create multiple line items for the same physical page in various reports.

For example, the URLs *http://www.cutroni.com/default.asp* and *http://www.cutroni.com/Default.asp* will generate the same page for the visitor, but Google Analytics will create two line items in the Top Content report, one for *default.asp* and one for *Default.asp*. Obviously, these are the same page and should be tracked as a single line item. A lowercase filter forces the filter field—in this case, the request URI—to a consistent case, thereby consolidating all versions of the same page into a single line item in the Google Analytics reports.

 Another good use of the lowercase/uppercase filter is for keywords. Many users want to see "Analytics," "analytics," and "ANALYTICS" as the same keyword, not three different keywords. An uppercase or lowercase filter, applied to the Campaign Term field, will change the keyword case.

Advanced Profile Filters

Advanced filters can alter data fields by combining elements from multiple filter fields, removing unnecessary parts of filter fields, or replacing one filter field with another.

Unlike most filters, advanced filters have two filter fields: Field A and Field B. Along with each filter field, there is an Extract field. The Extract field is synonymous with the filter pattern; it is the regular expression that is applied to the filter field. You don't have to use both fields.

So, Extract A is applied to Filter A, and Extract B is applied to Filter B. The reason the filter patterns are named Extract for advanced filters is that you can remove, or extract, certain parts of Field A and Field B from each field. You specify the part of the filter field to extract using a regular expression.

In Figure 6-7, two fields are referenced: the Request URI for Field A and the Hostname for Field B. The pattern applied to filter Field A means, "capture all the characters in the request URI and retain those characters." The pattern applied to filter Field B means, "match all the characters in the Hostname and retain those characters."

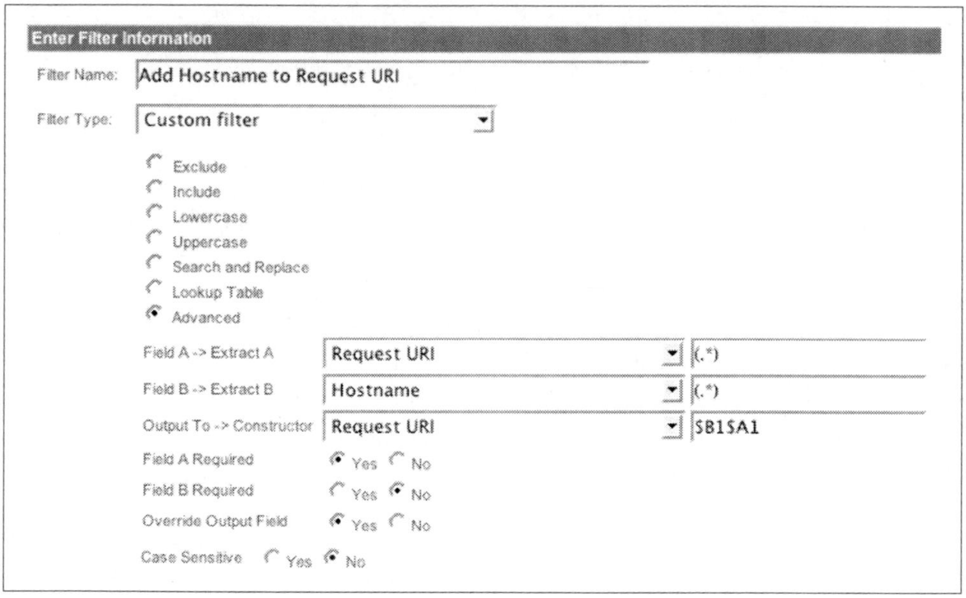

Figure 6-7. Advanced filters have two filter fields, Field A and Field B; you can extract a portion of each filter field using regular expressions

What happens to characters that are captured in the Extract fields? Google Analytics allows you to combine the extracted pieces of data and output them to another field, called a constructor. The constructor is simply a field. After capturing a part of the field, Google Analytics stores it in memory. Data extracted in Extract A starts with A, and data extracted from Extract B starts with B.

You can configure Google Analytics to permanently change the value of the constructor field using the Override Output Field setting (Figure 6-7). When you select Yes, the data in the constructor overwrites the Output Field value, so any reports that are created using that field will be modified. Table 6-2 shows the process of combining two extracts and exporting them to a constructor.

Table 6-2. Combining two extracts to modify an existing field

Captured part of request URI [$A1]	Captured part of hostname [$B1]	Output to constructor: request URI [$B1$A1]
/pages/index.html	www.websharedesign.com	www.websharedesign.com/pages/index.html

If this filter is applied to a profile, all the reports based on the request URI change; they will include the hostname as well as the directory path, filename, and query-string variables. Figure 6-8 shows the results in the Top Content report.

blog.websharedesign.com/blog-post-jun-17-2008.html

www.websharedesign.com/main-site-about-us.html

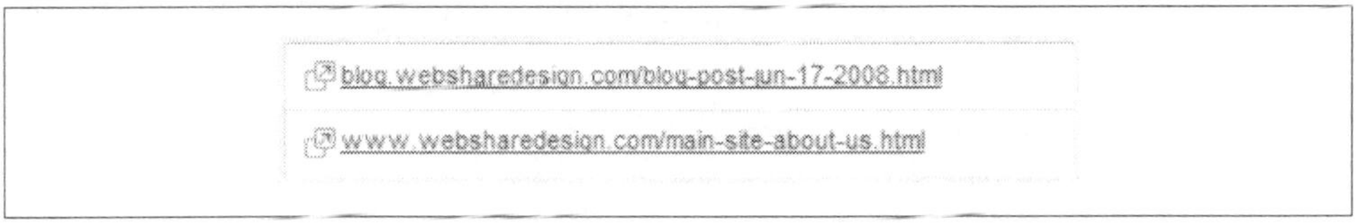

Figure 6-8. Results of an advanced filter in the Top Content report

 Modifying the Request URI field using an advanced filter, or any filter, can affect other settings in Google Analytics, most notably goal settings (goals are calculated using the request URI). So, if any filter changes the request URI, check the effect on your goal settings.

There are two other settings specific to an advanced filter: Field A Required and Field B Required. These settings control the logic of an advanced filter. When you set either one of these options to Yes, Google Analytics will place some constraints on when the filter takes action. If Field A does not match the pattern in Extract A, the filter will not execute. The same goes for Field B.

Now let's take a look at another example. Let's say we'd like to modify how some of our campaign data looks in the reports. We want to concatenate a number of different fields so we can see more data in a single report.

We can use a series of filters, passing data from one filter to the next, to modify a constructor.

This first filter will be an advanced filter to add the Campaign Name field to the Campaign Medium field. Don't worry about the function of the fields I'm referencing, I'll explain them in more detail later. Just know that they are pieces of data that identify where visitors came from.

While this filter is similar to the previous filter, there is one main difference. The constructor used in this filter, shown in Figure 6-9, is Custom Value 1. This is a temporary field that is not used by any reports; it is used only when you need to pass data from one filter to another.

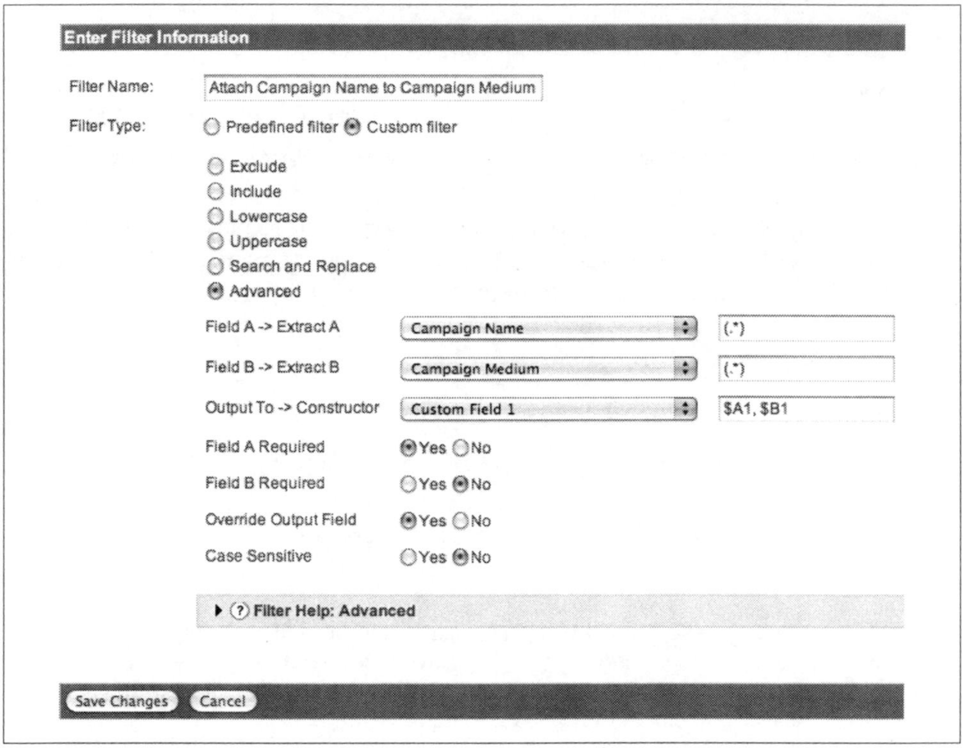

Figure 6-9. Advanced filter that stores data in a temporary variable

The second filter, shown in Figure 6-10, adds another piece of campaign information, the Campaign Source, to the value we previously created and stored in Custom Value 1. I've used a comma in the constructor to separate the Campaign Name and Medium from the Campaign Source. I like using the comma to separate values because if I export the data from Google Analytics into Excel, I can easily import it as a comma-separated file and Excel will place each value in a new column.

I've chosen to use the User Defined field as the constructor for the second filter, because I want to place the data in a field that is not used by any major reports. If we use one of the campaign fields here, like Campaign Name, all of the reports based on the Campaign Name will contain the new value rather than the Campaign Name. So, by using User Defined, we only change the User Defined report. If you use the User Defined report, consider using a different field for the constructor, creating an additional profile for this filter, or creating a duplicate profile and applying this filter to the new profile.

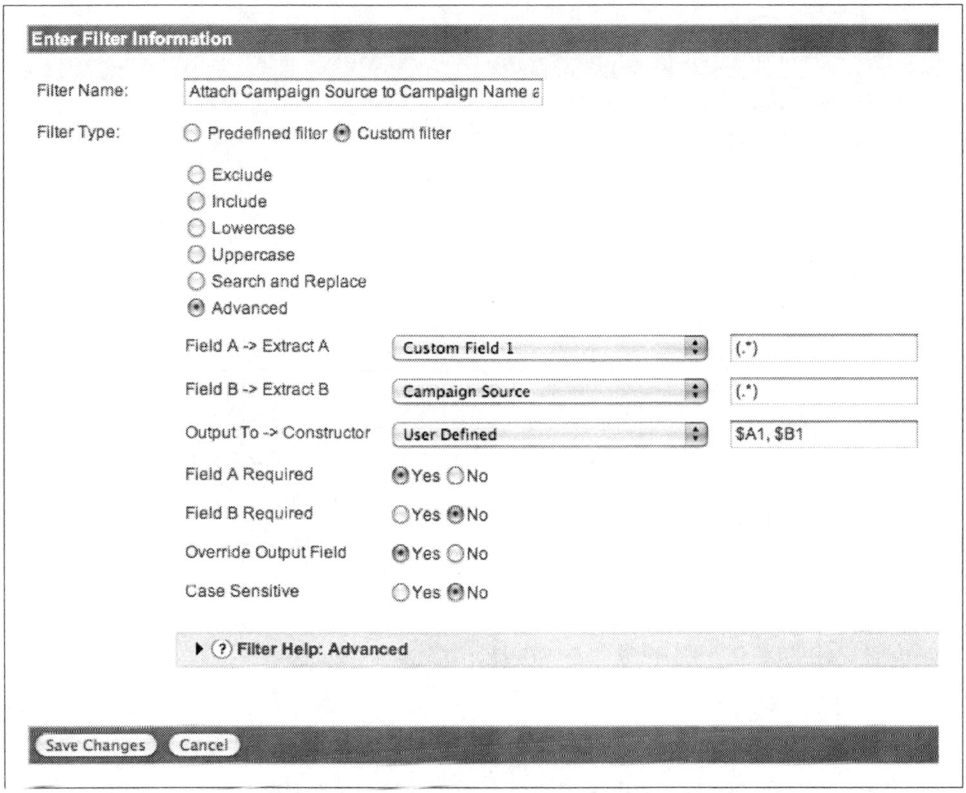

Enter Filter Information

Filter Name: Attach Campaign Source to Campaign Name a

Filter Type: ○ Predefined filter ● Custom filter

                    ○ Exclude
                    ○ Include
                    ○ Lowercase
                    ○ Uppercase
                    ○ Search and Replace
                    ● Advanced

                    Field A -> Extract A   [Custom Field 1 ▼]   [(.*)]

                    Field B -> Extract B   [Campaign Source ▼]   [(.*)]

                    Output To -> Constructor   [User Defined ▼]   [$A1, $B1]

                    Field A Required   ● Yes ○ No

                    Field B Required   ○ Yes ● No

                    Override Output Field   ● Yes ○ No

                    Case Sensitive   ○ Yes ● No

                    ▶ (?) Filter Help: Advanced

[Save Changes] [Cancel]

Figure 6-10. Advanced filter that modifies a value stored in a temporary variable

Remember, for these filters to work correctly, the filters must be in a specific order.

Google Analytics does not limit the number of extracts for each field. It can capture multiple parts of Extract A and Extract B. If more than one part of an extract is captured, then Google Analytics will retain multiple variables for that extract field. Figure 6-11 shows multiple values extracted from a filter field.

The filter shown in Figure 6-11 will capture all of Extract A (the entire hostname) and two parts of Extract B. The first part of Extract B that will be captured is *v* followed by any character. The second extract from Field B will be everything after */23/*.

Next, the filter will combine the hostname with the two extracts from Field B. It will separate the values in *$A1*, *$B1*, and *$B2* with slashes. The characters entered in the Output To field are literal characters, meaning they appear exactly as you type them, except for those that begin with *$A* or *$B*.

This type of filter is especially useful if you want to remove part of your request URI.

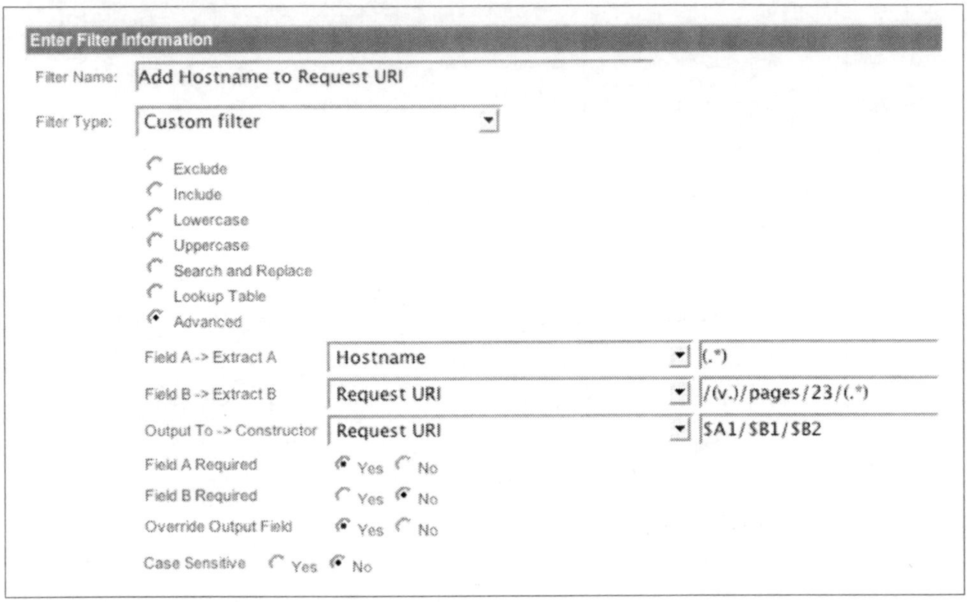

Figure 6-11. Multiple extracts using an advanced filter

Predefined Filters

Before we conclude our discussion on filters, I should mention that Google Analytics includes a number of predefined filters that encapsulate the most common filters. Google has simplified the implementation by changing the form interface and limiting the functionality. But predefined filters, like custom filters, work the same way. A pattern is applied to a piece of information (a field) and if the pattern matches any part of the field, the filter will execute.

There are basically two types of predefined filters: include filters and exclude filters. Like the standard include and exclude filters, these filters will include or exclude data from a profile. Unlike custom filters, predefined filters only offer three fields, shown in Figure 6-12:

- The *traffic from the domains* filter uses a reverse lookup to identify the domain of site visitors. The visitor domain excluded is the domain associated with the visitor's IP address.

- The *traffic from the IP addresses* filter removes all data coming from the addresses entered into the filter pattern. This filter is used primarily to exclude internal company resources.

- The *traffic to the subdirectories* filter isolates data for a specific directory on the website. This filter is usually used to create profiles that focus on one part of the website.

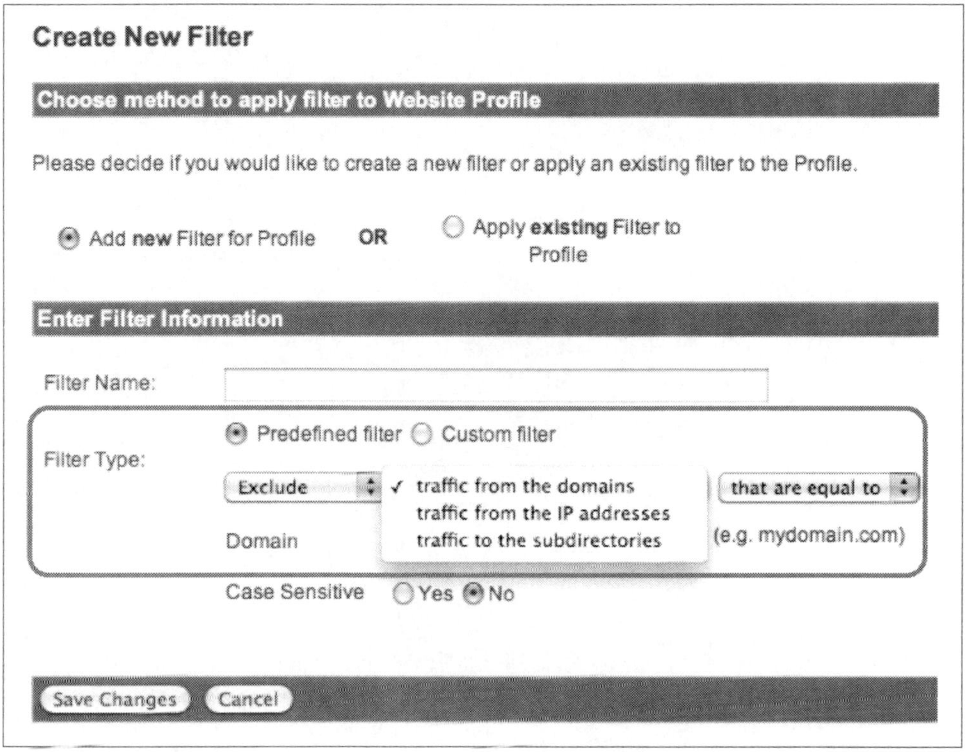
Create New Filter
Choose method to apply filter to Website Profile
Please decide if you would like to create a new filter or apply an existing filter to the Profile.
Add new Filter for Profile
OR
Apply existing Filter to Profile
Enter Filter Information
Filter Name:
Filter Type:
Predefined filter
Custom filter
Exclude
traffic from the domains
traffic from the IP addresses
traffic to the subdirectories
that are equal to
Domain
(e.g. mydomain.com)
Case Sensitive
Yes
No
Save Changes
Cancel

Figure 6-12. Predefined filters

In addition to choosing a field, you must also enter a value or pattern for Google Analytics to apply to the field. You enter the pattern in the text box below the field. If you choose the domain field, Google Analytics will change the name of the field to Domain.

Once you enter the pattern, you must specify how Google Analytics applies it to the field. Unlike custom filters, where you can use a regular expression to specify how the pattern must match the field, predefined filters have simple match-type options in a drop-down list. These options include:

- Are equal to (the pattern must match the field exactly)
- Begin with (the field must start with the pattern)
- End with (the field must end with the pattern)
- Contain (the field must contain the pattern)

You'll notice that regular expressions are nowhere to be found. Regular expressions are complicated, and Google offers these options to make filters accessible to those who don't know how to use regular expressions.

CHAPTER 7

Tracking Conversions with Goals and Funnels

Another common profile configuration is the creation of goals and funnels. Goals provide a way to measure conversions in Google Analytics. Hands down, specifying goals is the most important configuration step because they directly align business outcomes on your website with your Google Analytics configuration.

A conversion occurs when a site visitor completes a task on your website. Why is this important? Every website exists for a reason. It is not enough to measure traffic to your website, you want to measure how often visitors complete the tasks and processes that you create.

While it is not necessary to create any goals or funnels, it is highly recommended. How else will you measure business outcomes on your website if you do not configure goals?

Goals

A goal can be almost any visitor activity on your website. This includes viewing a specific page, spending a certain amount of time, or viewing a minimum number of pages during a visit.

Time on Site

Time on Site goals are triggered when a visitor's visit reaches or does not reach a certain length of time on your site. Time on Site goals are useful when trying to understand if visitors are engaging with your content.

Figure 7-1 shows the configuration page for Time on Site goals. All you need to do is define a time and whether the visit must be greater than or less than that time.

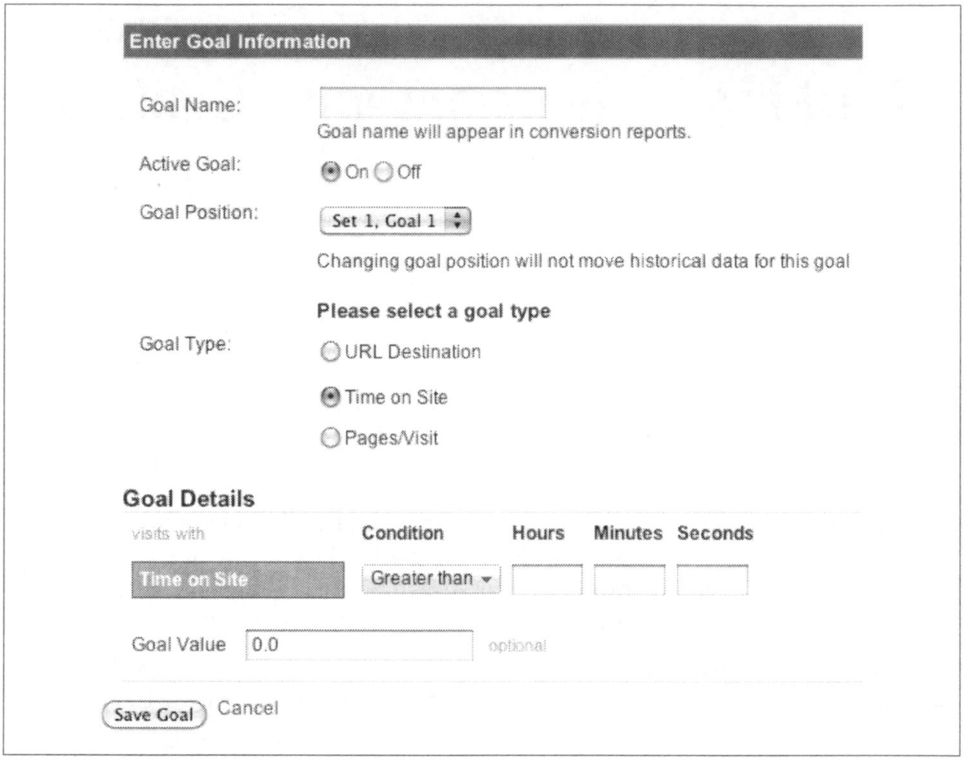

Figure 7-1. Creating a Time on Site goal

How Google Analytics Calculates Time

Google Analytics measures time based on communications from the visitor's browser to the Google Analytics server. Google Analytics calculates time on site by subtracting the first timestamp it receives from the last timestamp it receives. Timestamps are sent with each pageview, event, and transaction.

This does not take into account the amount of time the visitor might spend on the final page of a session. As a result, the time-on-site metric may not be 100% accurate. Unfortunately, this is a natural limitation of how Google Analytics calculates time.

Pages per Visit

Like Time on Site goals, pageview goals are triggered when a visitor's visit reaches a specific threshold. For Pages per Visit goals, the conversion is triggered when a visit exceeds or does not exceed a certain number of pageviews.

Figure 7-2 shows the configuration page for a Pages per Visit goal. You need to specify a number of pages and whether the visitor must view more or fewer than that number of pages to trigger the goal. That's it.

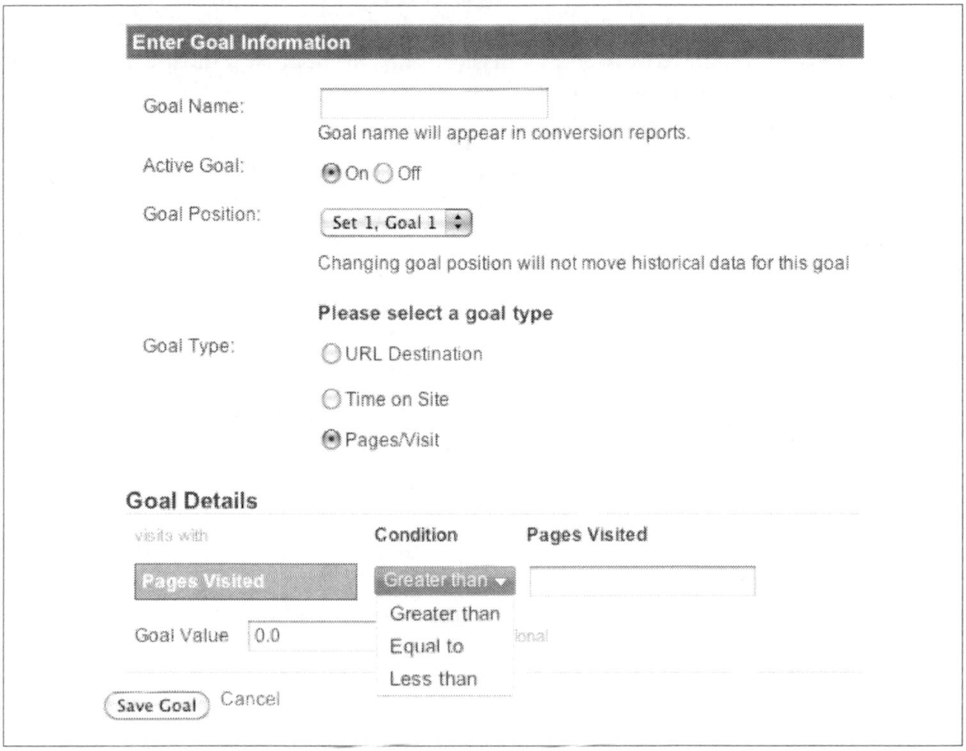

Figure 7-2. Creating a Pages Visited goal

Google Analytics can trigger a pageview goal if the visitor reaches a certain number of pages or if the visitor fails to reach a certain number of pages. I like to think of the latter as a negative goal, which identifies what percentage of traffic did not view a minimum number of pages.

Measuring a negative goal can often be handy when reporting data. Normally, we report how successful the website is. For example, we commonly say the website has a 5% conversion rate. In the case of a publisher, this may mean that 95% of website visitors view 6 pages on the site. Managers and other decision makers need this data, but may react differently to being told that 95% of website traffic does not convert, or does not view a certain number of pages. Showing a "negative" value can really help stress the opportunity that is being missed.

URL Destinations

A URL destination goal is simply a pageview that indicates the visitor has completed some type of high-value task. This process could be filling out a contact form, purchasing a product, or downloading a file. Each process usually concludes with some type of thank-you page. In Google Analytics, this is called the goal page.

As Google Analytics processes site data, it increments the goal counter each time a goal page is viewed. If the goal page is viewed multiple times during a single session, the goal counter is incremented only once. This is important, because it means that a visitor can convert only once during a visit.

There are multiple ways to define a URL destination goal, depending on the complexity of your website. The easiest way to create a goal is to paste the URL of your goal page into the Goal URL field. Next, eliminate the domain name until all that is left is the information after the *.com*, *.net*, or *.org*. Figure 7-3 shows the goal setup form and the Goal URL field.

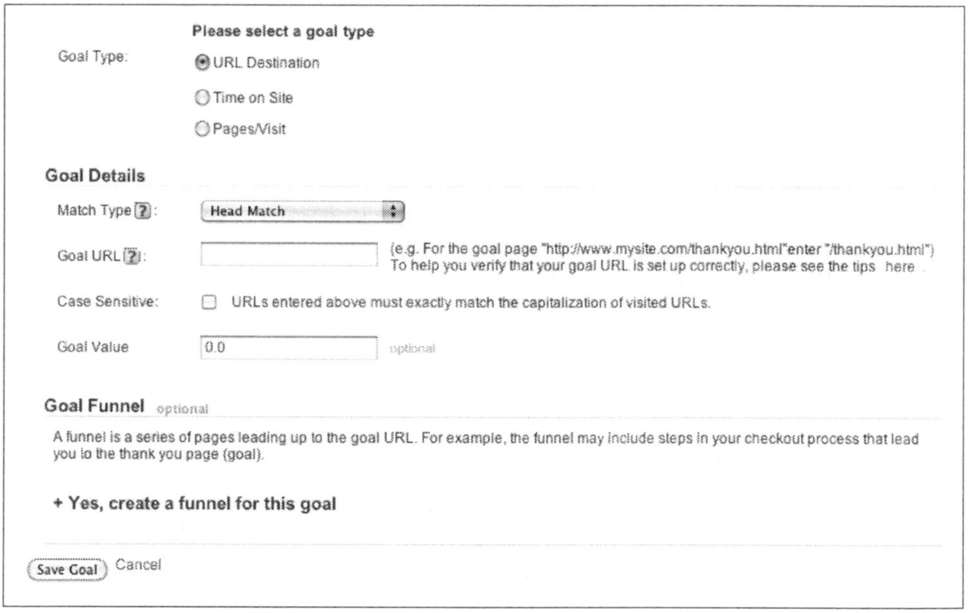

Figure 7-3. Paste the URL for a goal page in the Goal URL text field

So, if your checkout process ends with *http://www.cutroni.com/thankyou.php*, enter *http://www.cutroni.com/thankyou.php* in the Goal URL field and delete *http://www.cutroni.com*.

Additional Goal Settings

When creating any type of goal, you can specify a goal name. This name will identify the goal in the reports.

You can also start and stop goal tracking using a goal's Activate Goal setting. Selecting Off will stop tracking for the goal. Why would you want to turn a goal off? Google Analytics will calculate an overall website conversion rate using all of the goals you define for the site. If you create a goal that is temporary, say for a specific campaign, it could artificially skew the overall site conversion rate if you leave the goal on after the campaign ends.

The Goal Value field will monetize non-e-commerce goals. For example, if each contact form submitted by a user is worth $100, enter 100 in the Goal Value field. Google Analytics will use 100 to calculate ROI and other revenue-based calculations. If e-commerce tracking is active for a profile and you would like to use e-commerce data for your goals, simply leave this field blank. Google Analytics will insert a zero and use the value from e-commerce transactions as the goal value.

The Match Type setting can facilitate goal tracking for sites with complicated URLs. For example, if each goal page contains a unique customer identifier, it will be impossible to paste a single URL into the Goal URL field. Because each URL will be unique, your website will not have a single URL that represents the goal page. Google Analytics provides three different match types that you can use to match multiple URLs and resolve goal setup issues. Each match type changes how Google Analytics applies the value in the Goal URL field to the data it processes:

Exact Match
> The value in the Goal URL field must exactly match the URL in the location bar of the visitor's browser.

Head Match
> Use the Head Match setting when a small part of the goal URL differs from one visitor to another. When using a head match, the URL in the visitor's browser must exactly match the value in the goal URL. However, if there is any additional data at the end of the visitor's URL that does not appear in the Head Match value, the goal will still count. The head match will match both path data and query-string variables.

Regular expression
> This setting defines a goal using a regular expression rather than a static URL. If the regular expression entered into the goal URL matches any part of the URL in a visitor's browser, the goal is counted. This includes path information and query-string variables. To learn more about regular expressions, see the Appendix B.

In reality, Google Analytics uses the Request URI field when calculating goals. So, even if you specify the entire URL as the goal URL with an exact match, Google Analytics will use only the request URI. This also means if you modify the request URI using a filter (like an uppercase or lowercase filter), you may need to change your goal URL.

For example, if a goal is defined as */pages/html/thankyou.html*, but an advanced filter has been applied to the profile and changes the request URI to */pages/thankyou.html*, the goal will not work.

The Case Sensitive and Match Type settings are applied to the values in both the Goal URL and funnel steps. It is impossible to use a match type of Exact Match for your funnel steps and a Regular Expression match type for the Goal URL.

If you're not seeing any URL destination conversions in your reports, try checking the Top Content report. Remember, destination URL goals simply reflect a visitor viewing a page on a website. Google Analytics only counts one conversion per visit. This means that the number of unique pageviews for a particular page should match the number of conversions for the goal defined with the same URL. If you can't find your goal URL in the Top Content reports, the page is probably not tagged.

If you can't find the goal URL in the Top Content report, you may have defined the goal incorrectly. Make sure there are no leading or trailing whitespaces in the Goal URL field. If you're using a regular expression to define the goal, make sure the regular expression is correct.

Google Analytics calculates conversion rate based on the number of visits that completed a goal divided by the total number of visits. Some organizations prefer to calculate conversion rate based on unique visitors. Unfortunately, the conversion rate calculation methodology cannot be changed. Google Analytics will always calculate conversion rate based on visits.

Tracking Defined Processes with Funnels

A *funnel* is a series of predefined steps, or pages, that a visitor must pass through before reaching a goal. Not every goal will have an associated funnel, so defining a funnel is optional. You should set up a funnel if you have a predefined process that the visitor must go through before reaching the goal. This can be as simple as specifying the form used on a Contact Us page or as complicated as a multistep checkout process. The funnel is an excellent way to visualize problems in the conversion process (Figure 7-4).

I absolutely love funnel analysis. Why? It is a very simple way to identify problems related to conversions. Think about it: if a visitor is in a funnel process, you have already spent a lot of money on that visitor! You've spent marketing dollars to get him to the site and more money developing the site and content to convince him to convert. Once he's in the funnel, he's literally a few clicks away from conversion. Don't blow it now! Make sure your funnel works. Improvements to the funnel process can pay immediate dividends.

Setting up a funnel is very similar to setting up a destination URL goal. Each step in a funnel is a pageview. To create a funnel, paste the URL for each page in your process into the setup form (shown in Figure 7-5) and remove the domain name and extension.

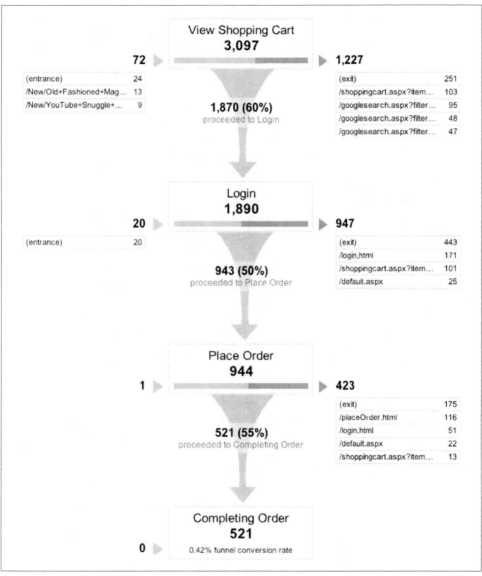

Figure 7-4. The Funnel Visualization report shows where visitors left a defined process

If you enable the Required step feature, visitors who complete the goal without starting at the first step in the defined funnel will not be shown as completing the goal in the funnel visualization report. However, the conversion will be recorded in other conversion reports.

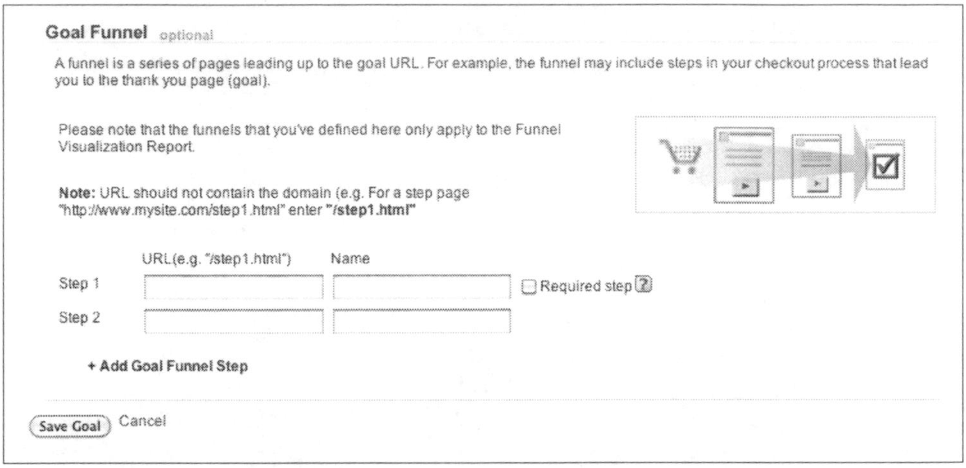

Goal Funnel optional

A funnel is a series of pages leading up to the goal URL. For example, the funnel may include steps in your checkout process that lead you to the thank you page (goal).

Please note that the funnels that you've defined here only apply to the Funnel Visualization Report.

Note: URL should not contain the domain (e.g. For a step page "http://www.mysite.com/step1.html" enter "/step1.html"

	URL (e.g. "/step1.html")	Name	
Step 1			☐ Required step ⑦
Step 2			

+ Add Goal Funnel Step

(Save Goal) Cancel

Figure 7-5. The funnel setup form

In reality, the Required step means that the visitor *must* go through step 1 of the funnel prior to conversion. This can be an incredibly powerful tool. For example, if you want to identify the influence that a certain page has on conversion, you can create a one-step funnel in which step 1 is the page you want to evaluate and the goal is the page that you want to understand step 1's influence on. When the Required step is enabled, Google Analytics will only track a conversion when the visitor sees step 1 at some point prior to conversion.

Google Analytics will backfill your predefined funnels. For example, if you have a four-step funnel and a visitor completes only the first step and the final step, Google Analytics will indicate that the visitor actually hit every step in the funnel process.

You can define destination URL goals and funnels for data created by _trackPage view(). Remember, if you pass a value to _trackpageview(), that data becomes a pageview in Google Analytics. These pageviews can then be defined as goals by placing the value passed to _trackPageview() in the Goal URL field. This is very handy if you want to configure Google Analytics to track a visitor's action as a goal. For example, you may want to create a goal for a visitor clicking on a button or an outbound link.

It is also common to use _trackPageview() to create virtual pageviews for the steps in the funnel. If all the steps in your funnel process have the same URL, you will need to create a virtual pageview for each step and use those virtual pageviews in the funnel settings.

CHAPTER 8

Must-Have Profiles

There are some filters and profiles that you should be using regardless of how you have configured Google Analytics. Each additional profile can help create segmented sets of data that can aid in analysis. Remember, you cannot create a new profile and reprocess historical data, so it's best to create these profiles during the initial setup, even if you don't need them right away. As you use Google Analytics, you will become a better analyst, your data needs will change, and these profiles will become useful.

Profile Roles

You should create several different profiles to perform different functions, such as protecting your data and controlling access.

Raw Data Profile

The raw data profile should have no configuration. It should be an unmodified set of data that you can use if other profiles fail. Hopefully you will never need to use it!

Master Profile

The master profile should not be altered or changed. You should initially refine the data within this profile as much as possible using filters and profile settings, and once the data is considered accurate, you should not change the profile unless absolutely necessary. If you must make any changes to a master profile, test them first using a test profile.

Test Profile

I recommend you create at least one test profile within your Google Analytics account. Use this profile to test goal settings, profile settings, and filters before you apply them to a master profile. Remember, an incorrect profile setting will forever change the data in your Google Analytics reports. Take the time to test all of your settings before applying changes to a production set of data.

Access-Based Profiles

Access to data in Google Analytics is controlled at the profile level. If there are certain employees who should only see certain data, you must create a filtered profile and assign access to the appropriate users.

For example, if a specific sales team should only see web traffic from a certain part of the country, you can create a profile with an include filter for the specific geographic region, then grant access to the appropriate users.

Using Profiles to Segment Data

There are some reports in Google Analytics, like the Funnel Visualization report, that you cannot segment, even with the advanced segmentation feature. However, it is often helpful to segment this data to identify issues and patterns related to a particular segment of traffic. For example, you may discover that paid search traffic navigates the funnel more successfully than organic traffic.

You can collect this kind of information by creating profiles for specific campaigns, sources, or mediums. By applying a filter to a profile, like the one shown in Figure 8-1, you can segment the data in every report for the profile.

You should include filters to perform the following operations on your master data profile:

- Exclude internal traffic
- Include valid traffic
- Force request URI to lowercase
- Force campaign parameters to lowercase

Exclude Internal Traffic

Any profile that analyzes visitor data should have a filter that excludes internal company traffic. Traffic generated by you or your employees dilutes true visitor data. A simple predefined filter (exclude all traffic from an IP address range), shown in Figure 8-2, will remove internally generated traffic.

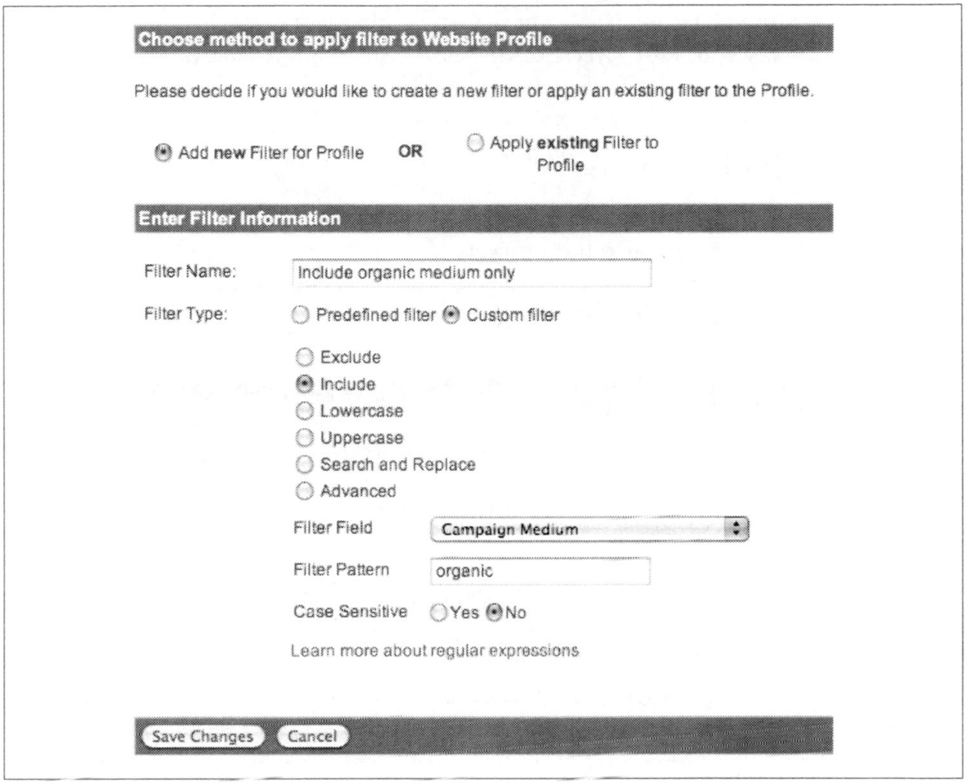

Figure 8-1. An include filter for a specific medium

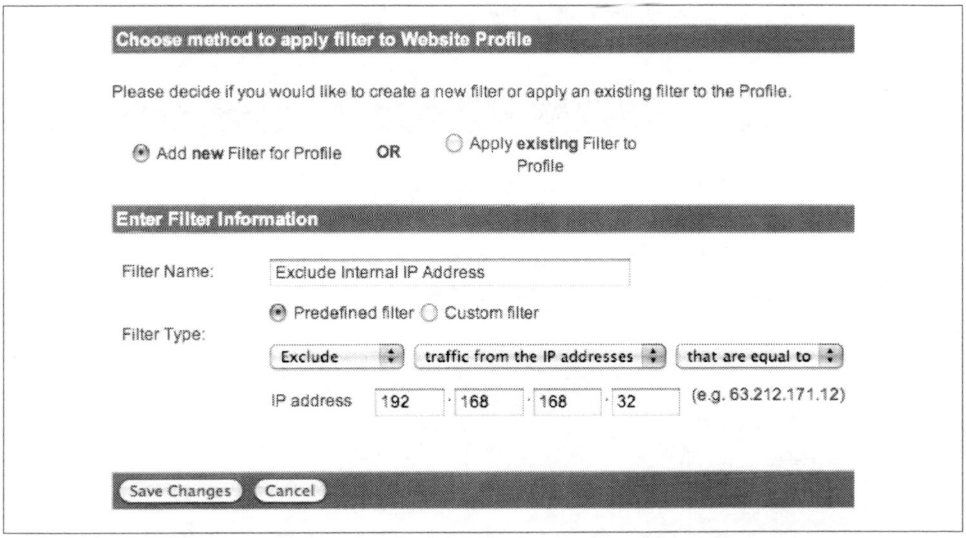

Figure 8-2. A predefined filter to exclude internally generated traffic from an IP range

Remember, you may have external contractors or other workers who do not have the same IP address as your employees. In this case, set up additional filters for each IP address.

Include Valid Traffic

The Google Analytics tracking code is plain text, and visitors can copy it by viewing your website HTML. A visitor could copy your tracking code and install it on a different website. This would artificially inflate the data within your profiles. To prevent this, use a simple include filter (Figure 8-3) based on your website hostname.

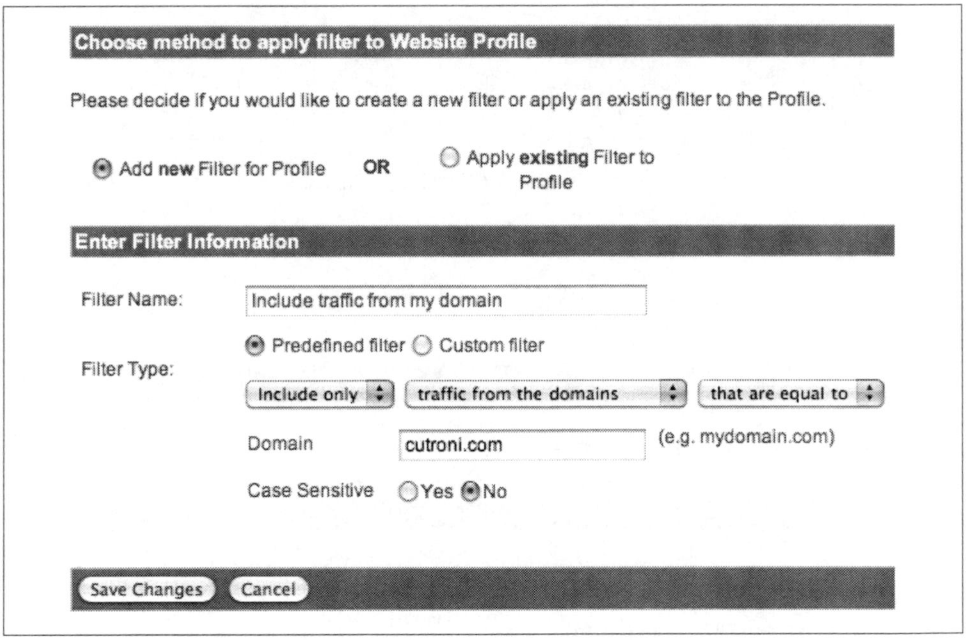

Figure 8-3. An include filter that ensures valid website traffic

The hostname attached to data coming from the perpetrator's site will have a different hostname. This filter will remove it from the profile.

While it is highly unlikely that this will happen, it is best to ensure the quality of your data using this filter. If you do not wish to use this filter and your data seems abnormally high, check the Visitors→Network Properties→Hostnames report. If any inappropriate hostnames are listed, it may be that your tracking code was hijacked and installed on an unrelated website.

Force Request URI to Lowercase

A lowercase filter (Figure 8-4) applied to the Request URI field is a simple way to ensure consistent, normal data in your content reports. Remember, the GATC is case-sensitive, so if your website has mixed-case URLs, you may have duplicate data in your Top Content report.

Choose method to apply filter to Website Profile

Please decide if you would like to create a new filter or apply an existing filter to the Profile.

◉ Add **new** Filter for Profile   **OR**   ○ Apply **existing** Filter to Profile

Enter Filter Information

Filter Name: Force Request URI to lowercase

Filter Type: ○ Predefined filter ◉ Custom filter

     ○ Exclude
     ○ Include
     ◉ Lowercase
     ○ Uppercase
     ○ Search and Replace
     ○ Advanced

     Filter Field   Request URI

     ▶ (?) **Filter Help: Lowercase > Request URI**

(Save Changes) (Cancel)

Figure 8-4. Filter to force the Request URI to lowercase, thus normalizing the Top Content report

Force Campaign Parameters to Lowercase

Just as we applied a lowercase filter to the Request URI, it is also a good idea to apply a lowercase filter to your campaign parameters. This helps normalize campaign parameters, which can be configured by multiple users. Figure 8-5 shows the basic settings for lowercase campaign filter. You should also force the following fields to lowercase:

- Campaign Name
- Campaign Medium
- Campaign Source
- Campaign Term
- Campaign Content

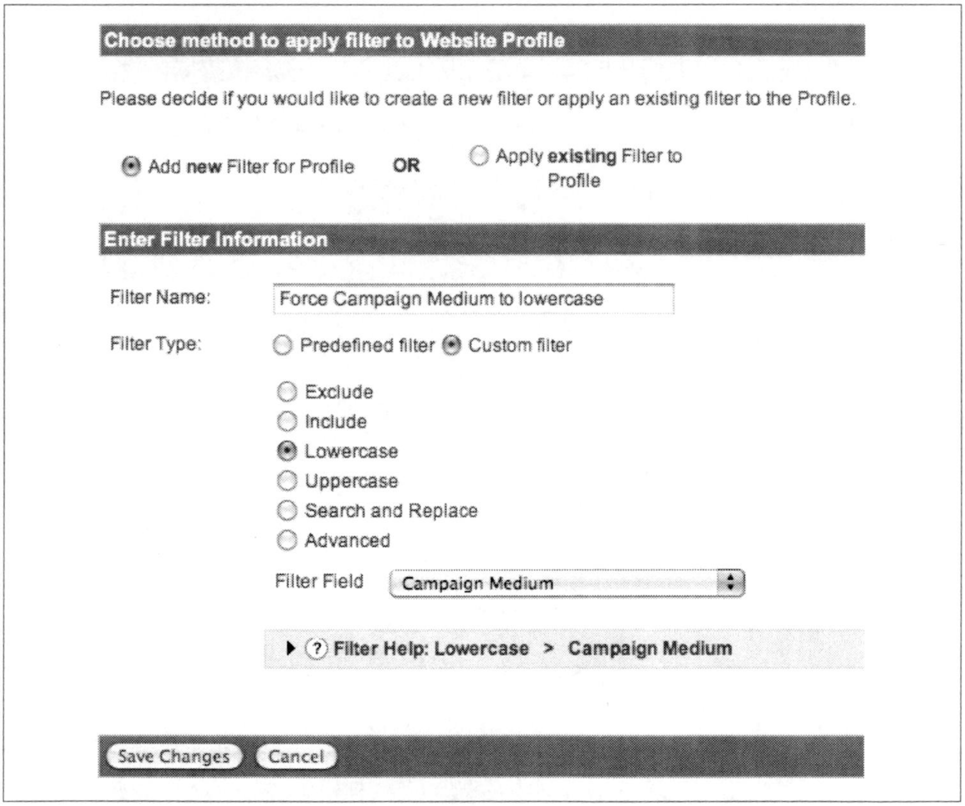

Figure 8-5. A lowercase filter to force the campaign medium to lowercase

In addition to these above filters, there are many other profile settings you should configure on the master data profile. Make sure you've configured the following profile settings for accurate data:

- Exclude query-string parameters
- Default page
- Website URL

Keeping Track of Your Configuration Changes

There are many things that can change the data in your Google Analytics account, such as new marketing campaigns and website changes. For example, if you launch a new cost-per-click (CPC) campaign, your website traffic will probably increase. Understanding why the data changes is the reason we do web analytics. It is imperative that you know if any nonbusiness forces are affecting your data. Specifically, did modification to your Google Analytics settings cause the data to change?

There are two basic ways to track changes to your Google Analytics configuration. The first is to use a simple *change log* to track the changes made to your Google Analytics settings. Create a very basic spreadsheet and record every modification that you and other employees make to a profile configuration. The change log does not need to be complicated. Start with the following columns:

- Date
- Profile name
- Name of the person who made the change
- Description of the change

It may also be useful to create a business activity log to record major business events that could affect the data. Such activities might be when you launch or stop an AdWords campaign or send an email blast to your email list. A spreadsheet is an easy way to determine if a business decision changed site traffic.

An alternate way to track changes is to use the Annotations feature in Google Analytics (shown in Figure 8-6). The Annotations feature lets you add small notes to your Google Analytics data.

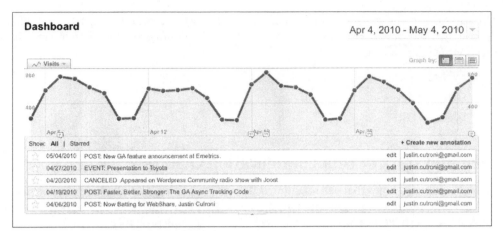

Figure 8-6. The Google Analytics Annotations feature

Annotations that you create are listed under the data over time graph. Simply enter a note (in fewer than 160 characters) and choose the visibility (Figure 8-7). Shared annotations are visible to anyone who has access to the profile. Private annotations are visible only to you. When tracking configuration changes, it's best to make the annotations public.

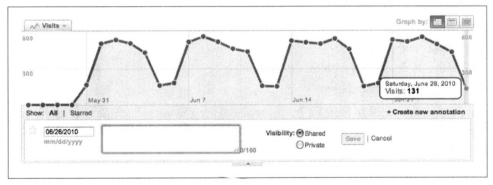

Figure 8-7. Creating an annotation

CHAPTER 9

Marketing Campaign Tracking

Another important part of setting up Google Analytics correctly is configuring online marketing campaign tracking. Unlike other configuration steps, you don't perform marketing campaign tracking in the Google Analytics administrative interface or on your website. Marketing campaign tracking involves changing the links used in your marketing activities. I'll discuss this more in a moment.

The reason marketing campaign tracking is so important is that, by default, Google Analytics places your visitors in three basic referral segments:

Search Engines
  Visitors who access your site by clicking on a search engine result (both organic search and paid search)

Referral
  Visitors who access your site by clicking on a link on some other website

Direct
  Visitors who go directly to your website by typing the URL in their browsers

While these segments are useful, they do not identify paid marketing activities. You want to measure paid marketing activities so you can better understand if they're successful, and you can only do this via marketing campaign tracking. Using marketing campaign tracking adds a fourth segment to the list above: campaigns.

How It Works

Marketing campaign tracking is based on the process of link tagging, which is adding extra information to the destination URLs used in your online ads. The extra information is actually a number of query-string parameters that describes a marketing activity. Figure 9-1 illustrates how link tagging identifies your marketing activity.

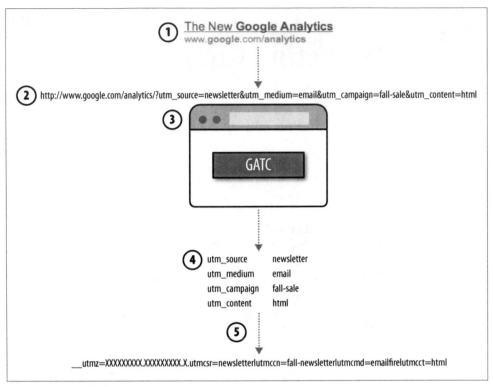

Figure 9-1. How link tagging works

It all begins with the ad that the visitor sees (step 1). In this example, the ad is an email message. When the visitor clicks on the link in the email message, she is sent to a destination URL. Within the destination URL there are additional query-string parameters that Google Analytics uses to identify the ad (step 2).

When the visitor arrives on the website landing page, the `_trackPageview()` method begins to execute. It examines the URL in the browser's location bar and identifies the query-string parameters that identify the URL as a campaign URL. `_trackPageview()` then copies the query-string parameters (step 3). Next, it splits the query-string parameters into their name-value pairs, reformats them (step 4), and finally stores them in the `__utmz` cookie (step 5). Because the values are now stored in a cookie, any actions the visitor performs can be linked to the ad that drove her to the site. This includes conversions and transactions.

Let's dig a bit deeper and learn about the specific query-string parameters used in link tagging. Table 9-1 shows how the tagged link in Figure 9-1 was created.

Table 9-1. A destination URL before and after link tagging

Link before tagging	Link after tagging
www.amazon.com/	www.amazon.com/?utm_campaign=fall-sale&utm_medium=email&utm_source=newsletter&utm_content=html

Parsing the tagged link in Table 9-1 identifies the query-string parameters used for identifying the ad. Table 9-2 identifies each parameter and value.

Table 9-2. The name-value pairs extracted from a destination URL

Parameter	Value
utm_source	newsletter
utm_medium	email
utm_campaign	fall-sale
utm_content	html

Now I'll describe what each parameter actually represents:

utm_campaign
> The name of the marketing campaign. Think of this as a bucket. It holds all of the marketing activities in some bigger effort. For example, buying some keywords on Google, running some banner ads, and sending out an email blast may all be part of the marketing plan for some type of sale. These three activities, which are all part of the same campaign, can be grouped together for easy reporting.

utm_medium
> The medium is the mechanism, or how the message is delivered to the recipient. Some popular mediums are email, banner, and cost-per-click (CPC).

utm_source
> Think of the source as the "who." With whom are you partnering to distribute the message? If you're tagging CPC links, the source may be Google, Yahoo!, or MSN. If you're using banner ads, the source could be the name of the website where the banner ad is displayed.

utm_term
> The search term or keyword that the visitor entered into the search engine. This value is set automatically for organic links, but must be set manually for CPC links. By default, Google Analytics will track the bid term and not the search term.

utm_content
> The version of the ad. This is used for A/B testing. You can identify two versions of the same ad using this variable. This parameter is not included in Figure 9-1.

Not all parameters are required. In fact, the only required parameter is utm_source. However, the core parameters are utm_campaign, utm_source, and utm_medium. To get the most value out of campaign tracking, you should always use these three when tagging a marketing link. You should use `utm_term` for tracking paid search advertising and use `utm_content` for A/B testing of different variations of ads (different banners, paid search ads, types of email, etc.) or collecting any additional information.

You must set the value for each parameter. In reality, it does not matter what value you use. Whatever data you use will appear in Google Analytics. However, it is important to follow some basic guidelines:

- Keep the value short.
- Use alphanumeric characters and avoid whitespaces.
- Make sure you and other Google Analytics users can understand the value when it shows up in a report.
- Be consistent with your naming and capitalizations.

The value of each parameter becomes a field or dimension in Google Analytics. Table 9-3 lists each query-string parameter and the field and dimension created from each.

Table 9-3. Google Analytics campaign parameters and the fields and dimensions created from the parameters

Query-string parameter	Field	Dimension
utm_campaign	Campaign name	Campaign
utm_medium	Campaign medium	Medium
utm_source	Campaign source	Source
utm_content	Campaign content	Ad content
utm_term	Campaign term	Keyword

We all know that Google Analytics creates reports by comparing a dimension to various metrics. The reports display the dimension values exactly as they appeared in the query-string parameter. For example, the Traffic Sources report is built from the Campaign Source dimension and the Campaign Medium dimension. These reports segment website traffic and conversions, thus providing insight into which marketing activities are working.

The Traffic Sources report, shown in Figure 9-2, shows website data based on Campaign Source and Campaign Medium.

The Source/Medium column contains all values for `utm_source` and `utm_medium`. But also notice that it contains other values that look familiar, specifically referral and source. Google Analytics actually assigns a medium and source value even if the visitor did not arrive via a campaign. The Traffic Sources report is a good way to look at marketing partners and evaluate their performance across all campaigns.

Table 9-4 shows the default values for direct, organic, and referral traffic.

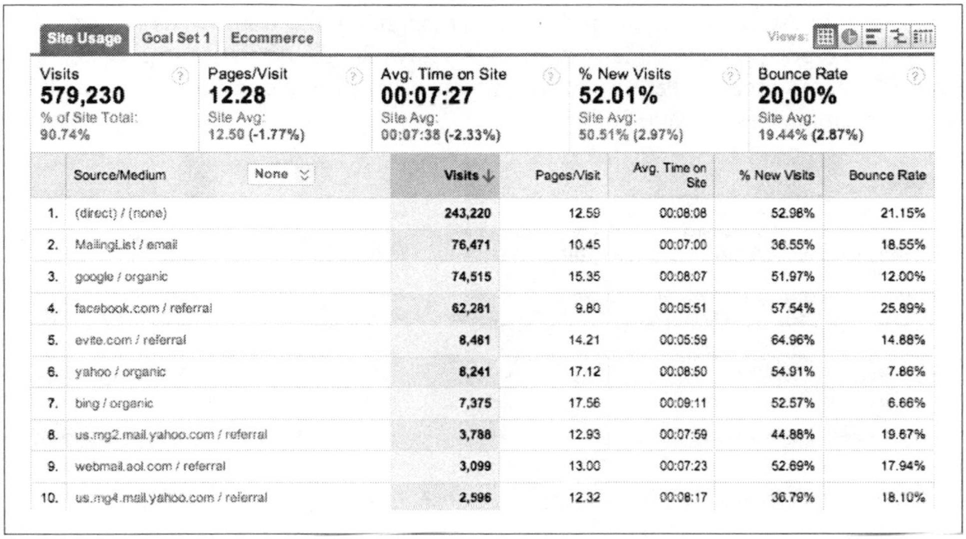

Site Usage | Goal Set 1 | Ecommerce | Views:

Visits	Pages/Visit	Avg. Time on Site	% New Visits	Bounce Rate
579,230	12.28	00:07:27	52.01%	20.00%
% of Site Total: 90.74%	Site Avg: 12.50 (-1.77%)	Site Avg: 00:07:38 (-2.33%)	Site Avg: 50.51% (2.97%)	Site Avg: 19.44% (2.87%)

	Source/Medium (None)	Visits ↓	Pages/Visit	Avg. Time on Site	% New Visits	Bounce Rate
1.	(direct) / (none)	243,220	12.59	00:08:08	52.98%	21.15%
2.	MailingList / email	76,471	10.45	00:07:00	36.55%	18.55%
3.	google / organic	74,515	15.35	00:08:07	51.97%	12.00%
4.	facebook.com / referral	62,281	9.80	00:05:51	57.54%	25.89%
5.	evite.com / referral	8,481	14.21	00:05:59	64.96%	14.88%
6.	yahoo / organic	8,241	17.12	00:08:50	54.91%	7.86%
7.	bing / organic	7,375	17.56	00:09:11	52.57%	6.66%
8.	us.mg2.mail.yahoo.com / referral	3,788	12.93	00:07:59	44.88%	19.67%
9.	webmail.aol.com / referral	3,099	13.00	00:07:23	52.69%	17.94%
10.	us.mg4.mail.yahoo.com / referral	2,596	12.32	00:08:17	36.79%	18.10%

Figure 9-2. The Traffic Sources report

Table 9-4. Default values for various traffic types

Traffic type	Campaign value	Source value	Medium value
Direct	(Not set)	(Direct)	(None)
Organic	(Not set)	The name of the search engine	Organic
Referral	(Not set)	The domain that referred the visitor	Referral

Why Link Tagging is Critically Important

Google Analytics will *always* try to place an untagged link in one of the default traffic source buckets (direct, referral, or organic). All CPC links that are *not tagged* will be categorized as organic. This can artificially inflate organic traffic volume, leading to incorrect analysis.

All untagged links that appear in email marketing will appear as direct traffic or referral traffic. Visitors who click on email links using a mail application like Outlook or Outlook Express will appear as direct traffic, while those who use a hosted mail application like Gmail or Yahoo! Mail will appear as a referral. Check your Traffic Sources→Referring Sites report. Do you see a large number of referrals from mail.yahoo.com or mail.google.com?

If you're using Google AdWords, it is highly recommended that you enable autotagging. If you are using other paid search systems, like Yahoo! Search Marketing or Microsoft adCenter, you must tag the destination URLs manually. This is absolutely vital to configuring Google Analytics correctly.

If you're interested in a single marketing campaign, try the Campaigns report. The Campaign report, shown in Figure 9-3, shows how Google Analytics segments visitation data based on a marketing campaign, which have been identified using the link-tracking parameters in Table 9-3.

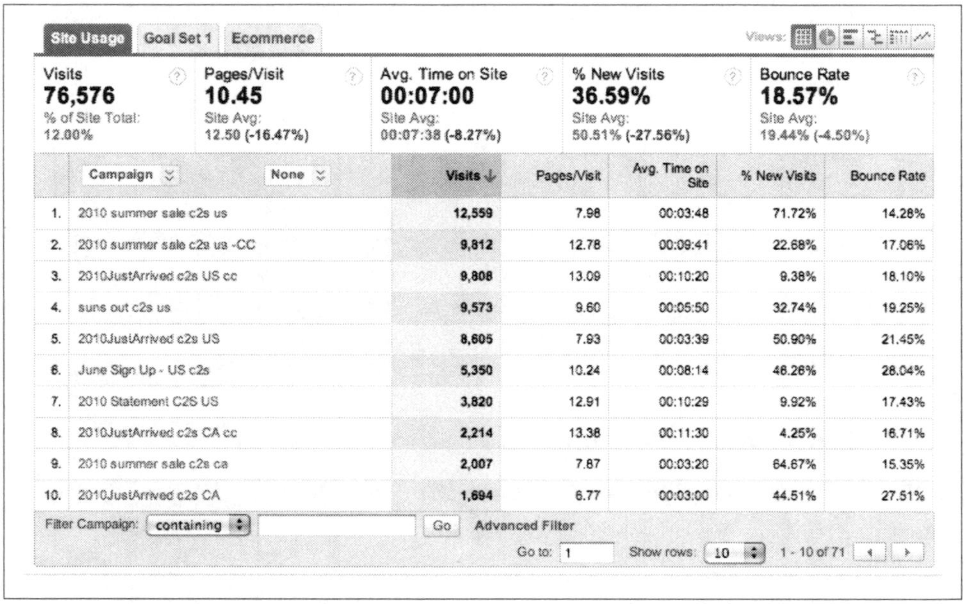

	Campaign	None	Visits ↓	Pages/Visit	Avg. Time on Site	% New Visits	Bounce Rate
1.	2010 summer sale c2s us		12,559	7.98	00:03:48	71.72%	14.28%
2.	2010 summer sale c2s us -CC		9,812	12.78	00:09:41	22.68%	17.06%
3.	2010JustArrived c2s US cc		9,808	13.09	00:10:20	9.38%	18.10%
4.	suns out c2s us		9,573	9.60	00:05:50	32.74%	19.25%
5.	2010JustArrived c2s US		8,605	7.93	00:03:39	50.90%	21.45%
6.	June Sign Up - US c2s		5,350	10.24	00:08:14	46.26%	28.04%
7.	2010 Statement C2S US		3,820	12.91	00:10:29	9.92%	17.43%
8.	2010JustArrived c2s CA cc		2,214	13.38	00:11:30	4.25%	16.71%
9.	2010 summer sale c2s ca		2,007	7.87	00:03:20	64.67%	15.35%
10.	2010JustArrived c2s CA		1,694	6.77	00:03:00	44.51%	27.51%

Figure 9-3. The Campaign report automatically segments site data based on the utm_campaign value

How to Tag Links

The process of link tagging is simple. Start by identifying the marketing information to be placed in the query-string parameters. Specifically, you need to identify the campaigns, mediums, sources, and potential keyword and content values. Remember, you use the keyword parameter only for tracking search-based ads, and you use the content parameter to identify different variations of an ad. I recommend using some type of spreadsheet to organize the information.

Once you have identified all the parameter values, modify the destination URLs to include the parameters and values. Place a question mark at the end of the destination URL followed by the query-string parameter. Separate each name-value pair using an ampersand (&).

If the destination URL already has query-string parameters, simply add the Google Analytics parameters at the end of the URL. Separate the Google Analytics parameters from the existing parameters using an ampersand (&).

Link tagging works for any destination URL. So, if you are sending out email messages or using banner ads, you should be tagging the destination URLs. In general, anytime you pay for advertising on the Web, you should try to tag the URL used in the ad.

A very simple way to tag your advertising links is to use the Google Analytics URL Builder (Figure 9-4), a free tool on the Google Analytics support site (*http://troni.me/ 9VYkUN*).

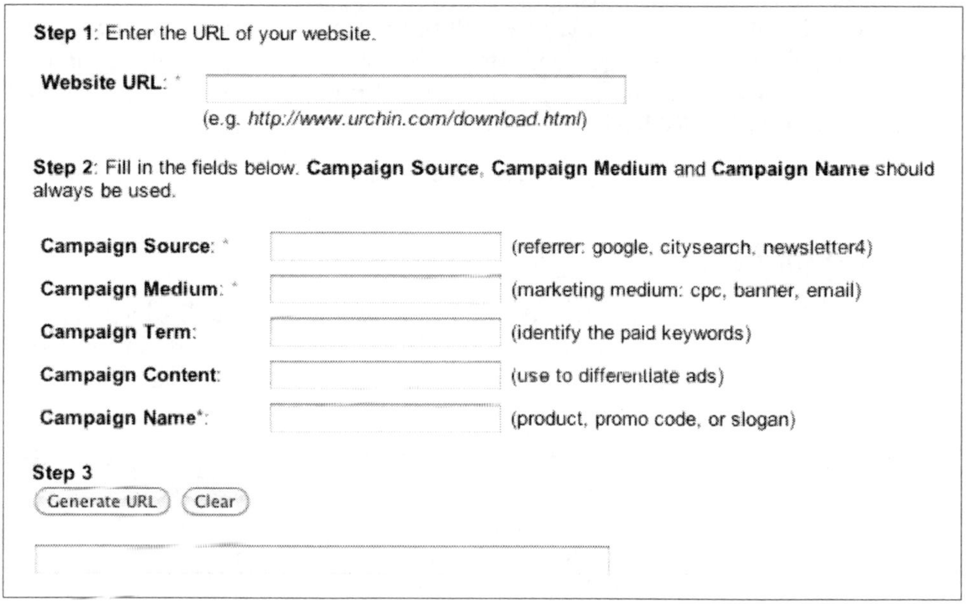

Step 1: Enter the URL of your website.

Website URL: *

(e.g. *http://www.urchin.com/download.html*)

Step 2: Fill in the fields below. **Campaign Source**, **Campaign Medium** and **Campaign Name** should always be used.

Campaign Source: *   (referrer: google, citysearch, newsletter4)

Campaign Medium: *   (marketing medium: cpc, banner, email)

Campaign Term: (identify the paid keywords)

Campaign Content: (use to differentiate ads)

Campaign Name*:   (product, promo code, or slogan)

Step 3

(Generate URL) (Clear)

Figure 9-4. Google Analytics URL Builder

Simply enter your desired values for each campaign tracking parameter and a destination URL. Then click Generate URL and the tool will return a tagged URL. This process works, but it has two issues.

First, this process can be incredibly time-consuming if you have a lot of links to tag. Second, the URL Builder does not store or record any previous values used for the campaign tracking parameters. Remember, it is critical to be consistent when choosing values for your campaign parameters. A better method is to use a Google spreadsheet to record campaign tracking values. I like using a Google spreadsheet, as you can share it among different teams within an organization. You can find a sample spreadsheet at *http://troni.me/cyXEOh*.

If your website uses redirects on the landing pages, there may be trouble with link tagging. The Google Analytics campaign tracking parameters must be present in the URL of the landing page. If the URL does not physically contain the tracking parameters, the visit will not be attributed to the correct ad.

It is recommended that you test your campaign tracking. Before sending out an email blast, send it to a group of coworkers and ask them to click on the links. Check your Google Analytics data in one to three hours and look for the data.

Some destinations URLs, especially those used in email marketing, can be very long even before the addition of the Google Analytics campaign tags. One trick is to create a custom URL on your website and direct all traffic from the email campaign to the custom URL. Then, when a visitor lands on the custom URL, dynamically append the campaign tracking variables to the URL. You can do this using application-level code or a simple HTML META refresh tag.

Another option is to use a URL-shortening tool, like bit.ly, TinyURL.com, or Cli.gs.

Tracking AdWords

The Google Analytics and Google AdWords systems are connected, which leads to some wonderful data. To take advantage of this interconnectivity, you must link the AdWords account to the Analytics account. There are two steps to linking an AdWords and Analytics account: enable autotagging and apply cost data.

The Auto-tagging feature (shown in Figure 9-5) automates the link tagging process that you can use to track a CPC campaign. When Auto-tagging is enabled, Google AdWords automatically adds a query-string parameter to the destination URL that identifies Google AdWords as the referring site. While this parameter is different than the standard link tagging parameters, it does the same thing. The query-string parameter is named gclid and contains a random value.

The second benefit of linking an AdWords account to an Analytics account is the Apply Cost Data feature (Figure 9-6). If you enable this option, Google Analytics imports your AdWords cost data and uses it in ROI and other calculations. You must enable the Apply Cost Data feature to correctly track AdWords traffic.

If you have inadvertently linked a Google AdWords account to a Google Analytics account, you can manually unlink the accounts in AdWords. Log in to your AdWords account, select the reporting tag, and choose Google Analytics. Choose "Edit account settings" at the top of the page and use the Unlink AdWords Account link to unlink the entire account, including all profiles, from the AdWords account.

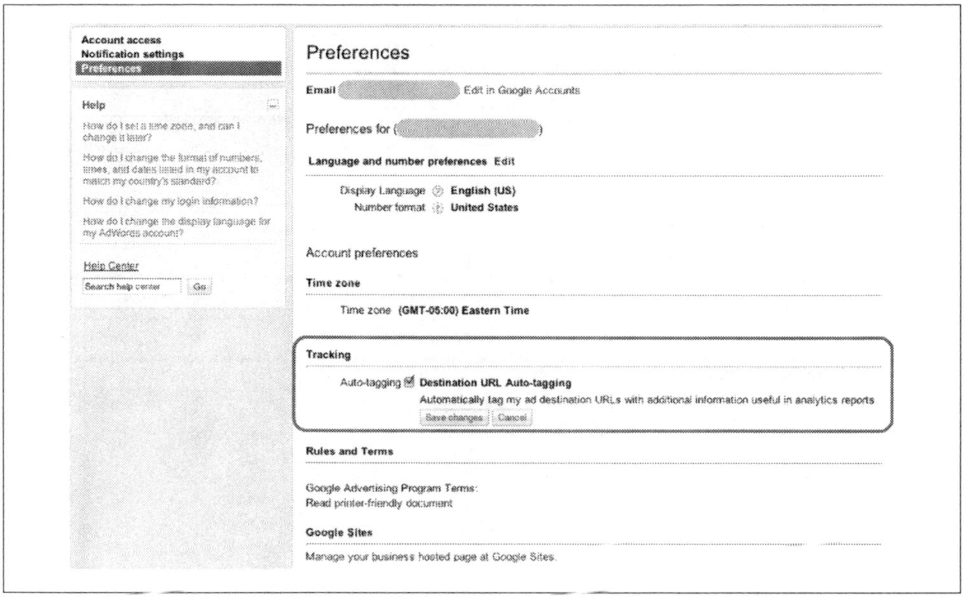

Figure 9-5. Activate the Auto-tagging feature in the Account preferences section of the My Account tab

In some cases, you may want to unlink a specific profile within your account from AdWords but keep other profiles linked to the AdWords account. This can be very useful if you need to keep certain employees or contractors from seeing your ad expenditure.

To unlink a profile from AdWords, navigate to the Profile Information page. There is an option, shown in Figure 9-7, to apply cost data. You can remove the cost data from the profile by removing the check from the checkbox. Cost data will no longer appear in this profile.

Tracking Other CPC Sources

While tracking Google AdWords with Google Analytics is fairly easy, tracking other paid search engines can be challenging, to say the least. The problem with tracking Yahoo! Search Marketing, Bing Search Advertising, and other search tools is that they use keyword-level tracking.

Remember, Google Analytics has a specific parameter, utm_term, to track keywords. However, creating a destination URL for each keyword can be close to impossible if you have a large number of keywords.

To simplify the process, you can use a common feature that most search platforms have: dynamic insertion. Dynamic insertion is a way to replace, in real time, a piece of the destination URL with some piece of information from the visitor's search. This can make it much easier to populate the destination URL with a utm_term tag.

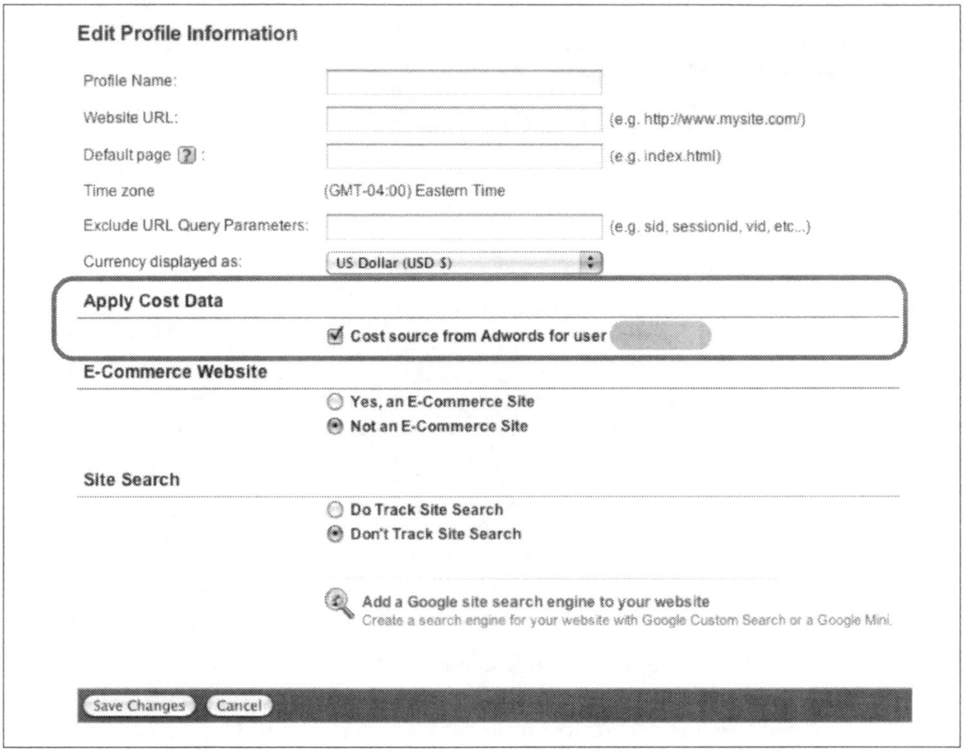

Edit Profile Information

Profile Name:

Website URL: (e.g. http://www.mysite.com/)

Default page ? :   (e.g. index.html)

Time zone   (GMT-04:00) Eastern Time

Exclude URL Query Parameters: (e.g. sid, sessionid, vid, etc...)

Currency displayed as: US Dollar (USD $)

Apply Cost Data

☑ Cost source from Adwords for user

E-Commerce Website

○ Yes, an E-Commerce Site
◉ Not an E-Commerce Site

Site Search

○ Do Track Site Search
◉ Don't Track Site Search

🔍 Add a Google site search engine to your website
    Create a search engine for your website with Google Custom Search or a Google Mini.

(Save Changes) (Cancel)

Figure 9-6. Use the Apply Cost Data option to add your AdWords cost data to Google Analytics

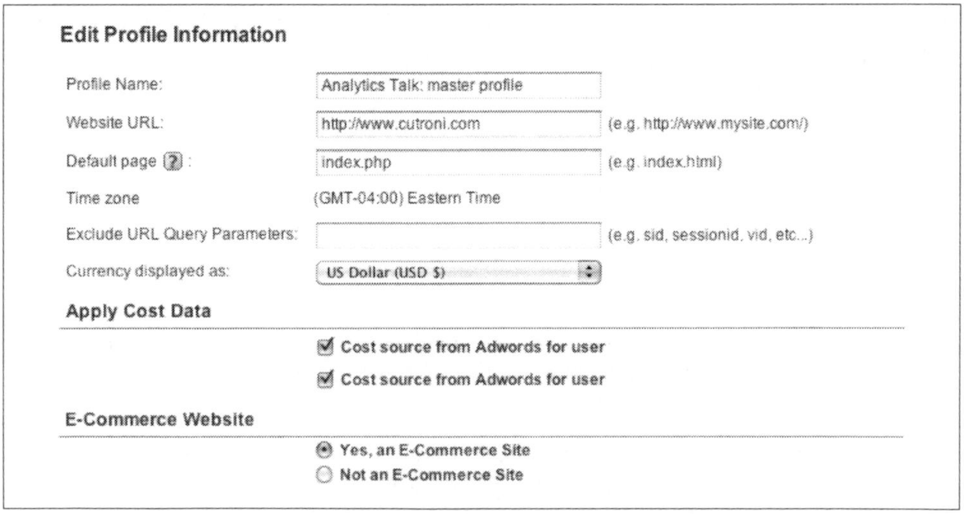

Edit Profile Information

Profile Name: Analytics Talk: master profile

Website URL: http://www.cutroni.com   (e.g. http://www.mysite.com/)

Default page ? :   index.php   (e.g. index.html)

Time zone   (GMT-04:00) Eastern Time

Exclude URL Query Parameters: (e.g. sid, sessionid, vid, etc...)

Currency displayed as: US Dollar (USD $)

Apply Cost Data

☑ Cost source from Adwords for user
☑ Cost source from Adwords for user

E-Commerce Website

◉ Yes, an E-Commerce Site
○ Not an E-Commerce Site

Figure 9-7. You can remove AdWords cost data from an individual profile on a profile-by-profile basis

Each search engine has its own convention for dynamic insertion. Tables 9-5 and 9-6 show some suggestions for values you can use in link tagging.

Table 9-5. Suggested link tagging parameters and values for tracking Bing Search Advertising

Tracking parameter	Value
utm_campaign	YOUR-CAMPAIGN-NAME-HERE
utm_content	m{AdID}
utm_source	msn
utm_medium	cpc
utm_term	{keyword}

Table 9-6. Suggested parameters and values for Yahoo! Search Marketing

Tracking Parameter	Value
utm_campaign	YOUR-CAMPAIGN-NAME-HERE
utm_content	Y{YSMADID}
utm_source	yahoo
utm_medium	cpc
utm_term	{YSMKEY}

If you use a bid management tool, like ClickEquations or SearchRev, to manage your paid search ad expenditure, you can simplify the process. These tools can automatically place certain pieces of information in the destination URL. They can also place a lot of garbage in the campaign tracking parameters.

It's important to understand how your bid management tool integrates with Google Analytics campaign tracking. For example, when using Click Equations, the Campaign name will appear the same way in Google Analytics as it does in ClickEquations. However, when using a tool like SearchRev, the campaign names will be modified, as shown in Figure 9-8.

Tracking Email

Email, like all marketing activities, is a process. This process includes reaching out to an individual with an email message, hoping the recipient opens the message and responds by clicking on a link in the message. You can measure each step in this process. However, Google Analytics can only measure how much website traffic the email message generates. It cannot measure how many people received or opened the message.

You can use link tagging to track email with Google Analytics. As mentioned above, Google Analytics cannot measure what happens in the recipient's inbox. It can only measure what visitors do on the website after clicking on a link in an email message.

	Site Usage	Goal Set 1	Clicks							Views:

Visits	Pages/Visit	Avg. Time on Site	% New Visits	Bounce Rate	Total Goal Completions	Revenue
15,972	**1.30**	**00:00:42**	**91.95%**	**78.92%**	**1,081**	**$0.00**
% of Site Total: 50.55%	Site Avg: 1.28 (1.51%)	Site Avg: 00:00:38 (10.16%)	Site Avg: 92.75% (-0.86%)	Site Avg: 81.34% (-2.98%)	% of Site Total: 60.83%	% of Site Total: 0.00%

	Campaign	None	Visits ↓	Pages/Visit	Avg. Time on Site	% New Visits	Bounce Rate	Total Goal Completions	Revenue
1.	SBUS_____NOSET/G...		5,912	1.32	00:00:34	88.97%	77.33%	496	$0.00
2.	SBUS_____NOSET		1,485	1.17	00:00:33	95.89%	86.46%	81	$0.00
3.	SBUS_____NOSET/SXUS...		618	1.29	00:00:56	94.66%	77.83%	67	$0.00
4.	SBUS_____NOSET/S...		617	1.39	00:00:57	85.25%	72.77%	72	$0.00
5.	SBUS_____NOSET/GXUS...		493	1.33	00:01:00	94.12%	77.48%	63	$0.00
6.	SBUS_____NOSET		436	1.33	00:00:49	88.99%	76.61%	25	$0.00
7.	SBUS__GEO_____NOSET		424	1.26	00:00:57	95.52%	80.90%	0	$0.00
8.	SBUS_____Branded__NOSET		396	1.32	00:00:39	85.35%	78.03%	31	$0.00
9.	SBUS__GEO_____NOSET		372	1.27	00:00:39	95.43%	82.80%	0	$0.00
10.	SBUS_____NOSET/GBUS...		363	1.26	00:00:51	92.84%	83.20%	15	$0.00

Filter Campaign: containing ▢ ▢ Go   Advanced Filter

Go to: 1   Show rows: 10 ▢   1 - 10 of 58 ◄ ►

Figure 9-8. Some tools, like SearchRev, will modify the utm_campaign parameter, making it difficult to read certain reports

Creating a link tagging strategy for tracking email depends on your email marketing strategy. Email marketers often segment their email lists many different ways depending on the type of marketing activity. For example, a company may target parents in a back-to-school campaign and send a parent-themed message to members on the email list who are parents. The Google Analytics measurement strategy should follow this overall marketing strategy and track how well or poorly the "parents" segment of email traffic performed.

When creating your link tagging strategy for email, remember you have four query-string parameters to track email. Try to stuff as much information as you can into these parameters to increase your ability to segment data in Google Analytics.

utm_campaign
: You can send email communications as part of a large marketing effort or independently. It depends on what the organization is using email messages for. This has a direct impact on the value of the campaign parameter. If the email message is sent out as part of a larger campaign, you can use the name of the main campaign. This will provide the ability to segment the main campaign by the different marketing mediums within the campaign. If the email message is sent as a standalone campaign, use something that clearly identifies the campaign.

utm_medium

> This parameter is easy. I find the best value for utm_medium is email. That's it, nice and simple.

utm_source

> The source parameter is useful for tracking the type of email and the segment receiving the email message.

utm_content

> You can use the content parameter to identify different variations of an email message. For example, parents of high-school-aged children receiving a back-to-school campaign message may get a different themed email message than parents with grade-school-aged children.

 Some organizations like to use the utm_term parameter when tracking email. This provides a fifth parameter to hold more information about the email campaign. I personally do not like this method, as it adds non-keyword data to keyword reports. If you choose to use utm_term to track email, be sure to add an include filter to any profiles that are used for search engine optimizations (SEOs) or CPC analysis.

With the rise in popularity of Google Analytics, many email vendors have integrated Google Analytics tracking. Most of the integrations include automatically adding the campaign tracking parameters to the links in your email message. Figure 9-9 shows the integration of Mail Chimp with Google Analytics.

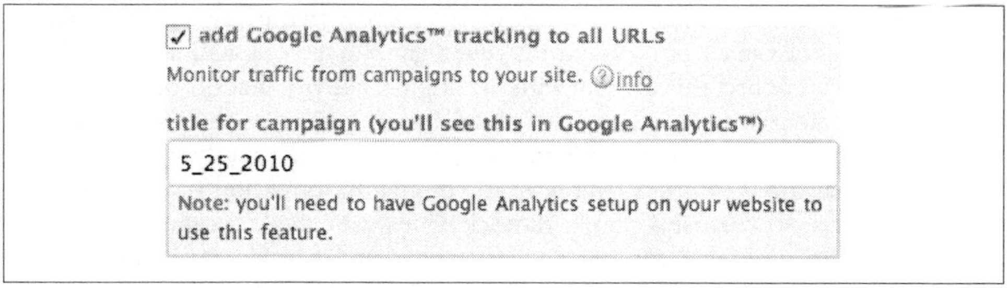

☑ add Google Analytics™ tracking to all URLs

Monitor traffic from campaigns to your site. ②info

title for campaign (you'll see this in Google Analytics™)

5_25_2010

Note: you'll need to have Google Analytics setup on your website to use this feature.

Figure 9-9. Some tools, like Mail Chimp, will automatically tag email links for you

By default, Mail Chimp will use the current date for the campaign name, the email list name for the source, and a value of "email" for the medium. It will not use a value for utm_content. While this can be enormously helpful and save you much time, make sure the default values used by your email provider jive with your overall link tagging strategy. Check with your email provider to determine if it integrates with Google Analytics.

If you host and run your own email marketing tool, it may be worth your time to modify the tool to automatically tag the links with the link tagging parameters. If you use some type of email tool, check to see if there is a plug-in or extension that provides the functionality.

Email Messages to Complete Conversion Activities

Some website conversions, like signing up for an email newsletter, have an email confirmation component. In these cases, the visitor must complete the conversion process by clicking on a link in some type of confirmation email message. Many people wonder if this email message should be tracked with campaign tracking and what the optimal solution is for understanding the overall conversion process.

In this type of situation, it's best to remember that you want to measure the visitor's progression through a process. As such, we want to generate metrics at each step to better understand where there may be issues. In reality, this has very little to do with using campaign tracking for email tracking and more to do with goals.

Step one is to create a goal to track how many visitors submit the original email form. This goal will track when visitors submit their email address. After the visitor submits her email address, she usually gets some type of thank-you page. This thank-you page should be configured as a goal. The visitor also gets some type of confirmation email message, indicating she must click on a link to confirm her subscription.

The next step in tracking this process is to track when someone clicks a link in the confirmation email message. This message usually contains a link that will bring the visitor to a confirmation page on the website. We know that every time this page is viewed, the visitor came from a "confirm your signup" type of email message. What we want to do is connect this activity with the original activity that brought the visitor to the site. As mentioned above, we can't track visitor actions in their inbox. But we can track what happens when they land on the site if we tag the links in the email message. To ensure we do not overwrite the original information that brought the visitor to the site, we can use a campaign tracking feature called no_override. This is a query-string parameter that you can add to destination URLs in email messages and other marketing materials. It's very similar to the standard link tagging parameters. Here's how a link in an email message might look with the no_override parameter:

www.cutroni.com/newsletter/signup/confirm.php?no_override=1

You can also use a funnel to track a visitor's progress through this process. However, the visitor may not immediately return to the site. There may be some interval of time between when the visitor submits his email address and when he confirms his subscription. If the visitor does not confirm his subscription within the visit timeout limit (30 minutes by default), Google Analytics will create a new visit. This will result in an abandonment from the funnel report. In reality, the visitor did not abandon the process; he just took his time.

Embedding Campaign Tags Within a Page

In some cases, it may not be possible to use link tagging. For example, there may be some redirects between the visitor's click and the landing page that remove the campaign tracking parameters. Or perhaps you're involved with an offline campaign that is driving traffic to an online landing page.

To dynamically add campaign parameters to the landing page, we can use as bit of JavaScript wizardry to manipulate the URL. Specifically, we can utilize a method known as _setAllowAnchor(). This command will instruct Google Analytics to look for the campaign parameters after a hash or pound symbol (#) rather than behind the question mark. The code below shows the standard page tag that has been modified to dynamically add link tagging parameters using JavaScript:

```
<script type="text/javascript">

  var _gaq = _gaq || [];
  _gaq.push(['_setAccount', 'UA-XXXXXX-YY']);
  _gaq.push(['setAllowAnchor',true]);

  location.hash = "#utm_source=my-source&utm_campaign=my-campaign&utm_medium
    =my-medium";

  _gaq.push(['_trackPageview']);

(function() {
    var ga = document.createElement('script'); ga.type
    = 'text/javascript'; ga.async = true; ga.src = ('https:'
    == document.location.protocol ? 'https://ssl' : 'http://www') +
    '.google-analytics.com/ga.js';
    var s = document.getElementsByTagName('script')[0];
    s.parentNode.insertBefore(ga, s);
  })();

</script>

<script>
```

When the JavaScript executes, the browser will refresh with the same URL and add the campaign parameters specified in the code. Be aware that if you try to send traffic to this page and you tag the links with the Google Analytics tracking code, the information in the JavaScript will overwrite the information in the link tags. You need to determine when it is appropriate to use this type of hack and how it could interfere with other campaign tracking.

Understanding Conversion Attribution

Visitor campaign information is stored in the __utmz cookie on the visitor's machine. This cookie not only stores campaign information, but also all referral information, including organic referrals, untagged referral links, and direct visits.

Each time a visitor visits the website, the `_trackPageview()` function updates the __utmz cookie with the appropriate campaign information. When the cookie is updated, Google Analytics discards the previous campaign information. As a result, Google Analytics tracks only the current campaign information, not previous campaign information.

With that said, there is a hierarchy of data importance that Google Analytics references before it updates the __utmz cookie and overwrites the referral information. Google Analytics buckets traffic in four basic ways:

Campaigns
   Links that are tagged with campaign information.

Referrals
   Visitors who click on an untagged link residing on a web page.

Direct
   Visitors who type the URL directly into the browser.

Search Engines
   Visitors who click on a search engine result.

Here is how Google Analytics updates the campaign tracking cookie based on the referrer:

- Direct traffic is always overwritten by referrals and by organic and tagged links.
- Referrals and organic or tagged links always overwrite existing information.

This is called *last click attribution*.

For example, a user may visit a site via a tagged link in a newsletter. When the visitor leaves the site, the campaign tracking cookie persists for six months and indicates that the visitor arrived via the newsletter.

Now suppose the same visitor decides to come back to the site one day later and types the website URL into the browser. This is a direct visit. The campaign cookie will still indicate that the visitor arrived via the newsletter, because the second visit was a direct visit, and direct traffic does not overwrite existing campaign information. If, one day later, the visitor clicks on a tagged CPC link, the __utmz cookie is updated to indicate the visitor clicked on a paid search link, and the visit is attributed to the CPC link.

 The timeout value for the campaign cookie is set to six months, by default. You can change this value for by using the `_setCookieTimeout()` method. Normally this is not required.

You can configure Google Analytics to retain the original campaign data stored in the __utmz cookie. To enable this feature, add an additional query-string parameter to a destination URL. The query-string parameter, `utm_nooverride=1`, will alert Google

Analytics that it should retain the existing campaign information. This essentially changes Google Analytics to use first-click attribution.

While helpful, this technique does not prevent the GATC from updating the campaign cookie if a visitor arrives by organic search or untagged referral link. This technique is helpful only in preventing tagged campaign links from overwriting existing referral information.

Tracking Internal Marketing Campaigns

Internal campaigns are marketing efforts that you run on your site to promote your products and services. Companies should track how people react to these campaigns and which ones are most successful. But what's the best way to do this with Google Analytics?

Some people use the standard campaign tracking to track internal campaigns. This is incorrect and you should never do it. Using the standard campaign tracking for internal campaigns will cause problems with your source data in the __utmz cookie.

There are a few ways to track internal campaigns using various Google Analytics features. You can use event tracking, custom variables, or virtual pageviews. I prefer to use the Google Analytics Site Search feature. You can easily configure Site Search to track internal campaigns. Let's walk through the steps to set up Site Search to track internal campaigns and then walk through the data and analysis.

Step 1: Create a New Profile

Because we're using Site Search for an unintended purpose, it's best to configure these settings on a new profile. It's not possible to use Site Search for tracking both internal campaigns and internal site searches within the same profile—you need to have a separate profile to track internal campaigns.

Step 2: Tag Your Internal Campaigns

Once you've created your new profile, it's time to tag your internal campaigns. Internal campaigns must be tagged in a similar manner to external campaigns: you need to add query-string parameters to your internal ad.

Unlike external campaigns, you do not use the standard link tagging parameters (utm_campaign, utm_medium, etc.)—you get to make up your own parameters.

You can use one or two parameters for internal campaign tracking and you can name them anything you want. The reason you can use one or two parameters is that the Google Analytics Site Search configuration uses two parameters, one for the search phrase and one for the search category. Whichever you choose, make sure you do not use the parameters for anything else.

Check your Top Content report for a complete list of your site's query-string parameters. Verify that the parameters you create are *not* in this list.

For example, we can use the parameter `icn` (short for internal campaign name). This parameter will hold the name of the internal campaign. We can use the following format for the value of the campaign name parameter:

```
icn=[internal-campaign-name]
```

I mentioned that you can use two parameters. You don't need to use two, but you can configure Site Search to track the internal site search phrase and a site search category. We'll use the category parameter to track the internal campaign name.

Let's name the second parameter `ici` (short for internal campaign info). Again, make sure the parameter you're using does not already exist. This second parameter lets us collect details about the ad the visitor clicked on and the location of the ad.

Here's a basic format:

```
ici=[ad-creative]_[location-on-the-page]
```

You can see that we're stuffing a lot of information into the parameter. You can put whatever you want and Google Analytics will gladly suck it in. By adding more information, we'll get a granular view of how the internal campaigns perform and which locations and variations lead to the most conversions.

If you don't have different types of internal ads or just don't care about this level of detail, you can ignore the `add ici` parameter.

Now define the values for all the ads. This can get messy if you're running a lot of internal campaigns, but you can do it—just be organized! Use a spreadsheet to keep track of all the values you use.

Once you've got all your parameters, it's time to tag your links. The exact process depends on your site. You may need to change static links, like this:

```
< a href="/internal-page.php?icn=2010-spring-sale&ici=stubs_home-roller >
```

Or, if you have complicated Flash ads, you may need to get inside the Flash code. It depends on your site.

The bottom line is when someone clicks on an internal ad, you want to see your internal campaign parameter on the next page. If you don't see the parameter in the URL, you did something wrong.

You can use the sample spreadsheet to track the different parameters you use for your internal campaigns. The spreadsheet also has a formula in column D to automatically add the parameters to your URLs.

Once you have added the parameters to your links, it's time to configure the Site Search settings.

Step 3: Configure Site Search Settings

Remember, we're configuring these settings on a new profile so we don't break the site search in our main reporting profile.

Site search has three settings. First, turn Site Search on (Figure 9-10).

Next, enter the name of the parameter that contains the site search phrase (in this case, it's our internal campaign name) into the Query Parameter field.

Next, choose Strip Query String Parameters. This setting will remove the parameter from the URL after Google Analytics processes the data. This is a good idea, because it reduces duplicate pages in your Top Content reports.

You will probably want to exclude your internal campaign name parameter and internal campaign information parameter from your other profiles. It can really mess up your pageview data.

If you're using an internal campaign information parameter, configure the Site Search Category settings the same way. Just make sure you use your internal campaign information parameter in the Category Parameter setting.

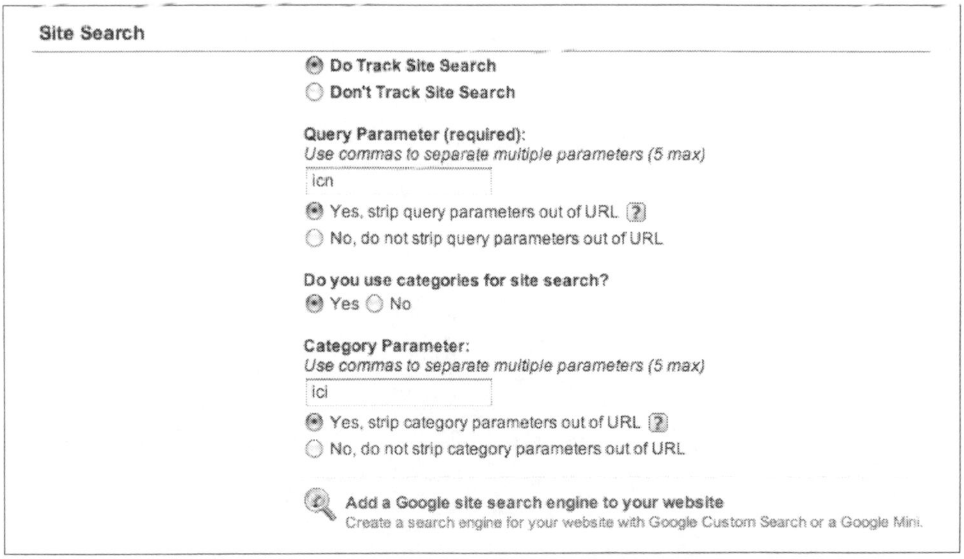

Site Search

⦿ Do Track Site Search
◯ Don't Track Site Search

Query Parameter (required):
Use commas to separate multiple parameters (5 max)

> icn

⦿ Yes, strip query parameters out of URL ?
◯ No, do not strip query parameters out of URL

Do you use categories for site search?
⦿ Yes ◯ No

Category Parameter:
Use commas to separate multiple parameters (5 max)

> ici

⦿ Yes, strip category parameters out of URL ?
◯ No, do not strip category parameters out of URL

🔍 **Add a Google site search engine to your website**
Create a search engine for your website with Google Custom Search or a Google Mini.

Figure 9-10. Site Search settings for tracking internal marketing campaigns

The Reports

Let's start by answering a simple question: do people who respond to internal campaigns convert more or less than those who do not respond to internal campaigns? To answer this question, use the Content→Site Search→Usage report. Figure 9-11 shows that there were only eight visitors who clicked an internal campaign. Sad! But it's just test data.

Now let's drill deeper and identify which internal campaigns are most effective. Use the Content→Site Search→Search Terms report, as shown in Figure 9-12. This report contains the names of all internal campaigns. Again, what was the response to the campaign? Was it worth the effort? Don't forget to check the Goals tab and the Ecommerce tabs (if applicable) to measure outcomes!

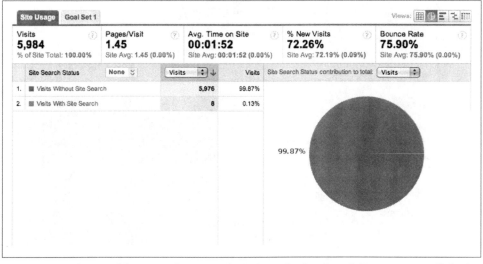

Figure 9-11. When used for internal site search tracking, the Site Search Usage report will display clicks on internal campaigns

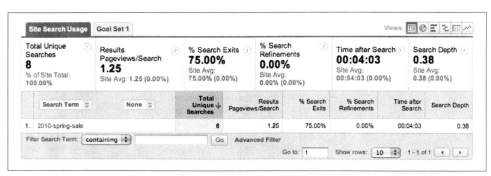

Figure 9-12. The Search Terms report shows which internal campaigns visitors responded to

---

Let's drill deeper to understand which ads within those campaigns are working. Click on a campaign name and choose Category from the Analyze drop-down list.

Now we're looking at all of the information that we put into the `ici` query string parameter for this particular campaign name (Figure 9-13). If we had multiple internal ads, we'd be able to differentiate ad placements and creative variations.

Don't forget to use the Goals and Ecommerce tabs to measure outcomes! This is what most people want to know: which, if any, internal campaigns generated revenue and conversions?

But we can do more. Change to the Content→Site Search→Start Pages report (Figure 9-14). Now we can see which page people were on when they clicked on an internal ad. Again, more insight into where visitors responded to an internal campaign.

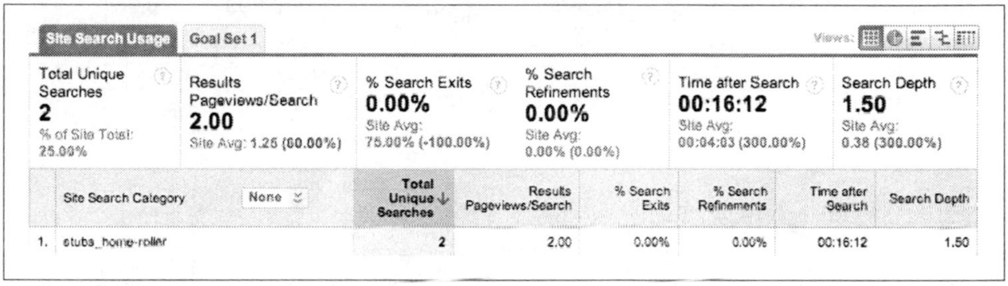

Figure 9-13. Analyzing the internal campaign by Site Search Category shows which internal campaign creative was most popular

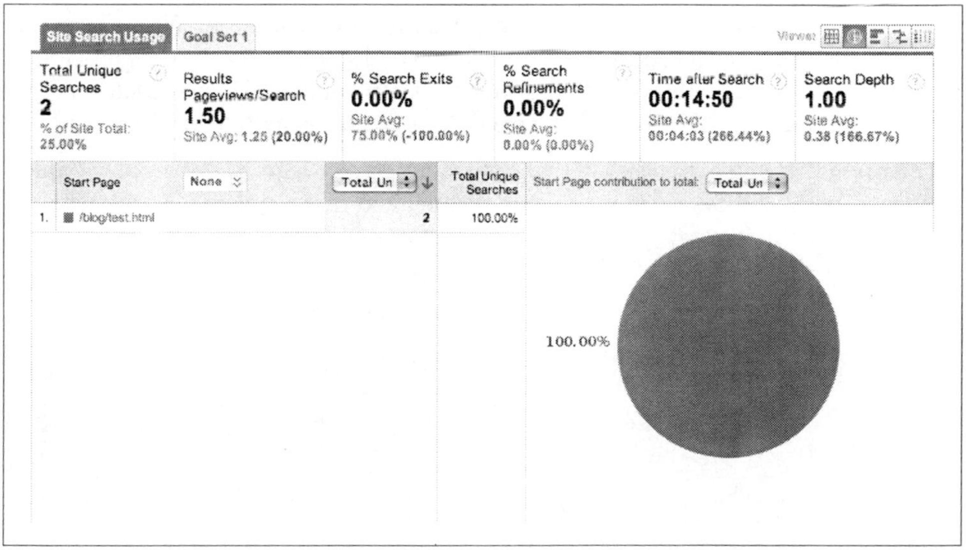

Figure 9-14. The Start Pages report shows which pages visitors were on when they clicked on an internal campaign

For all those marketing folks who are so concerned with internal campaigns, how about creating a nice custom report and automating the delivery or, better yet, using the Custom Report Sharing feature to share this report with others? People will love this because you can change the wording so it does not say "Site Search," but rather "Internal Campaigns Report."

We can also use a secondary dimension to view the external marketing campaigns (or sources, or mediums) that drive visitors to react to internal campaigns (Figure 9-15). Perhaps the external marketing campaign has some influence over how visitors react to the internal campaign creative.

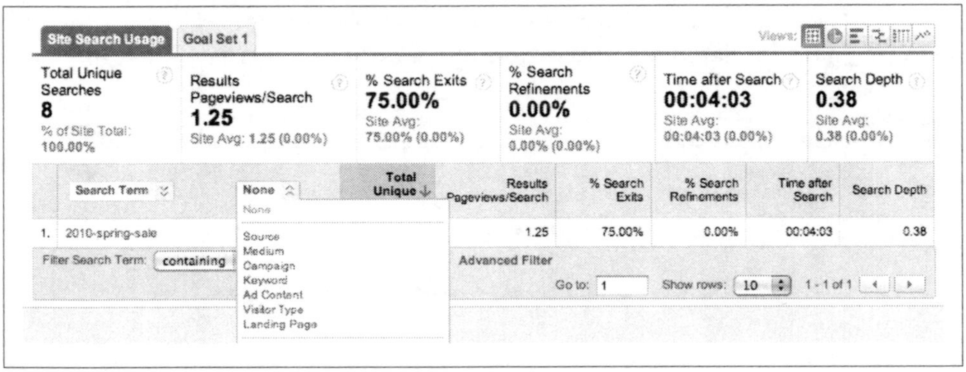

Figure 9-15. Use a secondary dimension to view which external campaigns are driving users to respond to internal campaigns

And finally, the ultimate in analysis: internal campaign attribution. We can use the Search Term Refinement feature if visitors click on multiple internal campaigns. Google Analytics will track all subsequent site searches, but in our case, follow-up site searches are actually additional internal campaigns that the visitor responded to.

I'll mention that you can track internal campaigns using events and custom variables. However, both of these solutions require coding, and that requires working with IT. Using Site Search, in most cases, will not require any code changes to your site.

CHAPTER 10

Advanced Tracking Techniques

This chapter addresses common website architectures that can cause problems with the Google Analytics tracking. Remember, the technology that Google Analytics uses to track visitors, called page tagging, is based on JavaScript and cookies. So any website architecture, like multiple domain names, that affects cookies or JavaScript can interfere with tracking. You usually make most of the changes required to deal with these website configurations to your website and not Google Analytics directly.

If your website contains a small number of static HTML pages, it is very likely that this chapter will not apply to you. However, if you have a dynamic website that crosses multiple domains and subdomains, this chapter will offer valuable information about how, and why, you should configure Google Analytics.

Tracking Across Multiple Domains

Google Analytics can track visitors across multiple domains. This functionality is primarily used on websites that have a third-party shopping cart, but you can use this capability for other purposes. If your website traverses multiple domains, you will want to track your visitors as they move from one domain to another. If you do not track them across domains, each visitor will appear as a new visitor each time she moves from one of your websites to another. It will also be difficult to attribute conversions to different marketing activities.

You should implement tracking across multiple domains only if there is some functional connection between the websites. If there is no business relationship between the sites, there may not be a need to track visitors between domains. Only you can decide if you need to track visitors between multiple domains.

Critical to cross-domain tracking is the concept of first-party cookies. First-party cookies are cookies whose domain is the same as the website that the visitor is currently visiting. For example, cookies for a user visiting *www.cutroni.com* have a domain of *cutroni.com*.

Google Analytics uses first-party cookies. Therefore, the GATC on *www.cutroni.com* can interact only with cookies that have a domain of *cutroni.com*. If the visitor leaves *www.cutroni.com*, as is the case when a website uses a third-party shopping cart, the GATC cannot access the tracking cookies on the shopping cart pages.

How It Works

When a visitor arrives at the website for the first time, the GATC sets a number of cookies that uniquely identify the visitor. No matter where the visitor goes on the website, he can always be identified by the cookies.

Things change if the visitor leaves the website. The tracking cookies are first-party cookies, which means they can be used only by the website that sets them. If the visitor leaves the site to use a shopping cart located on a different domain, the tracking cookies will no longer work. There needs to be some mechanism to transfer the cookies, along with the visitor, from one domain to another. This is shown in Figure 10-1.

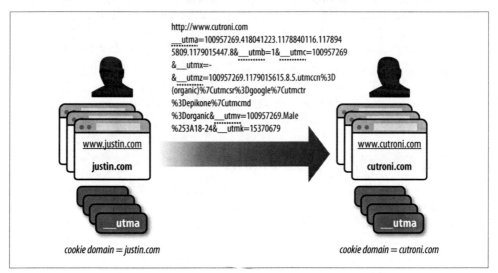

Figure 10-1. When a visitor moves from one domain to another, his tracking cookies must move with him

Google Analytics provides two methods to transfer the tracking cookies between domains: `_link()` and `_linkByPost()`. Both functions operate in the same manner. They extract the tracking cookie values from the cookies and place the data in the destination page URL as query-string parameters. The tracking cookies, shown in code in the middle of Figure 10-1, are passed in the query string as the visitor moves from *justin.com* to *cutroni.com*. The name of each tracking cookie has a dotted line beneath it.

When the visitor lands on *cutroni.com*, the GATC copies the cookie values from the query string and resets the tracking cookies on *cutroni.com* with the same values. When the process is complete, the visitor has two sets of cookies with the same values. One set of cookies is for *justin.com* and one set is for *cutroni.com*.

Two critical conditions must be met for this technique to work:

- Both domains must have the GATC installed.
- The third-party domain must accept query-string parameters.

If the third-party domain prohibits either of these conditions, Google Analytics will not track visitors from one domain to the other.

Implementation

First, make sure the pages on both websites have the GATC installed. Before you can tag your pages, you must modify the tracking code. To modify the code, use the radio buttons in the code configuration tool (Figure 10-2). Choose "Multiple top-level domains" and Google Analytics will add two lines of code to the page tag.

Figure 10-2. Use the code configuration tool to modify the tracking code for cross-domain tracking

It is my belief that the tracking code generated by the code configuration tool is not the best configuration. Specifically, I do not believe it should use the following line of code:

```
_gaq.push(['_setDomainName', 'none']);
```

The _setDomainName() method sets the domain for the tracking cookies. The code above is actually different than what is in the Google Analytics support documentation. The support documents recommend that you pass a value of none to the _setDomain Name() method. I disagree with this recommendation, because it causes the tracking code to use the entire hostname for the cookie domain.

This can cause multiple instances of the Google Analytics tracking cookies. It is possible to get a cookie with a domain of both *www.website.com* and *.website.com*. More than one set of cookies per visitor is bad!

Rather than using the code that Google provides, modify it by replacing none with the primary domain of your website. I've modified the code below to work with *www.cutroni.com*. Notice that I changed none to .cutroni.com.

```
<script type="text/javascript">

  var _gaq = _gaq || [];
  _gaq.push(['_setAccount', 'UA-XXXXXX-YY']);
  _gaq.push(['_setDomainName', '.cutroni.com']);
  _gaq.push(['_setAllowLinker', true]);
  _gaq.push(['_setAllowHash', false]);
  _gaq.push(['_trackPageview']);

(function() {
    var ga = document.createElement('script'); ga.type
    = 'text/javascript'; ga.async = true;
    ga.src = ('https:' == document.location.protocol ?
    'https://ssl' : 'http://www') + '.google-analytics.com/ga.js';
    var s = document.getElementsByTagName('script')[0];
    s.parentNode.insertBefore(ga, s);
  })();

</script>
```

The _setAllowLinker() method is a switch that activates a security feature within the tracking code. This feature creates a key that ensures the tracking variables are set with the same values on both domains. You can see the key in the URL. It is stored in a query-string parameter named _utmk.

Once you have modified and installed the tracking code, add _link() or _linkBy Post() to your website. As mentioned above, these methods extract the tracking cookie values and add them to the landing page URL as query-string parameters.

If the website transfers the visitor between domains using standard anchor tags, add _link() as follows:

```
<a href="http://www.b.com" onclick=
    "_gaq.push(['_link','http://www.cutroni.com']);return false;">Buy Now</a>');
```

If the website uses a form to transfer the visitor between domains, add _linkByPost() to the necessary forms. Modify all appropriate forms as follows:

```
<form name="post_form" action="http://www.b.com" method="post"
    onsubmit="_gaq.push(['_linkByPost', this]);">
```

_linkByPost() will change the form action by adding query-string parameters to the value in the action attribute when the visitor submits the form.

The above code will not work unless the _gaq is loaded into the browser. If the _gaq has not been loaded, the link to the other domain will not work, because the _gaq needs *ga.js* to load in the browser to establish the _link() and _linkByPost() methods.

You may need to tag the links and forms on both websites. Why? Every page on both websites should be considered a search engine results page and thus a starting point for a visitor's visit. However, if there is no chance that the visitor's visit will start on website *b* and then move to website *a*, there is no need to change the links or forms on website *b*.

Many people have been experimenting with DOM scripts to dynamically call _link() or _linkByPost() rather than manually adding the functions to the HTML. While these scripts will work some of the time, success has been inconsistent due to variations in the DOM from one browser to another. You should take care when experimenting with this customization.

Once you have modified the tracking code and added _link() or _linkByPost(), visitors will be tracked between domains. To aid in reporting, it is a good idea to add a filter that attaches the website hostname to the request URI. This makes it easier to identify common content on each domain. The settings for the filter are shown in Figure 10-3.

Tracking Across Multiple Subdomains

Like tracking across multiple domains, the primary issue with tracking across multiple subdomains has to do with the cookie domain.

By default, the GATC includes the website subdomain in the cookie domain. This means that a cookie set by the GATC while the visitor is visiting one subdomain cannot be utilized by the GATC on a different subdomain. So, a visitor who visits multiple

```
┌─────────────────────────────────────────────────────────────────────────┐
│ Enter Filter Information                                                  │
│                                                                           │
│  Filter Name:      ┌──────────────────────────────────────┐              │
│                    │ Attach Hostname to Request URI         │              │
│                    └──────────────────────────────────────┘              │
│  Filter Type:      ○ Predefined filter ◉ Custom filter                    │
│                                                                           │
│                    ○ Exclude                                              │
│                    ○ Include                                              │
│                    ○ Lowercase                                            │
│                    ○ Uppercase                                            │
│                    ○ Search and Replace                                   │
│                    ◉ Advanced                                             │
│                                                                           │
│           Field A -> Extract A    ┌────────────────┐   ┌──────────┐       │
│                                   │ Hostname      ▼│   │ (.*)     │       │
│                                   └────────────────┘   └──────────┘       │
│           Field B -> Extract B    ┌────────────────┐   ┌──────────┐       │
│                                   │ Request URI   ▼│   │ (.*)     │       │
│                                   └────────────────┘   └──────────┘       │
│           Output To -> Constructor┌────────────────┐   ┌──────────┐       │
│                                   │ Request URI   ▼│   │ $A1$B1   │       │
│                                   └────────────────┘   └──────────┘       │
│           Field A Required        ◉Yes ○No                                │
│           Field B Required        ○Yes ◉No                                │
│           Override Output Field   ◉Yes ○No                                │
│           Case Sensitive          ○Yes ◉No                                │
│                                                                           │
│           ▶ ⑦ Filter Help: Advanced                                       │
│                                                                           │
│  ( Save Changes )  ( Cancel )                                             │
└─────────────────────────────────────────────────────────────────────────┘
```

Figure 10-3. Advanced filter to add the hostname to the Request URI

subdomains on a website will receive a different set of tracking cookies for each sub-domain. Table 10-1 includes some examples that illustrate this issue.

Table 10-1. How subdomains affect cookie domains

Domain	Cookie domain	Can be accessed by
support.website.com	*.support.website.com*	*support.website.com* only
secure.website.com	*.secure.website.com*	*secure.website.com* only

To resolve this issue, the cookie domain must be consistent from one subdomain to another. This means removing the subdomain from the cookie domain. Once you have removed the subdomain, the GATC can access the cookie that appears on any subdomain, as shown in Table 10-2.

Table 10-2. Changing the cookie domain enables tracking across different subdomains

Domain	Cookie domain	Can be accessed by
support.website.com	.website.com	support.website.com or secure.website.com
secure.website.com	.website.com	support.website.com or secure.website.com

You can change the tracking cookie domain using the _setDomainName() method. _setDomainName() is not used in the default configuration; this is what causes the inclusion of the subdomain in the cookie domain.

Implementation

You can configure Google Analytics to track visitors across multiple subdomains with the following process:

1. Modify the tracking code to include the _setDomainName() method.
2. Apply a filter to clarify Google Analytics reports.
3. Segment traffic into multiple profiles for improved reporting (this step is optional but recommended).

Begin by modifying the GATC to include the _setDomainName() method. You can pass _setDomainName() a specific value, which will in turn be used for the cookie domain. So, using _setDomainName() to force the cookies to use the website's primary domain lets the tracking code access the cookies on various subdomains.

Add the primary domain of the website to the setDomainName().Pass method (be sure to include a leading period):

```
<script type="text/javascript">

  var _gaq = _gaq || [];
  _gaq.push(['_setAccount', 'UA-XXXXXX-YY']);
  _gaq.push(['_setDomainName', '.cutroni.com']);
  _gaq.push(['_trackPageview']);

(function() {
    var ga = document.createElement('script'); ga.type = 'text/javascript';
    ga.async = true;
    ga.src = ('https:' == document.location.protocol ? 'https://ssl'
    : 'http://www') + '.google-analytics.com/ga.js';
    var s = document.getElementsByTagName('script')[0];
    s.parentNode.insertBefore(ga, s);
  })();

</script>
```

No need to do this manually: you can use the tracking code configuration tool, as shown in Figure 10-4.

Tracking Code

Instructions for adding tracking

Standard | **Advanced** | **Custom**

❶ What are you tracking?

❷ Paste this code on your site

Copy the following code, then paste it onto every page you want to track immediately after the opening <body> tag. Learn more

○ A single domain (default)

◉ One domain with multiple subdomains

Examples: apps.cutroni.com
           store.cutroni.com
           video.cutroni.com

○ Multiple top-level domains

☑ **Your account is already receiving data from AdWords**

```
<script type="text/javascript">

var _gaq = _gaq || [];
_gaq.push(['_setAccount', 'UA-          ']);
_gaq.push(['_setDomainName', '.cutroni.com']);
_gaq.push(['_trackPageview']);

(function() {
    var ga = document.createElement('script'); ga.type = 'text/javascript'; g
    ga.src = ('https:' == document.location.protocol ? 'https://ssl' : 'http://
    var s = document.getElementsByTagName('script')[0]; s.parentNode.ins
})();

</script>
```

Figure 10-4. Using the code configuration tool to alter the tracking code for subdomain tracking

Once you have modified and installed the tracking code, add a filter to the appropriate profile (Figure 10-5). The filter will differentiate pages that appear on multiple subdomains. For example, the page *index.html* may appear on multiple subdomains but will appear as *index.html* in the reports. Adding the hostname to the request URI will differentiate multiple versions of the same page.

The final step in configuring multiple subdomains is optional but recommended. It is a good idea to create a separate profile for each subdomain. This provides a greater level of reporting and more insight into visitor actions on each subdomain.

This filter, or any filter that modifies the Request URI field, will break the Site Overlay report. The reason is that the Site Overlay report uses the request URI to identify which links in the Site Overlay report correspond to specific data (like clicks and visits).

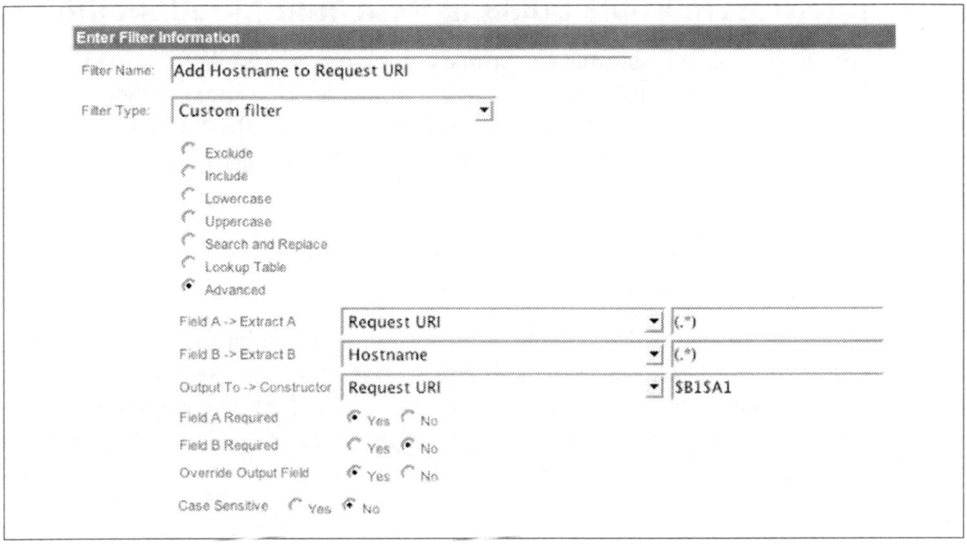

Figure 10-5. An Advanced filter that concatenates the hostname and the Request URI

To create the subdomain-specific profiles, use an include filter (Figure 10-6) based on the Hostname field. When complete, there should be one main profile that contains summary data for all subdomains and individual profiles for each subdomain.

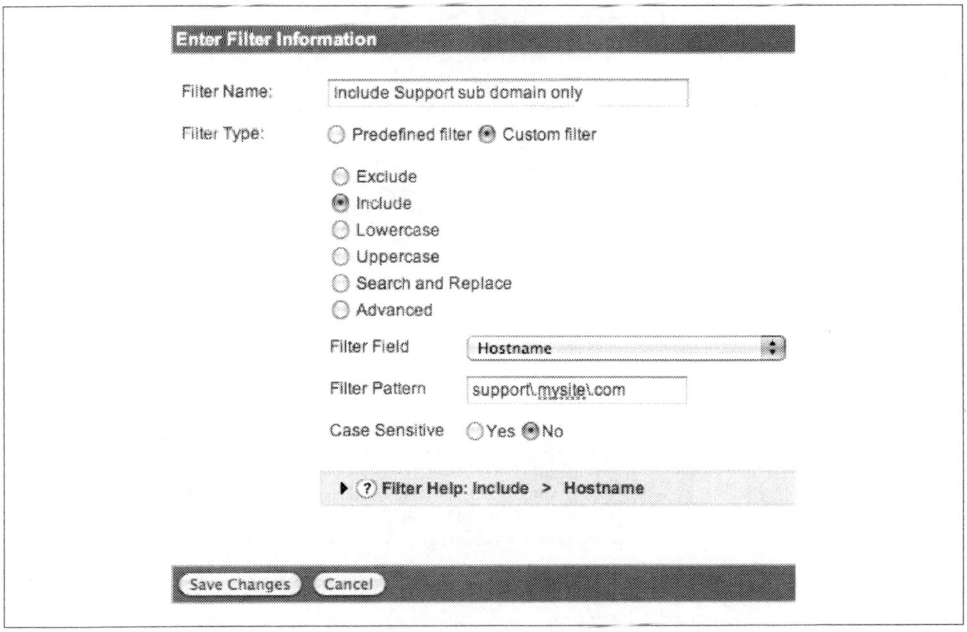

Figure 10-6. An include filter used to create a profile for a specific subdomain

Tracking Across Multiple Domains with Multiple Subdomains

You can track visitors across multiple primary domains that each contain multiple subdomains. The key to a successful implementation is making sure the Google Analytics tracking cookies are set with the correct domain and that the cookies are passed between the primary domains. There are three steps to configuring this type of tracking:

1. Modify the tracking code on each subdomain and primary domain.
2. Modify links and forms on both sites to use _link() or _linkByPost().
3. Add a filter to clarify the data in the reports.

Many of the GATC modifications for this configuration are similar to the settings used in the multiple domains and multiple subdomain tracking. Use _setDomainName() to remove the subdomain from the cookie domain, thus making tracking across each subdomain possible. Use _setAllowLinker() to trigger certain actions in the tracking code necessary for cross-domain tracking. Table 10-3 lists tracking code modifications for each domain.

Table 10-3. The GATC configuration for a website that uses multiple domains and multiple subdomains

Site	Hostnames	Tracking code

Site 1	*secure.website1.com*
	products.website1.com
		```<script type="text/javascript">```
		
		```var _gaq = _gaq || [];```
		```_gaq.push(['_setAccount', 'UA-XXXXXX-YY']);```
		```_gaq.push(['_setDomainName', '.website1.com']);```
		```_gaq.push(['_setAllowLinker', true]);```
		```_gaq.push(['_setAllowHash', false]);```
		```_gaq.push(['_trackPageview']);```
		
		```(function() {```
		``` var ga = document.createElement('script'); ga.type =```
		```'text/javascript'; ga.async = true;```
		``` ga.src = ('https:' == document.location.protocol ?```
		```'https://ssl' : 'http://www') + '.google-analytics.com/ga.js';```
		``` var s = document.getElementsByTagName('script')[0];```
		```s.parentNode.insertBefore(ga, s);```
		```})();```
		
		```</script>```

Site 2	*secure.website2.com*
	support.website2.com
		```<script type="text/javascript">```
		
		```var _gaq = _gaq || [];```
		```_gaq.push(['_setAccount', 'UA-XXXXXX-YY']);```
		```_gaq.push(['_setDomainName', '.website2.com']);```
		```_gaq.push(['_setAllowLinker', true]);```
		```_gaq.push(['_setAllowHash', false]);```
		```_gaq.push(['_trackPageview']);```

Site	Hostnames	Tracking code
| | | ```
(function() {
    var ga = document.createElement('script'); ga.type =
'text/javascript'; ga.async = true;
    ga.src = ('https:' == document.location.protocol ?
'https://ssl' : 'http://www') + '.google-analytics.com/ga.js';
    var s = document.getElementsByTagName('script')[0];
s.parentNode.insertBefore(ga, s);
})();
``` |
| | | `</script>` |

In reality, this is the same code format that I suggest using for standard cross-domain tracking.

In addition to changing the tracking code, you must modify each site to use _link() or _linkByPost(). Remember, these modifications pass the Google Analytics tracking cookies between the domains via the query string. If the cookies are not passed between domains, the visitor's session will not be tracked between websites.

Finally, to help clarify the data in your reports, use an advanced filter to attach the Hostname field to the Request URI field.

To aid in analysis, it is wise to create separate profiles for each primary domain and subdomain. Do this by using a simple include filter based on the Hostname field.

Theoretically, there is no limit to the number of primary domains or subdomains that you can track a visitor across. However, it may be impractical to track across more than two or three primary domains.

For businesses that have multiple domains, take the time to evaluate the need to track individual visitors across all domains in the network. Unique visitors is the primary metric that is affected by cross-domain tracking. Because a cookie identifies each unique visitor, it is necessary for the cookie to accompany the visitor from one domain to the next. If you're looking to track an individual visitor across 50 domains, you'll need to propagate that cookie across all domains. While it is impractical to do this using the standard Google Analytics cross-domain tracking, it may be possible using a custom solution developed for your particular situation. Other metrics can also be affected by cross-domain tracking: visits can appear inflated, time on site can be too short, and bounce rate may be abnormal. Again, take the time to understand the impact to the business.

Frames and iFrames

You can use Google Analytics on sites that have frames. However, take care during installation and configuration. The most common problem with sites that use frames is that the original referral information can become distorted. This can lead to problems when tracking online marketing.
```

Frames

When implementing Google Analytics on a site that uses frames, make sure both the frameset and the pages within the frame are tagged with the Google Analytics tracking code. If both pages are not tagged, Google Analytics does not track referral information correctly.

The reason for this is that the browser sets referral information using information in the main frame DOM. All pages contained within the main frame identify the main frame as the referring website. If only one page within the main frame contains the Google Analytics tag, the referral information for a visit will be set to the main site rather than the true referral information.

A side effect of tagging both the frameset page and the pages within the frameset is that there will be an artificially high number of pageviews for some pages, specifically the frameset. If the frameset page is not critical (i.e., it is simply a navigation menu or page header), consider removing it from the profile using an exclude filter.

 If your website uses frames and the number of pageviews is a critical metric for your business, be sure you filter your profile data appropriately to ensure accurate metrics.

iFrames

The effect of iFrames on Google Analytics tracking is similar to that of standard frames. If the outer page is not tagged with the Google Analytics tracking code, the original referral information will be lost.

Another common issue with iFrames is the use of third-party shopping carts. If you are using a third-party shopping cart and embedding the shopping cart pages in an iFrame, it will be difficult to track the visitor session from originating website to the shopping cart website, because the tracking cookies must be passed to the shopping cart domain.

This process is very different from the normal third-party domain setup. In the standard third-party setup, we use the _link() and _linkByPost() methods to pass the tracking cookie values in the URL. However, you cannot use these methods with an iFrame, because both _link() and _linkByPost() redirect the browser, which can cause problems with an iFrame.

Fear not, there is a solution. In this type of configuration, use the _getLinkerUrl() to dynamically add the tracking cookie values to the source of the iFrame:

```
var iFrame = document.getElementById("iFrame");
iFrame.src = "_gaq.push(['_getLinkerUrl', 'http://www.iFrame-domains.com/']);
```

We have seen some tracking issues with Internet Explorer (version 6 and later) and with Safari when using this type of implementation. The problem is that some browsers require a P3P privacy header to be passed to the iFrame when requesting content from a third-party domain. While it is possible to send a P3P header, it can be difficult to create cross-browser code. If you're looking for more information on generating a P3P header, check *http://www.p3ptoolbox.org/guide/*.

E-Commerce Tracking

The Google Analytics e-commerce tracking feature provides a rich set of reports that you can use for product and customer analysis. If you are part of an e-commerce company, it is recommended that you implement the e-commerce tracking code to collect transaction data. The resulting report is very valuable and helps you gain additional insight into the performance of your online business.

As with most things, understanding how Google Analytics collects, processes, and stores e-commerce data is key to a proper implementation.

You should not use Google Analytics e-commerce tracking in place of an accounting or order management tool package. While the tracking is fairly accurate, there are too many external forces that can affect the data quality. It is best to analyze larger sets of e-commerce data and look for trends that provide insight into customer actions. Do not rely on it for accounting tasks.

How It Works

Figure 10-7 illustrates the basic process used to track e-commerce transactions. Tracking begins when a visitor submits a transaction (step 1) and it is received by the web server (step 2). The web server usually passes the data to an application server, where it is processed (step 3). This processing may include adding the data to a database, validating a credit card, or emailing the customer. Once the application server has processed the transaction, it usually creates some type of receipt page for the visitor (step 4).

At this point in the process, you must make a modification to accommodate Google Analytics. Before the application server sends the receipt page back to the web server, the application must add information about the visitor's transaction to an e-commerce page tag on the receipt page.

So, if you are using PHP, Java, Ruby on Rails, or .NET, you must create application code that adds the transaction data in the e-commerce tag to the receipt page. This is the step that most people do not understand.

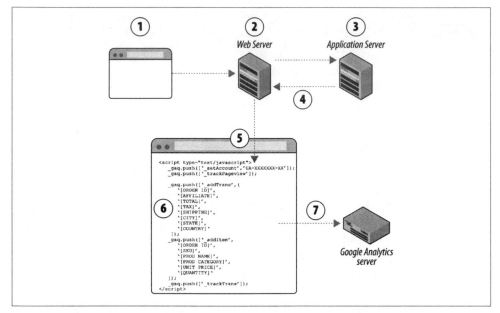

Figure 10-7. E-commerce transaction collection

The e-commerce tag looks like this:

```
<script type="text/javascript">
  _var _gaq = _gaq || [];  ❶
  gaq.push(['_setAccount','UA-XXXXXX-YY']);
  _gaq.push(['_trackPageview']);

  _gaq.push(['_addTrans',  ❷
    '{ORDER ID}',    // order ID - required
    '{AFFILIATE}',   // affiliation or store name
    '{TOTAL}',       // total - required
    '{TAX}',         // tax
    '{SHIPPING}',    // shipping
    '{CITY}',        // city
    '{STATE}',       // state or province
    '{COUNTRY}'      // country
  ]);
  _gaq.push(['_addItem',  ❸
    '{ORDER ID}',        // order ID - need to associate item with transaction
    '{SKU}',             // SKU/code - required
    '{PROD NAME}',       // product name
    '{PROD CATEGORY}',   // category or variation
    '{UNIT PRICE}',      // unit price - required
    '{QUANTITY}'         // quantity - required
  ]);
  _gaq.push(['_trackTrans']); //submits transaction to the Analytics servers ❹
</script>
```

All of the data in curly braces must be replaced with actual transaction information. Again, you must make this modification to your application server. Let's look at each section of code.

❶ The first part of the code contains the standard _setAccount() and _trackPage view() methods. You still need the standard page tag to create the queue and record a pageview for the receipt page.

❷ The second section is called the transaction section. This block contains summary information about the transaction. This includes the transaction ID, total, tax, shipping, etc. This information is contained in the _addTrans() method.

❸ The third section is an item section and contains the _addItem() method. There should be one item section for each distinct product purchased by the visitor. This usually means one item section per SKU or unique product ID. The data in an item section includes the product name, product category, unit price, quantity, etc. Tables 10-4 and 10-5 list all data in the transaction and item sections.

❹ The final part of the e-commerce code is the _trackTrans() method. Like _page Tracker(), _trackTrans() sends data back to the Google Analytics server. In fact, _trackTrans() uses a request for the invisible GIF file to send the data to Google Analytics. The primary difference is that _trackTrans() sends only e-commerce data. It sends one request for the transaction data and one request for each item in the transaction.

Returning to the e-commerce process diagram in Figure 10-7, once the application server completes processing, it sends the receipt page to the web server, which sends it back to the visitor's browser (step 5). As the receipt page renders and the browser hits the e-commerce page tag, it is added to the queue of Google Analytics commands (step 6) and eventually sent to Google's servers (step 7).

Once the e-commerce data has been sent to the Google Analytics server, the processing is similar to that of a pageview. Google Analytics processes the data at a regular interval, applies filters to the fields created during processing, and stores the data in a database. Special fields are created when an e-commerce transaction is processed. Like all other fields in Google Analytics, e-commerce fields can be used in filters.

Table 10-4. Description of transaction-line data variables

Variable	Description
Order id	The internal tracking ID for the order.
Affiliate	If the transaction was generated by a partner or specific store, that value can be stored here.
Total	Total amount of the transaction. This value should be an integer. Do not use a monetary symbol or comma in the value.
Tax	The amount of tax applied to the transactions. This value should be an integer. Do not use a monetary symbol or comma in the value.

Variable	Description
Shipping	The shipping charge applied to the transaction. This value should be an integer. Do not use a monetary symbol or comma in the value.
City	The city entered by the customer. This can be the ship-to city or bill-to city. Not used in reporting, this can be left blank.
State	The state (or region if used outside of the U.S.) entered by the customer. This can be the ship-to or bill-to state/region. Not used in reporting, this can be left blank.
Country	The country entered by the customer. This can be the ship-to country or bill-to country. Not used in reporting, this can be left blank.

Google Analytics generates the geographic location data for e-commerce transactions (City, State, and Country) in the same manner as other geodata. Google Analytics creates it using a network mapping of the visitor's IP address. So, the data in the City, State, and Country fields is not used to map a transaction to a geographic location. However, Google Analytics will still collect the data that is added to the geographic transaction fields of the JavaScript.

Table 10-5. Description of item-line data variables

Variable	Description
order id	This is the same order ID used in the transaction line. Google Analytics uses the order ID to group the products contained in a transaction.
sku	Product SKU.
product name	The name of the product purchased.
product category	The category the product belongs to.
price	The unit price for the product.
quantity	How many units were purchased.

Implementation

There are three steps to add Google Analytics e-commerce tracking to a website:

1. Verify the tracking code is installed on the receipt page. You must be sure that the receipt page is tagged. The e-commerce methods reside in the *ga.js* library. If the reference to the *ga.js* file is missing from the receipt page, the e-commerce code will not execute and the transaction data will not be sent to Google Analytics.

2. Enable e-commerce reports for the profile. By default, the e-commerce reports are disabled. This means the e-commerce menu does not appear in the left-hand navigation pane. You must modify the profile setting, as shown in Figure 10-8, and specify that the website is an e-commerce site.

3. Create the application logic to populate the e-commerce tag with transaction data. The actual implementation of this step differs from one website to another depending on the application architecture, but you must create some logic that formats the e-commerce data according to the format described above. Make sure the e-commerce page tag appears below the standard page tag. I prefer to group all of the code together—this makes it easier to find and maintain.

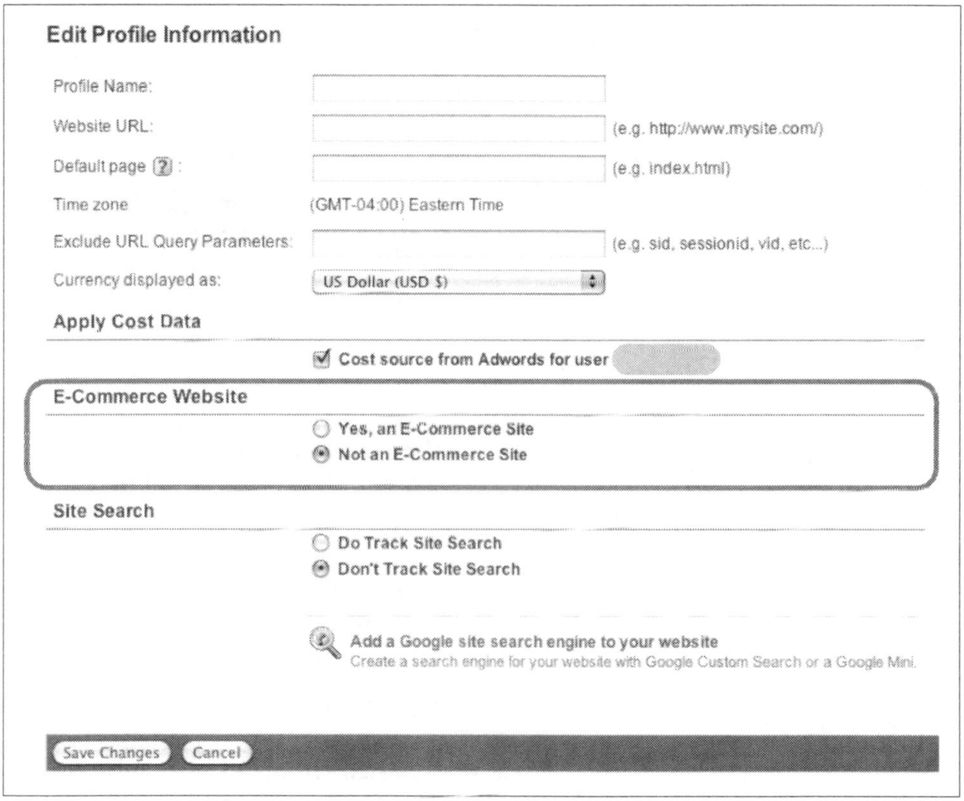

Figure 10-8. Enabling e-commerce reports in your website profile

If you are using an e-commerce platform, like Miva Merchant, Magento, or Zoovy, there is already a Google Analytics e-commerce plug-in. Check with your e-commerce provider to determine if there is a plug-in available. It will save you a lot of time.

Once you have formatted the e-commerce data and added it to the receipt page, e-commerce data should begin to populate the e-commerce reports. If it does not, there may be a problem with the installation.

Filtering e-commerce data is somewhat different than filtering standard pageview data. For example, you cannot filter e-commerce transactions by the Hostname field. If you are trying to filter e-commerce data, use the fields that are specific to e-commerce tracking like transaction ID or Affiliate Value. In these cases it may be necessary to add additional information to an e-commerce field, like "E-commerce Transaction ID."

Common E-Commerce Problems

Here are some of the most common e-commerce issues and their solutions.

Garbled data in e-commerce reports

If the data in the product performance reports (particularly the Product Overview and Product Categories report) is garbled or contains extra characters, there may be an issue with the data in your hidden form. Verify that the transaction line and product lines contain only alphanumeric characters. Monetary data should not include a dollar sign or commas.

All transaction sources are your website

This is a common problem for websites using a third-party shopping cart. The problem is normally not the implementation of the e-commerce tracking code. It is more likely that the cross-domain tracking is incorrect.

A simple way to identify the source of this problem is to examine the data in the All Traffic Sources report. Use the E-Commerce tab to identify which traffic sources are driving revenue. If your website's hostname is listed in the report, there is probably an issue with the cross-domain tracking.

Missing transactions

It is not uncommon for some transactions to be missing from Google Analytics. This usually occurs when visitors navigate away from the receipt page before the data is transmitted. If the number of transactions in Google Analytics is off by more than 10% when compared to your accounting software, there may be a bigger problem.

In general, Google Analytics should be tracking most transactions. If there is a significant number of transactions missing, double-check the implementation. You may want to move the e-commerce code to the top of the receipt page so the data is sent to Google Analytics immediately as the page loads in the visitor's browser.

Tracking third-party e-commerce platforms

E-commerce tracking may not be feasible for all third-party shopping carts. If the shopping cart provider does not permit modifications to the receipt page, the standard implementation of e-commerce tracking will not work, and you should try a workaround.

Each shopping cart is different, so there is no single workaround that will solve every problem. A quick search of your shopping cart provider's support documents should point you to the integration instructions.

Yahoo! store transactions

As of March 2010, the standard e-commerce implementation process will not work with Yahoo! stores. There are various companies that charge a monthly fee to integrate Yahoo! store e-commerce data and Google Analytics data.

I've used Monitus's Web Analytics Connector (*http://troni.me/9PcS1E*). Its service connects your Yahoo! store data with your Google Analytics data. Monitus charges a monthly fee for this service based on the number of pageviews your site generates. If you're using a Yahoo! store, you should consider using the Yahoo! service.

Inflated e-commerce revenue

There can be two causes for inflated revenue numbers in Google Analytics. The first cause is usually people bookmarking the receipt page and visiting multiple times. The only way to resolve this issue is to add some type of logic to stop the e-commerce code from executing when the receipt page is accessed directly rather than as part of a transaction.

Another cause of inflated revenue data is canceled transactions. Google Analytics collects e-commerce data when the receipt page renders in the visitor's browser. If the transaction is declined or modified at some point later, these changes will not be represented in Google Analytics.

The only way to modify transactions in Google Analytics is to erase the transaction by submitting a duplicate transaction with a negative value. While this will eliminate the revenue from the transaction, it will not eliminate the other information associated with the transaction. This is the only way to remove a transaction from Google Analytics.

Using E-Commerce Tracking on Non-E-Commerce Sites

There's a lot you can do with e-commerce tracking even if you're a non-e-commerce site. You can use the e-commerce reporting to monetize lead generation forms or contact forms and measure visitor interactions with a form. If you're working with a non-profit website, you can use e-commerce tracking to track donations.

Let's say we have a lead generation site that sells books, cars, and jets (a completely unlikely combination). The site has a very simple lead generation form that lets the users choose the items they are interested in and their timeframes for purchase.

We want to measure the fields visitors fill out, the values they choose, and the overall value of the form (Figure 10-9).

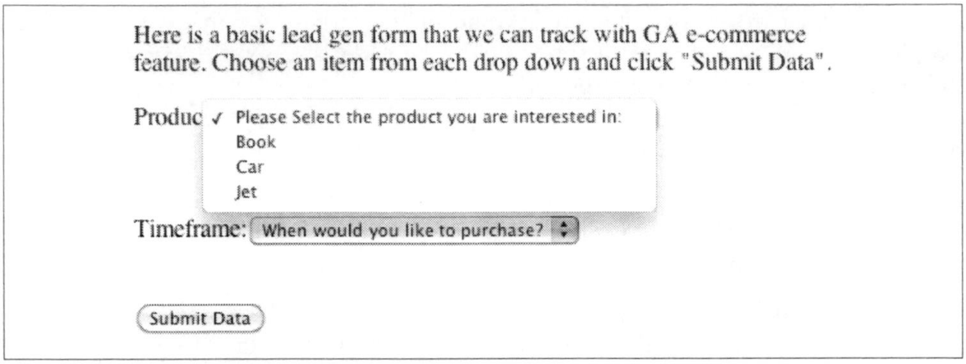

Here is a basic lead gen form that we can track with GA e-commerce feature. Choose an item from each drop down and click "Submit Data".

Produc ✓ Please Select the product you are interested in:

Book

Car

Jet

Timeframe: When would you like to purchase? ⬍

Submit Data

Figure 10-9. A fictional lead generation form

This page contains some JavaScript code that calculates the value of the form based on the visitor's choices. Here's the code:

```
<html>

<head>

<script type='text/javascript'>
    var _gaq = _gaq || [];
    _gaq.push(['_setAccount', 'UA-XXXXXX-YY']);
    _gaq.push(['_trackPageview']);

//
// Create a fake order ID using the current
// time and the unique identifier that GA uses to
// track this visitor.
//
var timeObj     = new Date;
var unixTimeMs  = timeObj.getTime();
var unixTime    = parseInt(unixTimeMs / 1000);
var orderID     = vID + '-' + unixTime;
var orderID     = Math.floor(Math.random()*1000000+1) + '-' + unixTime;

//
// This is the function that does all the work.
// It calculates a "total" based on form choices,
// manipulates the format of the data and finally
// sends the data to Google Analytics.
//

function recordData(f) {
//
// Assign a value to product selection
//
switch(f.product[f.product.selectedIndex].value) {
 case "book":
  productVal=10;
  productName="book";
  break;
```

```
      case "car":
       productVal=30;
       productName="car";
       break;
      case "jet":
       productVal=500;
       productName="jet";
       break;
      default:
       productVal=0;
       productName="NONE";
       break;
     }

     //
     // Assign a value to time selection
     //
     switch(f.time[f.time.selectedIndex].value) {
      case "today":
       timeVal=100;
       timeName="today";
       break;
      case "later":
       timeVal=50;
       timeName="later";
       break;
      default:
       timeVal=0;
       timeName="NONE";
       break;
     }

     //
     // Calculate a total value for the form by
     // summing the value for product and timeframe.
     //
     formVal = timeVal + productVal;

     //
     // Finally, format the data by concatenating the form selections
     // and send the data to GA.
     //
     _gaq.push(['_addTrans',
         orderID,              // Order ID
         '',                   // Affiliation
         formVal,              // Total
         '0.00',               // Tax
         '0.00',               // Shipping
         'Burlington',         // City
         'Vermont',            // State
         'USA'                 // Country
       ]);
```

```
_gaq.push(['_addItem',
    orderID,                        // Order ID
    productName+' : '+ timeName,    // SKU
    productName+' : '+ timeName,    // Product Name
    '',                             // Category
    formVal,                        // Price
    '1'                             // Quantity
]);

//
// Send the transaction to GA!
//
_gaq.push(['_trackTrans']);

alert("Done.  Thanks for submitting the form.");
}

</script>

</head>

<body>

<p>Here is a lead gen form that can be tracked with the e-commerce feature.
    Choose an item from each drop down and click "Submit Data".</p>

<form name="survey" action="" />
<p>Product:<select name="product">
<option value="choose">Select the product you are interested in:</option>
<option value="book">Book</option>
<option value="car">Car</option>
<option value="jet">Jet</option>
</select>
</p>
<br />
<p>Timeframe:<select name="time">
<option value="choose">When would you like to purchase?</option>
<option value="today">Today</option>
<option value="later">In the future</option>
</select>
</p>
<br />
<input type="button" name="submit" value="Submit Data"
    onclick="javascript:recordData(this.form);" />
</form>

</body>
</html>
```

When the visitor submits the form, the JavaScript code assigns a value to both the item the visitor chose and the timeframe for purchase. It then calculates a total value for the form by summing both values.

In this example, a form that includes a high-priced item (like a jet) and a short timeframe (buy now!) is worth more than a low-priced item with an unknown timeframe. I chose arbitrary values for each item and each timeframe, but you could derive these values from business data.

After manipulating the data, the code places both pieces of information in the GA e-commerce format, where they are happily whisked away to Google.

I decided to do all of the calculations in JavaScript because it was easy. You could create a "form calculator" on the server side, but you would still need to format the data like a transaction in order to send it to Google Analytics.

Remember, we're using the e-commerce framework to equate products to form choices, so any report that displays product information will really show form elements and their values.

The best example of this is the E-Commerce→Product Performance→Product Overview report. This report simply lists all of the products that were purchased in all of the transactions.

Based on the way I created the code, each "product" in the report (Figure 10-10) will be a combination of the item that the visitor is interested in and the timeframe for purchase.

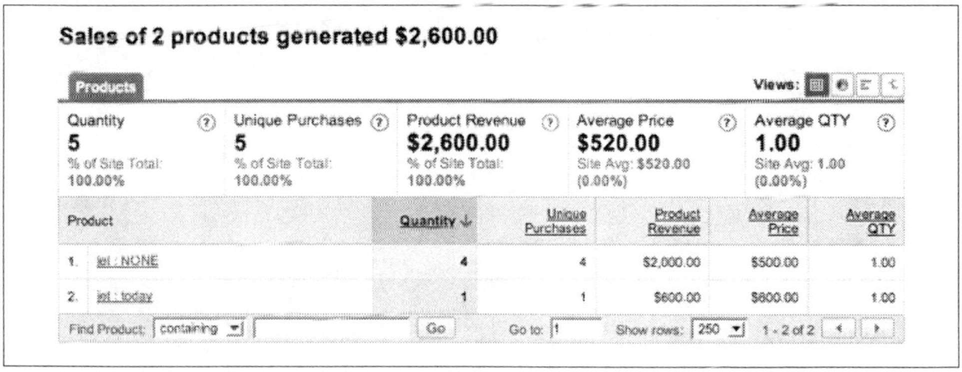

Figure 10-10. E-commerce Product report used to track lead generation form choices

How is this data actionable? This information is the direct voice of the visitor. The visitor is literally telling us what she wants and when she wants it.

From the report in Figure 10-10, we can see that everyone wants a jet. Most visitors did not specify a timeframe for purchase, but one visitor wants a jet today. I'd call that a hot lead!

Another report that is very useful is the E-Commerce→Transactions report (Figure 10-11). In our configuration, this report lists all of the forms that have been submitted and the value of each.

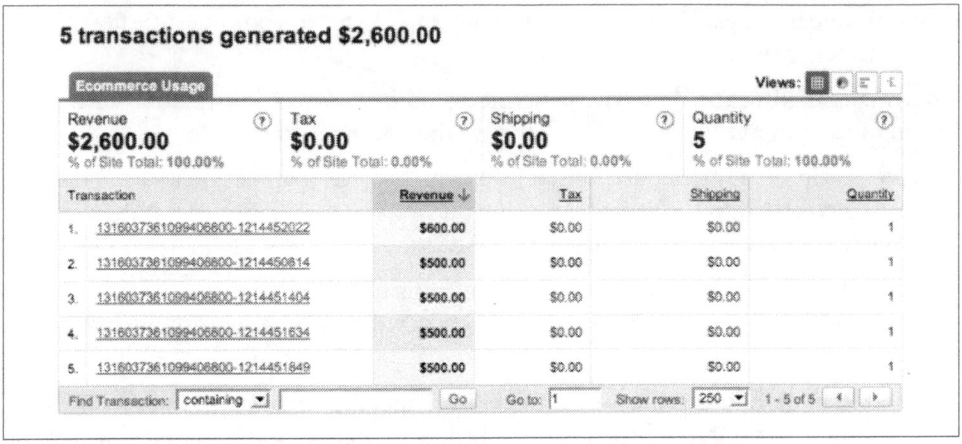

Figure 10-11. E-commerce Transactions report listing lead generation form submissions

The great thing about this report is we can drill into each transaction and review the specific form details. If we click on the first transaction in the report, we can get the details of the form (shown in Figure 10-12).

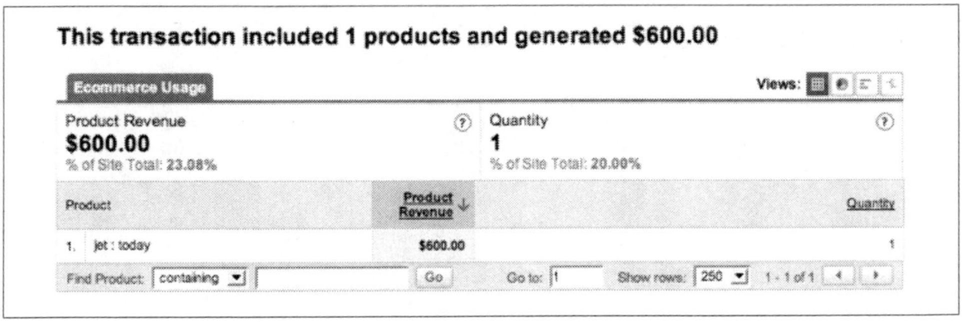

Figure 10-12. Visitor lead generation form choices

I know this example is not that exciting, but imagine a form with many, many fields. You would be able to see all of the visitors' choices and better understand what made a specific form valuable.

The effect of using e-commerce tracking for a lead generation form goes far beyond the e-commerce reports. Remember, many reports in Google Analytics have an Ecommerce tab that displays monetary metrics related to the data in a report.

For example, the Traffic Source→All Traffic Sources report shows metrics like average order value, transactions, and revenue for each traffic source (Figure 10-13). If you use standard goal tracking, you will only get the conversion rate. I think this is far more valuable.

Site Usage	Goal Conversion	**Ecommerce**							Views: ▦ ⊕ ⋿ ⊺

Visits ?	Revenue ?	Transactions ?	Average Value ?	Ecommerce Conversion ? Rate	Per Visit Value ?
4	**$3,520.00**	**15**	**$234.67**	**375.00%**	**$880.00**
% of Site Total: 100.00%	% of Site Total: 100.00%	% of Site Total: 100.00%	Site Avg: $234.67 (0.00%)	Site Avg: 375.00% (0.00%)	Site Avg: $880.00 (0.00%)

Source/Medium		Visits	Revenue ↓	Transactions	Average Value	Ecommerce Conversion Rate	Per Visit Value
1. (direct) / (none)		4	$3,520.00	15	$234.67	375.00%	$880.00

Find Source/Medium: containing ▾ [   ] Go   Go to: 1   Show rows: 10 ▾ 1 - 1 of 1 ◀ ▶

Figure 10-13. Lead values used on the Ecommerce tab

Event Tracking

There is a new paradigm taking shape in the world of web analytics. For a long time, the most granular piece of data we collected was the pageview (Figure 10-14). However, with the onset of new technologies, like Flash and Ajax, and the addition of new content types, like movies and widgets, pageviews no longer provide the necessary data to understand user actions.

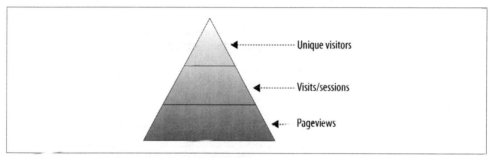

Figure 10-14. The old web analytics data hierarchy

We need a new, more granular piece of data that describes how visitors interact with our content. In Google Analytics, that new piece of data is called *events*.

Events are actions that visitors take on a web page that don't generate new pageviews. Interacting with a video player, a widget, or an audio player are all common events that you can track with Google Analytics.

In the old days (i.e., 2008!) we could track this data as a virtual pageview (see "Understanding Pageviews" on page 23), but this is really ineffective for two reasons. First, it creates lots of pageviews that pollute our true pageview numbers. Second, the reporting wasn't built to handle events, so it doesn't provide any real insight. That's why we have event tracking.

Event tracking adds another layer of data to the visitor data hierarchy, shown in Figure 10-15.

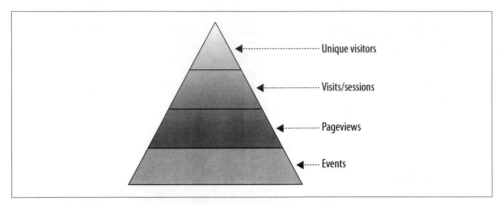

Figure 10-15. The new web analytics data hierarchy, which includes events

Now we can really get a good idea of how visitors are engaging our interactive content. This will be vital as web technologies, like Ajax and Flash and mobile apps, continue to evolve.

Events do not create a lot of new metrics in Google Analytics. Basically, Google Analytics counts how many events occur. All events, and the attributes of events, are recorded as dimensions in Google Analytics. This makes is possible to perform advanced analysis using events in custom reports and advanced segments.

If you're wondering how you might use events, consider the following:

Social media tools

If you're embedding social media tools on your site, you can use event tracking to measure whether people are using these tools. Figure 10-16 shows how REI allows visitors to share content using a number of different social media platforms. Capture clicks to evaluate whether visitors use this type of feature and the ways they like to share.

Embedded video

If your website uses video, you can measure almost all aspects of a video player using event tracking. Start with the basic commands—capture how many times the player loads and how many times the video ends, along with other interactions with the player features (play, pause, skip, etc.). Don't forget to measure which videos people watch and, if you run ads during the videos, use the value field to collect revenue information.

Calculators

Many financial sites contain some type of calculator, like the mortgage calculator shown in Figure 10-17. You can easily track these with event tracking. Use events to capture the various values visitors enter into the calculator, thus providing some insight into visitor needs. Remember, it is against the Google Analytics terms of service to capture any personally identifiable information.

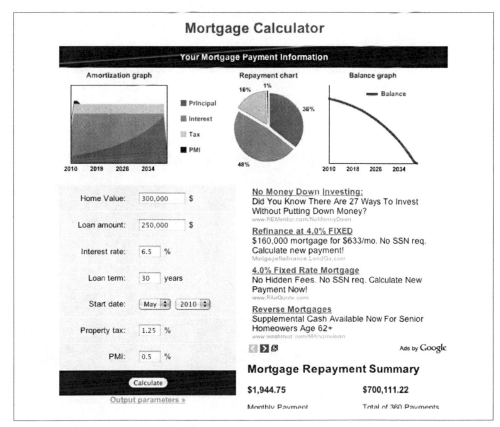

Figure 10-16. Capture different sharing options using event tracking

Figure 10-17. You can track online calculator activity with event tracking

Getting Started with Event Tracking

Before we get into the structure of event data, let's talk about analysis. All analysis starts with a business question. What is the most popular organic keyword that visitors searched for? How many sales did I have last week? What was the revenue for a specific campaign? Normally, when you're using Google Analytics, you don't need to do any special configuration to answer these questions. Google Analytics does most of it for you.

But with events, you need to create *all* of the data that will end up in Google Analytics. You literally need to define what data you want Google Analytics to collect both in name and in value. If you don't know what business questions you want to answer, you won't be able to collect the correct data.

As we continue this section, we'll use Google Maps (shown in Figure 10-18) as our example. If I was an analyst for Google Maps, I would want to answer a lot of questions:

- How many people use the zoom and do they zoom in or out?
- Which map view is most popular: map, satellite, hybrid, etc.
- How many people drag a map waypoint to a new location?

To make things easy, let's focus on one business question: which map view is the most popular? So, now that we know the question we want to answer, let's talk about the data we need to answer it.

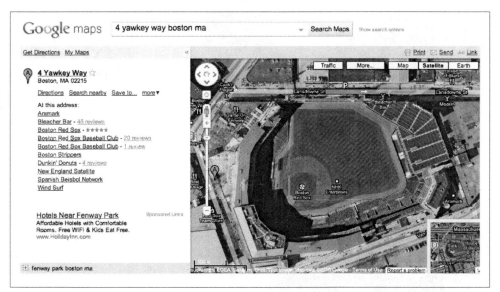

Figure 10-18. Event tracking is the perfect way to track page level objects, like the map in Google Maps

Understanding the data model

There are four parts to the events data model: categories, actions, labels, and values.

Categories are buckets that group the actions visitors perform on our web pages. This may be a video player or an Ajax widget. Using our Google Maps example, the category would be "Map." Remember, the business question we want to answer concerns a feature in the map part of the page.

You can alter the category to meet your reporting needs. Consider that Google Maps appears in multiple languages. If we need to report on the performance of each language version, we may create different values for the categories, specifically one for each language:

- Map – US English
- Map – UK English
- Map – FR French

The second part of the data model is actions. Actions represent the literal actions that visitors perform on our web pages and are grouped by categories. Actions literally tell us what the visitor did.

Lots of actions can occur on a web page. Just think about our map—here are a few actions that our map might have:

- Zoom
- Change view type
- Drag waypoint
- View traffic
- Print
- Send email
- Get a link to the map

Because we're focused on one business question, we're going to focus on one action: change view.

 Google Analytics will report on all actions independently of the categories they're associated with. This provides another way to slice the data and investigate how visitors are interacting with your content. However, there is a drawback to this functionality. If you have two actions with the same name that belong to different categories, Google Analytics will sum their data when you're viewing by action. Be careful when naming your actions. Try to use a unique name so the Actions report will make sense.

Labels describe the action that occurred. If the actions tell us what the visitor did, the value tells us the result. The label value is optional. For the 'Change view type' action listed in the types of actions above, we might have the following labels:

- Satellite
- Satellite with Labels
- Map
- Terrain

Labels are really important to understanding actions. If an action only has one value, it does not provide any insight into what the visitor did.

The final part of the data model is values. Values are optional, but can provide a lot of insight into certain events. Values can be any integer that indicates the value of the action/label combination. The values usually relate back to some type of measurement or a monetary value.

There are no good measurement values associated with our Google Maps data, so let's assign a monetary value to each action/label. Who knows, maybe someone viewing a hybrid map is worth more than someone viewing a regular map due to the ads Google displays:

- Satellite = 10
- Satellite with Labels = 15
- Map = 5
- Terrain = 0

Values have no units associated with them, so if some action/label combination has units of dollars and a different action/label combination has units of miles, Google Analytics will sum them indiscriminately. It's best to stick to one set of units.

Pulling It All Together

So now, let's look at our business question and the data model we're going to use to answer it:

> **Business question we want to answer**: Which view type do visitors use most?
> **Event category**: Map
> **Event actions**: View Change
> **Event labels & values**: Satellite = 10, Satellite with Labels = 15, Map = 5, Terrain = 0

Implementation

Now let's take the data we defined in the previous section and turn it into code.

Step 1: Tag your pages

I know this seems simple, but the first step is to make sure you tag your pages with the Google Analytics tracking code:

```
<script type="text/javascript">

  var _gaq = _gaq || [];
  _gaq.push(['_setAccount', 'UA-XXXXXX-YY']);
  _gaq.push(['_trackPageview']);

(function() {
    var ga = document.createElement('script'); ga.type = 'text/javascript';
    ga.async = true;
    ga.src = ('https:' == document.location.protocol ? 'https://ssl' :
    'http://www') + '.google-analytics.com/ga.js';
    var s = document.getElementsByTagName('script')[0];
    s.parentNode.insertBefore(ga, s);
  })();

</script>
```

In reality, it is not necessary to use the default tracking code, which creates a pageview. You do not need to create a pageview in order to track an event. This makes it possible to track events independently of page content, which can come in handy if you're tracking a widget or some other piece of distributed content.

If you do not want to track a pageview along with your event, you can make this modification to the tracking code:

```
<script type="text/javascript">

  var _gaq = _gaq || [];
  _gaq.push(['_setAccount', 'UA-XXXXXX-YY']);

(function() {
    var ga = document.createElement('script'); ga.type = 'text/javascript';
    ga.async = true;
    ga.src = ('https:' == document.location.protocol ? 'https://ssl' :
    'http://www') + '.google-analytics.com/ga.js';
    var s = document.getElementsByTagName('script')[0];
    s.parentNode.insertBefore(ga, s);
  })();

</script>
```

Step 2: Add code to create event data

You can create all event data using a single line of JavaScript code:

```
_gaq.push(['_trackEvent', category, action, optional_label, optional_value]);
```

You can see that we need to pass our defined values for category, action, label, and value to the _trackEvent() method. Place the above code where the actual actions happen. So, with the Maps example, add some code that tracks when the visitor clicks on the button to change the map view type. Here's how that code might look when someone clicks on the Satellite view button:

```
<a href="#" onclick="_gaq.push(['_trackEvent', 'Map', 'View Change',
    'Satellite', 10]);"
```

The event code can go anywhere you need to track a visitor action. Just be sure that the _gaq object has been created and the _setAccount() method has been added to the queue.

Also, Google Analytics will only collect 500 GATC requests per visit. This includes both pageviews and events. This limit is in place to protect Google Analytics against malicious attacks, and it's very rare for anyone to hit the limit. If you do need to send more than 500 combined requests to Google Analytics per visit, review the amount of data being sent to Google and determine what is truly necessary.

Reporting

The Google Analytics Events report is structured just like the data you create. You can view individual categories, actions, and labels using the report created for each. Figure 10-19 shows the Category report. It shows all the category values that you specify in your code.

35,906 total events were recorded via 3 event categories

Events	Site Usage	Ecommerce			Views:

Total Events	Unique Events	Event Value	Avg. Value
35,906	**19,406**	**73,453,763,566**	**2,045,723.93**
% of Site Total: 100.00%	% of Site Total: 100.00%	% of Site Total: 100.00%	Site Avg: 2,045,723.93 (0.00%)

	Event Category	None ⌄	Total Events ↓	Unique Events	Event Value	Avg. Value
1.	Time On Page		26,905	14,781	73,453,590,848	2,730,109.30
2.	YouTube Video Player		8,996	4,622	17,825	1.98
3.	Time+On+Page		5	3	154,893	30,978.60

Filter Event Category: containing ⌄ [____] Go   Advanced Filter

Go to: 1   Show rows: 10   1 - 3 of 3   ◄   ►

Figure 10-19. The Content→Event Tracking→Category report

You'll notice that Event reports have their own unique metrics. Google Analytics will count the total time this category was recorded, which is the Total Events metric. Unique Events is simply a measurement of visits that included this category, and the Event Value is a sum of all values collected with this category.

We can drill down into this category and view all associated actions and labels by clicking on the Category name (Figure 10-20).

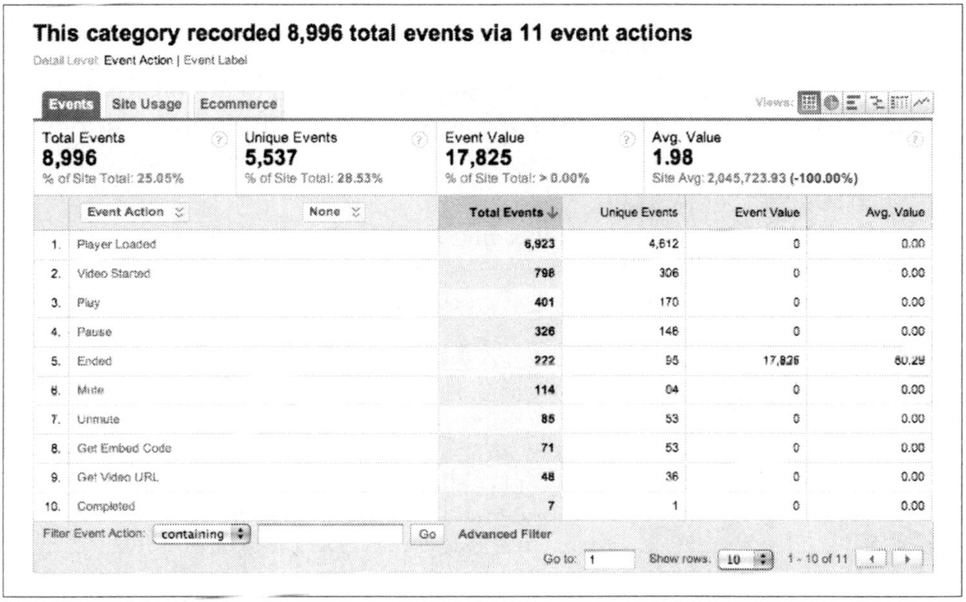

This category recorded 8,996 total events via 11 event actions

Detail Level: **Event Action** | Event Label

Events	Site Usage	Ecommerce				Views:

Total Events	Unique Events	Event Value	Avg. Value
8,996	**5,537**	**17,825**	**1.98**
% of Site Total: 25.05%	% of Site Total: 28.53%	% of Site Total: > 0.00%	Site Avg: 2,045,723.93 (-100.00%)

	Event Action ⌄	None ⌄	Total Events ↓	Unique Events	Event Value	Avg. Value
1.	Player Loaded		6,923	4,612	0	0.00
2.	Video Started		798	306	0	0.00
3.	Play		401	170	0	0.00
4.	Pause		326	148	0	0.00
5.	Ended		222	95	17,825	80.29
6.	Mute		114	64	0	0.00
7.	Unmute		85	53	0	0.00
8.	Get Embed Code		71	53	0	0.00
9.	Get Video URL		48	36	0	0.00
10.	Completed		7	1	0	0.00

Filter Event Action: containing ⌄ [   ] Go   Advanced Filter

Go to: 1   Show rows: 10 ⌄   1 - 10 of 11 ◄ ►

Figure 10-20. Viewing the actions and labels within a category

Figure 10-20 shows the actions associated with this category. We can view the labels by clicking the Event Label link.

You probably noticed that event reports have a Site Usage tab and an Ecommerce tab. The Site Usage tab shows a few metrics (visits, pages/visit, average time on site, and percent new visits) for the respective actions, label, or category (depending on the report you are looking at). The Ecommerce tab shows the results of a specific category, action, or label. Think of it this way, "What were the e-commerce results of my category, action, or label?"

You can also view actions and labels independently of the category using the Action report or Label report, respectively. Google Analytics cannot differentiate between two actions with the same name. For example, if you have a "Play" action for a video player and a "Play" action for an audio player, the Action report will list two line items, both with the value "Play."

Creating events will affect some metrics, like the bounce rate. Normally, if a visitor lands on your site and generates one pageview, Google Analytics will count that visit as a bounce.

However, if a person lands on your site, generates one pageview and an event, Google Analytics will not count that visit as a bounce. When an event is triggered on your website, Google Analytics makes the assumption that the visitor is engaging with your content.

Tracking a Distributed Object

You can use event tracking to track objects on your website, as well as objects on other websites. This can be especially useful if you need to measure a piece of distributed content, like a widget. When you create your widget, add the event tracking code to the necessary areas.

Once deployed, Google Analytics will begin to collect the standard data. In addition, Google Analytics will collect the hostnames of the websites on which your events executed. This information can be useful when evaluating which sites generate the most interaction with your content.

Tracking clicks as events

Tracking clicks as events is very similar to using pageviews to track clicks. Instead of adding the `_trackPageview()` method to HTML, add the Google Analytics event code, add `_trackEvent()`. Use a logical data hierarchy, as shown below, to categorize your clicks. If you don't know how event tracking works, see the section "Event Tracking" on page 135.

Category: Download
Action: [filename]
Label: NONE
Value: [optional, but you can apply a monetary value]

```
<a href="/schedule.pdf" onclick="_gaq.push(['_trackEvent','Download','
    /schedule.pdf','',15]);" />PDF</a>
```

Category: Outbound link
Action: [outbound link URL]
Label: NONE
Value: [optional, but you can apply a monetary value]

```
<a href="http://www.cutroni.com"
    onclick="_gaq.push(['_trackEvent','Outbound Link','',this.href,, 10]);"
    />www.cutroni.com</a>
```

If you would rather capture the outbound click as a virtual pageview, use the following function:

```
<script type="text/javascript">
function trackDownload(link, category, action) {
    _gaq.push(['trackEvent',category, action);
    setTimeout('document.location = "' + link.href + '"', 100);
}
</script>
```

Custom Variables

Custom Variables are an evolution of the Google Analytics User-Defined, or Custom Segmentation, feature. Like Custom Segmentation, Custom Variables provide a flexible way to add more information to Google Analytics. The big difference is that you can create multiple custom variables and you can create three different types of custom variables. With the ability to track multiple custom variables and different types of custom variables, you can use the Custom Variables feature for many different things, like:

- Segmenting members from nonmembers
- Segmenting customers from noncustomers
- Tracking all the campaigns a visitor sees prior to converting
- Content categorization
- Visitor segmentation based on demographic information
- Customer segmentation based on customer loyalty
- Measuring visitor lifetime value

As my friend Phil likes to say, custom variables are decorations that you hang on your data. Almost like holiday decorations hanging on a tree! We can use this additional information to segment our Google Analytics data and gain a deeper understanding of our website performance. The great thing is custom variables hold data that *you* define.

Before we get into how to implement custom variables, you need to understand how they're structured. There are three parts to a custom variable:

Name and Value
> Each custom variable is basically a name-value pair. You can create many different values, each with a different name. For example, if you want to track a visitor's favorite baseball teams, you can create a variable named fav_team. This variable could then have multiple values. This is totally different than the old Custom Segmentation feature, which limited you to one variable (i.e., one name) that could contain multiple values. Now you can create multiple variables, each of which can have multiple values.

The name of a variable plus the value for a variable must be fewer than 64 characters. Why? The data is sent to Google via a request for an image file. The actual length of the request is limited and Google wants to ensure that all of the data makes it to the server.

Index

Think of the index as a placeholder. From a programming standpoint, Google needs some type of structure to hold custom variables. The solution was to create an index with five slots. This means that at any one time you can set five custom variables. This does not mean that you can only set five custom variables, just five custom variables at one time.

 For those who want to dig deep into the *ga.js* tracking code, there is a specific method that you can use to increase the number slots in the index. While you can execute this code and increase the number of slots, Google will not process more than five custom variables at a time.

Scope

The real power of custom variables comes with something called the scope. Think of scope as the different levels of visitor data. When a visitor visits a website, Google Analytics collects custom variables at three levels:

Pageview-level

This is data associated with each page viewed during a visit. Page-level data can change from one page to the next.

Visit-level

This is data associated with the visitor's entire visit. This data can change from one visit to the next, but visit-level data is applied to every page within a visit. This data only exists for the *current* visits.

Visitor-level

This data is applied to the visitor for every visit and every pageview the visitor generates. This data persists across all visits that a visitor creates. Visitor-level custom variables are stored in the __utmv cookie on the visitor's machine.

The ability to control the scope of a custom variable makes this feature extremely flexible. For example, if you want to group all of the content on your site, you can add a page-level custom variable to every page that identifies the groups a page belongs to.

If you want to segment visitors by their purchase history, you can add a visitor-level custom variable containing information about the visitor's purchase history. The possibilities are truly endless.

However, things get complicated when we start to discuss scope and how it interacts with the index. Scope can influence which slots in the index are filled and how long they remain filled. If you try to place a value in a slot that is already being used, you may overwrite the data that was previously set. So, it's important to know which slots are open and which are filled. You can place multiple variables in the same slot, but you'll overwrite the existing variables and could lose valuable information.

Here is a simple way to understand how each scope (page-level, visit-level and visitor-level) can affect the slots in the index:

- When you set a *visitor*-level custom variable, you should *never* use that slot again.
- When you set a *visit*-level custom variable, you should *never* use that slot again *during the same visit*.
- When you set a *page*-level custom variable, you should *never* use that slot again *during the same visit on the same page*.

These suggestions are based on *not* overwriting existing variables.

Let's look at data from a visit and discuss the scope and index of the custom variables. Figure 10-21 shows four pages in a visitor's visit. On each page in the visit, we would like to set a page-level custom variable. Perhaps we're using the custom variable to group the site content. We also want to set visit- and visitor-level custom variables when the visitor performs certain actions, like adding a product to a shopping cart or logging in to his account. These last two custom variables are set when the actions are performed.

	Page 1	Page 2	Page 3	Page 4
Visit 1	Page [1]	Page [1]	Page [1] Page [2] Visit [3]	Page [1] Visitor [2]

Figure 10-21. Four pages from a visitor's visit and the custom variables set on each page

Looking at the progression of pageviews for this visit, the visitor views Page 1 and we set a page-level variable in slot 1. This variable is the category for the page. Next, the visitor moves to Page 2 and again we set a page-level custom variable in slot 1 to categorize the page. We can reuse slot 1, because it opened up after the visitor left Page 1.

Moving on to Page 3, we set three custom variables. We set a page-level custom variable to categorize the page in slot 1. This means that we cannot use slot 1 for any other variable on Page 3. Then we set a second page-level variable on Page 3 to place the content in a second category. This means we cannot use slot 1 or slot 2 again on Page

3. Finally, we create a visit-level custom variable on Page 3 to identify that the visitor added an item to his cart. This means we cannot use slot 3 again during the entire visit.

Finally, when the visitor arrives on Page 4, we set a page-level custom variable to categorize the page and a visitor-level custom variable to identify that the visitor shared some demographic information. Because we created a visitor-level custom variable in slot 2, we cannot use slot 2 on any subsequent visits, because it will be full. Remember, a visitor-level custom variable persists from one visit to the next. This means the slot containing the custom variable remains full.

Remember, this is just an example. The entire scenario could be broken if the visitor did not progress through the pages as described. What if the visitor saw page 4 before page 3?

Let's look at this cross-visit behavior a bit more by examining a second visit for this visitor (Figure 10-22).

	Page 1	Page 2	Page 3	Page 4
Visit 1	Page [1]	Page [1]	Page [1] Page [2] Visit [3]	Page [1] Visitor [2]
Visit 2 No slot 2	Page [1]	Page [1] Page [3]	Visitor[1]	

Figure 10-22. Two visits for a visitor and the custom variables set on each pageview

Before we discuss the custom variables that will be set during the second visit, remember that we can no longer use slot 2. This slot was filled with a visitor-level custom variable during the first visit, so it remains filled when the second visit begins. We can still use slots 1, 3, 4, and 5.

Looking at the pageviews and custom variables from visit 2, we can see that another visitor-level custom variable was set in slot 1 on Page 3. This means that slot 1 and slot 2 are now filled. If the visitor returns a third time, we can only work with slots 3,4, and 5.

From this very simple example, you can see it is critical to plan your custom variable implementation. Before you start the implementation, you must understand which data you want to track, which scope the data should occupy, and how you will manage the slots in the index.

As a best practice, try using the same scope for the same index. It will help ensure the same variable is always set in the same index.

Custom Variable Implementation

Let's move on and look at the actual code used to create the custom variables. Luckily, the implementation is fairly straightforward. Again, to reiterate, planning your custom variables is critical.

Like all things in Google Analytics, the data comes from JavaScript. There is a method named _setCustomVar() that creates the custom variable. You can see the name and value, along with the index and scope:

```
_gaq.push(['_setCustomVar', index, name, value, opt_scope]);
```

To create a custom variable, add the JavaScript to the appropriate place in your website with the desired values. Remember, the code is just JavaScript, so you can attach it to many different HTML event handlers, like onLoad, onclick, or onSubmit. You can also place it in Ajax and Flash. Where you place _setCustomVar() depends on when you have the business data available to set the custom variable.

If possible, it is best to place the custom variable code *before* any calls to _trackPage view(). Custom variable data is sent to Google Analytics with pageview or event. It is not sent when the _setCustomVar() method is called. If you set a custom variable and it is the last thing that happens during a visit, the data will never be sent to Google Analytics; another *__utm.gif* request must occur to transmit the custom variable data to Google.

The name and value passed into _setCustomVar() will be stored in the __utmv cookie. When Google Analytics processes your profile data, it creates five custom variable fields and populates it with the values in the __utmv cookie. This field is just like any other field in Google Analytics. You can create filters using this field or view reports constructed from this field.

For example, say you have a contact form on your site that contains a drop-down list that allows users to specify their gender. If you want capture their answers and segment your visitors by gender, call the _setCustomVar() method when the form is submitted. This creates the custom segment cookie and sets the user-chosen value as the value. Here's how the HTML code might look:

```
<form onsubmit="_gaq.push(['_setCustomVar',1,'Gender',this.gender.options
    [this.gender.selectedIndex].value,3);">
<select name="gender">
<option value="Female">Female</option>
<option value="Male">Male</option>
</select>
```

Remember, the index value and the scope are integers. The index will be 1, 2, 3, 4, or 5 to represent the slot that the custom variable will occupy. The scope will be 1 for a visitor-level custom variable, 2 for a visit-level custom variable, and 3 for a page-level custom variable.

Also remember that the combination of the custom variable name and the custom variable value must not exceed 64 characters.

Custom Variable Reporting

To be honest, the custom variable reporting is fairly basic. All of the custom variable names are listed in the Visitors→Custom Variable report, as shown in Figure 10-23. When you click on the name of a custom variable, you will see all of the values for that custom variable.

You have 13 unique custom variables

	Custom Variable	Visits ↓	Hits	Pages/Visit	Avg. Time on Site	% New Visits	Bounce Rate
1.	content	9,654	20,966	2.17	00:03:40	38.27%	44.01%
2.	content	8,206	19,061	2.26	00:03:53	41.03%	40.51%
3.	author	6,049	8,618	1.37	00:01:48	71.48%	74.95%
4.	year	6,011	8,481	1.35	00:01:49	71.85%	75.33%
5.	category	5,992	8,443	1.35	00:01:49	72.08%	75.57%
6.	Visitor%20Type	310	1,078	1.74	00:01:59	80.00%	0.00%
7.	channel	289	511	0.00	00:00:01	4.84%	0.00%
8.	usergroup	6	7	1.00	00:00:00	0.00%	83.33%
9.	Combination	2	2	1.00	00:00:00	0.00%	100.00%
10.	GWO	2	3	1.50	00:12:12	50.00%	50.00%

Figure 10-23. You can compare the performance of your custom segments using the Custom Variable report

So why has Google added a scope if we can't see it in the reports? I'm just going to let you speculate, but it's obviously a critical part of custom variables and we should see that data in reports.

Once the data is in Google Analytics, there are a number of ways to view how your custom segments perform. The easiest way is using the Visitors→Custom Variables report. This report shows a wealth of information for your custom segments, including basic visitation data (visits, average pageviews per visit, etc.) and conversion data.

Another way to utilize the custom segment value is to create advanced segments and custom reports. When Google Analytics collects custom segment data, it creates a number of custom variable dimensions that you can use when building an advanced segment or a custom report. Figure 10-24 shows the custom variable dimensions in a custom report.

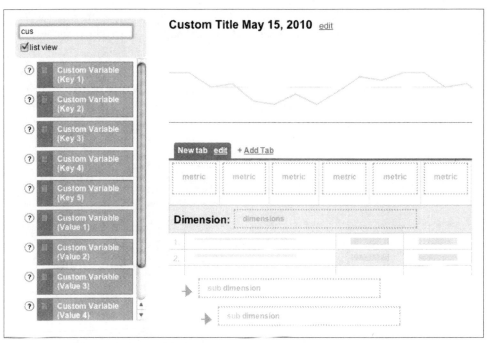

Figure 10-24. The Custom Variable dimensions in a custom report

Segmenting Members from Nonmembers

One way to use custom variables is to segment members from nonmembers. Why is this so important? Members and nonmembers are very different groups of people. Members are usually those who have already converted at some goal. Nonmembers are those you are trying to convert. Segmenting the two groups allows you to better understand each group and their needs.

It doesn't matter which analytics tool you use, if your website has some type of member's area, you need to segment out members to get an accurate view of your website performance and online marketing activities.

Custom variables provide a great way to segment members from nonmembers in Google Analytics. To do so, you need to call _setCustomVar() when a member identifies herself. You can put it on a "Thanks for logging in" page. Here's a perfectly good implementation of the code:

```
<script type="text/javascript">
  _gaq.push(['_setCustomVar',1,'Visitor_Type','Member',3]);
</script>
```

This example uses a visitor-level scope, as membership is a visitor attribute that is likely to persist from one visit to the next. I placed the variable in slot 1, but your implementation will likely be different due to the use of other custom variables.

Remember, if possible, place the above code snippet *before* the call to `_trackPage view()`, so the custom variable data is sent to Google Analytics when the pageview data is sent.

Once the cookie has been set on the visitor's machine, you can use the standard Custom Variable reports to view each segment, or you can create an advanced custom segment to perform a deeper analysis of each group. Figure 10-25 shows the settings for an advanced segment to identify members.

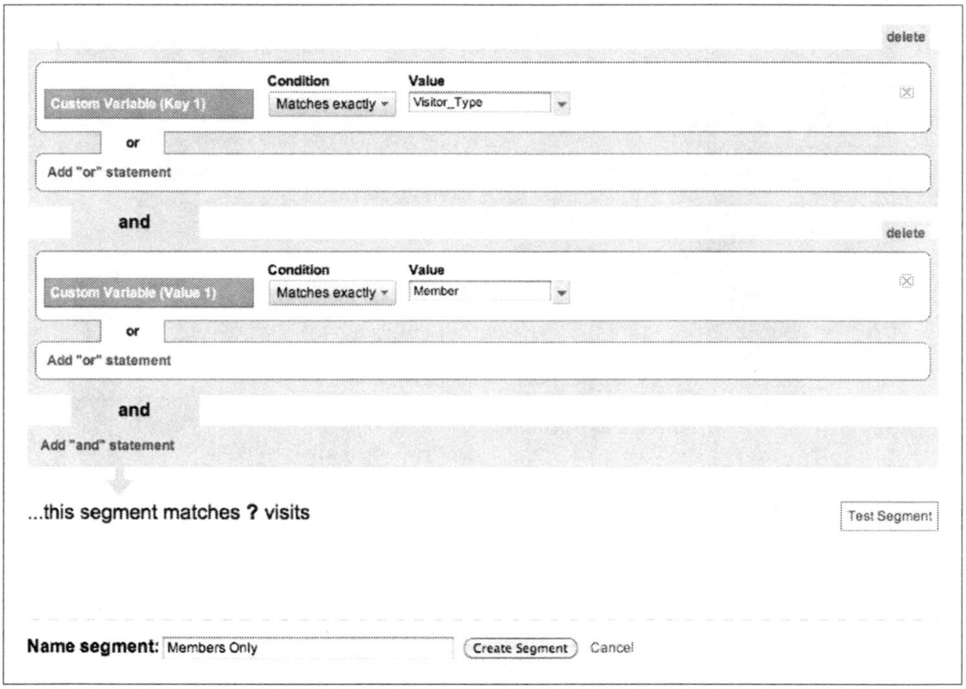

Figure 10-25. An advanced segment to identify members

Notice the dimensions in this advanced segment: Custom Variable (Key 1) and Custom Variable (Value 1). These relate back to the slot that we used when setting the custom variable. The membership custom variable was set in Slot 1, corresponding to Key 1 and Value 1 used in the advanced segment.

When you apply this advanced segment to a profile, it will help you identify what members are doing on the site. By creating a segment specifically for members, you can focus on their usage of the member's area. For example, the Top Content report will identify the content they find most engaging. You can also use some of the loyalty reports to see how often they use the website.

You can just as easily create a segment for nonmembers by changing the conditions in the second part of the advanced segment to identify those who are not members (Figure 10-26).

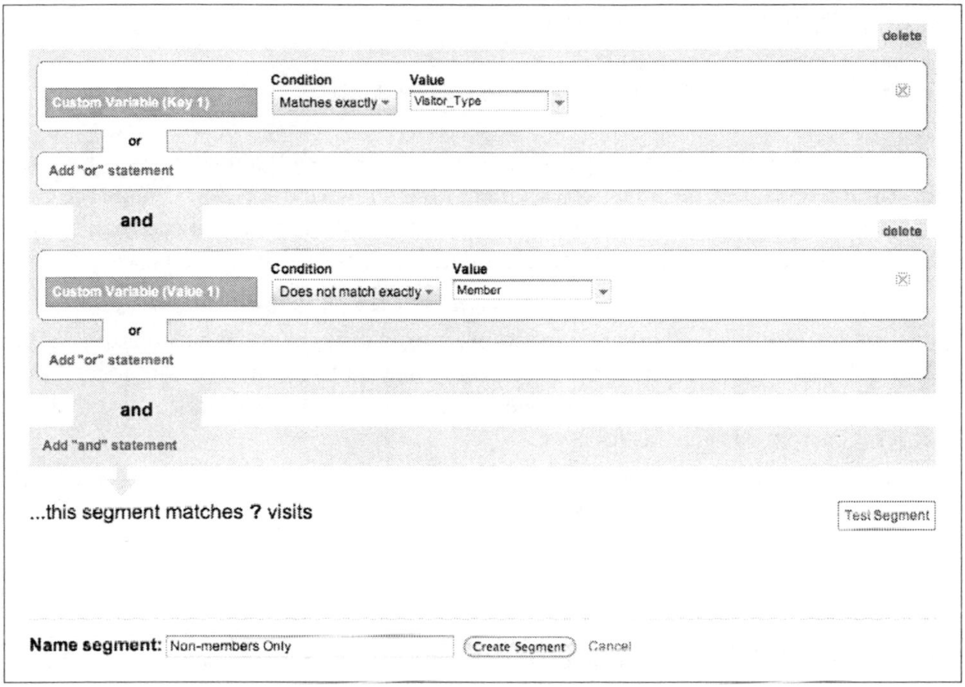
delete
Condition
Value
Custom Variable (Key 1)
Matches exactly
Visitor_Type
or
Add "or" statement
and
delete
Condition
Value
Custom Variable (Value 1)
Does not match exactly
Member
or
Add "or" statement
and
Add "and" statement
...this segment matches ? visits
Test Segment
Name segment:
Non-members Only
Create Segment
Cancel

Figure 10-26. An advanced segment to identify nonmembers

This advanced segment will show data for those visitors who are not members, thus providing a more accurate view of how effective the website is at converting visitors.

> You cannot use custom variables in profile filters. If you need to segment members from nonmembers at the profile level, you can still use the old Custom Segmentation feature, but you cannot use both Custom Segmentation and Custom Variables at the same time.
>
> At the time of this writing, the only way to segment using Custom Variables is through the Advanced Segmentation feature.

If your membership model has various levels, like Gold, Silver, and Bronze, you can include this information in an additional custom variable. This allows for a more detailed analysis of each membership level. For example, use the following code to set a Gold level:

```
<script type="text/javascript">
_gaq.push(['_setCustomVar',2,'Member_Level','Gold',1]);
</script>
```

Use the following to set a Silver level:

```
<script type="text/javascript">
_gaq.push(['_setCustomVar',2,'Member_Level','Silver',1]);
</script>
```

Use the following to set a Bronze level:

```
<script type="text/javascript">
_gaq.push(['_setCustomVar',2,'Member_Level','Bronze',1]);
</script>
```

After setting the custom variable cookie, you can create different segments for each subscription level. Use the advanced segment filter shown earlier, and change the Custom Variable Value to match one of the values in the code above. You can then use the advanced segments to analyze the member data and observe their habits.

In addition to tracking members and nonmembers, as well as the different membership levels, we can also track whether members are logged in to the site when visiting. While membership is a visitor trait that persists from one visit to the next, being logged in is a session attribute that changes from one visit to the next. As a result, it's best to use a visit-level custom variable, as follows:

```
<script type="text/javascript">
_gaq.push(['_setCustomVar',3,'Member_Status','Logged_In',2]);
</script>
```

This code should appear after the visitor logs in.

Custom Variables for E-Commerce

You can use custom variables on e-commerce websites for many different things, including measuring loyalty and customer value. Many organizations define customer loyalty based on purchasing frequency. You can implement this with some simple server-side code and custom variables.

The first step is to define the custom variables. For this example, we will use a single variable named Cust_Type (short for Customer Type) and assign it one of three values based on purchase history:

- New customers, 1 purchase
- Return customers, 2 or 3 purchases
- Loyal customers, 4 or more purchases

The next step is to create server-level code that identifies how many times a customer has made a purchase. The exact implementation will be specific to your site, but in most cases this will be some type of database query. Once the server-level code has determined the purchase history, it must create the appropriate custom variable JavaScript.

For a new customer, the final JavaScript will look like this:

```
<script type="text/javascript">
  _gaq.push(['_setCustomVar',5,'Cust_Type','New',1]);
</script>
```

For a return customer, the final JavaScript will look like this:

```
<script type="text/javascript">
  _gaq.push(['_setCustomVar',5,'Cust_Type','Return',1]);
</script>
```

And for a loyal customer, the final JavaScript will look like this:

```
<script type="text/javascript">
  _gaq.push(['_setCustomVar',5,'Cust_Type','Loyal',1]);
</script>
```

You can also track the value of a customer based on lifetime revenue from that customer using a custom variable. You can do this with a single variable that contains the total revenue from a customer. Every time the customer makes a new purchase, you can update the custom variable with the total revenue from the customer. The JavaScript might look something like this:

```
<script type="text/javascript">
  _gaq.push)['_setCustomVar',4,'Cust_Value','1,000.00',1]);
</script>
```

Notice that the dollar value is within quotes. This is because the value is a string and must always be in quotes. As is the case with the customer loyalty variables, most of the work for the customer value variable is server-level programming. You must create code that generates the value and inserts the Google Analytics code in the appropriate place.

One final idea for using custom variables with an e-commerce website is to measure coupon usage. You can create a visit-level custom variable that tracks coupon usage and segments traffic according to whether visitors used a coupon when completing a transaction:

```
<script type="text/javascript">
  _gaq.push(['_setCustomVar',1,'Coupon','Free_Ship',2]);
</script>
```

This code sets a visit-level custom variable called Coupon. The value of the custom variable is the type of coupon used. In this case, it was a free-shipping coupon. Again, a majority of the work is creating the server-side code that identifies that the visitor used a coupon (and which coupon he used), and then formats the custom variable JavaScript accordingly.

Custom Variables for Publishers

Many publishers have been waiting for custom variables to come to Google Analytics. Until now there has been no good way for publishers to logically categorize their content in Google Analytics. Many companies tried by creating custom URI structures using _trackPageview(), but the resulting data was less than optimal.

Page-level custom variables are ideal for categorizing content. Because a piece of content can live in many different categories, you can use a different custom variable for each category. For example, perhaps an article is part of the Sports category and the Opinion category. You may implement a page-level custom variable like this:

```
<script type="text/javascript">
  _gaq.push(['_setCustomVar',1,'Cat','Sports',3]);
  _gaq.push(['_setCustomVar',2,'Cat','Opinion',3]);
</script>
```

Publishers can also use custom variables to categorize content by author, publication data, or any other attribute that aids in analysis. Imagine segmenting all content based on publication year to gain a better understanding of the organic search value of old content. This is easy with a custom variable.

Roll-Up Reporting

Roll-up reporting is a technique used to gather data at different levels. For example, larger organizations may have many, many websites and it may be necessary to track all of these websites individually and then aggregate the data in order to understand how the organization is doing as a whole. There are two ways to do roll-up reporting, and the implementation you choose will depend on your business needs and site architecture.

Roll-up reporting for subdomains

Organizations that have all of their websites on a single primary domain can use a filter-based approach to roll-up reporting. Let's look at a scenario in which all of the websites for an organization reside on different subdomains:

- Data from *shop.mystore.com*
- Data from *support.mystore.com*
- Data from *products.mystore.com*
- Data from all three subdomains

Our goal is to provide metrics across all of the different subdomains and for each subdomain individually. To do this, we install the same tracking code on all of the websites and configure the tracking code for subdomain tracking. The code would look like this:

```
<script type="text/javascript">

  var _gaq = _gaq || [];
  _gaq.push(['_setAccount', 'UA-XXXXXX-YY']);
  _gaq.push(['_setDomainName', '.mystore.com']);
  _gaq.push(['_trackPageview']);

(function() {
    var ga = document.createElement('script'); ga.type = 'text/javascript';
    ga.async = true;
    ga.src = ('https:' == document.location.protocol ? 'https://ssl' :
    'http://www') + '.google-analytics.com/ga.js';
```

```
    var s = document.getElementsByTagName('script')[0];
    s.parentNode.insertBefore(ga, s);
  })();
```

```
</script>
```

Then, in Google Analytics, we create multiple profiles to segment the data based on subdomain. Refer to Chapter 3 for more information about creating the duplicate profiles. Once complete, you'll need to add the filters listed in Table 10-6 to the different profiles to include the necessary data to each profile.

Table 10-6. Profile filters to segment data when doing roll-up reporting

Profile	Filter
All data from all subdomains	Custom Filter
	Type: Advanced Filter
	Field A: Hostname
	Field B: Request URI
	Extract A: (.*)
	Extract B: (.*)
	Output To: Request URI
	Constructor: $A1$A2
Data from *shop.mystore.com*	Custom Filter
	Type: Include
	Field: Hostname
	shop\.mystore\.com
Data from *support.mystore.com*	Custom Filter
	Type: Include
	Field: Hostname
	support\.mystore\.com
Data from *products.mystore.com*	Custom Filter:
	Type: Include
	Field: Hostname
	products\.mystore\.com

 You should create raw data profiles and test profiles for each of the above.

There are certain things that can complicate this setup. Specifically, you cannot filter e-commerce data and event data. So, if the site uses events to track many different things and you need to segment these events by subdomain, this technique will not work. When looking at the profile for *products.mystore.com*, it will contain all of the events generated on all of the subdomains.

The same is true for e-commerce data. The profile for *products.mystore.com* will contain all e-commerce data for all of the subdomains. However, you *can* filter e-commerce data. You must create an additional filter that filters e-commerce data based on some field.

Normally when filtering e-commerce data, we add some type of identifier to the transaction ID to make it easier to identify where the transaction occurred. For example, for transactions occurring on the store subdomain, we modify the transaction ID by adding *store_* to the beginning of every transaction ID. This value is added by some server-side code.

Then, once the transaction ID has an identifier, we create an include filter, as shown in Figure 10-27, to include only transactions for that subdomain.

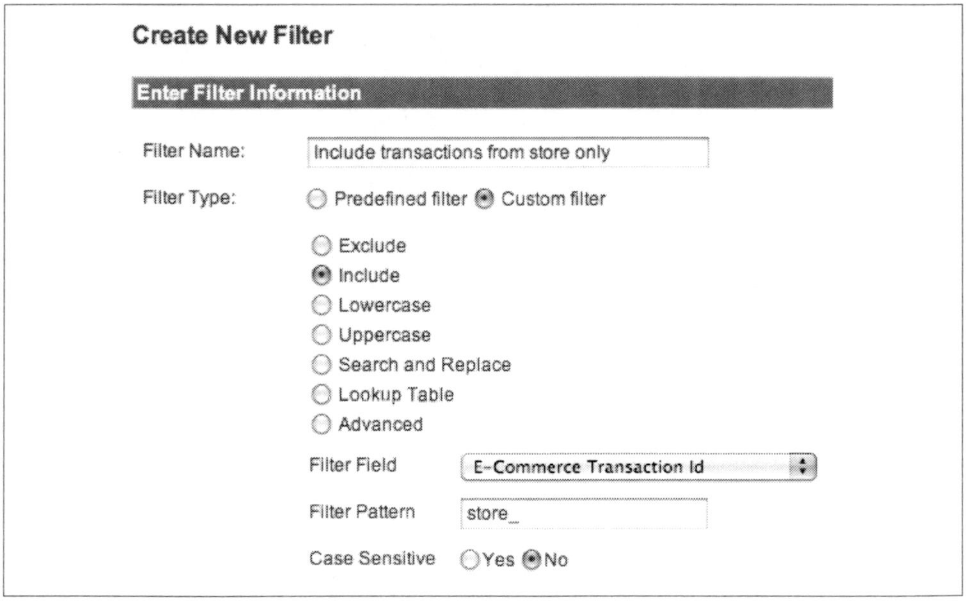

Figure 10-27. Include filter to only include transactions from the store subdomain

Obviously, this could be a very complicated implementation based on your ability to modify the transaction IDs coming from your site.

Roll-up reporting across multiple domains

The second type of roll-up reporting is tracking multiple unrelated websites that reside on different primary domains. This implementation can be much more challenging, as it involves adding different tracking code to each individual website. Each website will require two versions of the GATC: one version to track the individual site and a second version to track the site in a roll-up profile.

Let's look at an example in which we will track three sites individually but also at a roll-up level:

- Data from *www.site1.com*
- Data from *www.site2.com*
- Data from *www.site3.com*
- Data from all sites

The code placed on *www.site1.com* looks like this:

```
<script type="text/javascript">

  var _gaq = _gaq || [];
  _gaq.push(['site1Tracker._setAccount', 'UA-XXXXXX-1']);
  _gaq.push(['site1Tracker._setDomainName', '.site1.com']);
  _gaq.push(['site1Tracker._trackPageview']);

  _gaq.push(['rollupTracker._setAccount', 'UA-XXXXXX-2']);
  _gaq.push(['rollupTracker._setDomainName', '.site1.com']);
  _gaq.push(['rollupTracker._trackPageview']);

(function() {
    var ga = document.createElement('script'); ga.type = 'text/javascript';
    ga.async = true; ga.src = ('https:' == document.location.protocol ?
    'https://ssl' : 'http://www') + '.google-analytics.com/ga.js';
    var s = document.getElementsByTagName('script')[0];
    s.parentNode.insertBefore(ga, s);
})();

</script>
```

Notice that the first section of code (containing UA-XXXXXX-1) has been essentially duplicated in the second section (containing UA-XXXXXX-2). This code creates a second tracking object. The code in the first section collects data using a tracking object named siteTracker and sends that data back to profile ID 1. The second tracker, named rollupTracker, sends the data back to profile ID 2. Both blocks of code do exactly the same thing. The only difference is they send the data back to different profiles, thus allowing us to collect data for the individual profiles and at a roll-up level.

This type of roll-up tracking also has challenges. If the website is an e-commerce website and we would like to track transactions at both an individual site level and at an aggregate level, we must duplicate the tracking code. Remember, we need to send the data to two different profiles, identified by two different tracking objects. This means two sets of e-commerce code for every transaction:

```
<script type="text/javascript">
  _var _gaq = _gaq || [];
  _gaq.push(['site1Tracker._setAccount', 'UA-XXXXXX-1']);
  _gaq.push(['site1Tracker._setDomainName', '.site1.com']);
  _gaq.push(['site1Tracker._trackPageview']);

  _gaq.push(['rollupTracker._setAccount', 'UA-XXXXXX-2']);
  _gaq.push(['rollupTracker._setDomainName', '.site1.com']);
  _gaq.push(['rollupTracker._trackPageview']);

  //
  // Send the data to the individual site profile
  //
  _gaq.push(['site1Tracker._addTrans',
    '{ORDER ID}',   // order ID - required
    '{AFFILIATE}',  // affiliation or store name
    '{TOTAL}',      // total - required
    '{TAX}',        // tax
    '{SHIPPING}',   // shipping
    '{CITY}',       // city
    '{STATE}',      // state or province
    '{COUNTRY}'     // country
  ]);
  _gaq.push(['site1Tracker._addItem',
    '{ORDER ID}',       // order ID-needed to associate item with transaction
    '{SKU}',            // SKU/code - required
    '{PROD NAME}',      // product name
    '{PROD CATEGORY}',  // category or variation
    '{UNIT PRICE}',     // unit price - required
    '{QUANTITY}'        // quantity - required
  ]);
  _gaq.push(['site1Tracker._trackTrans']); //submits transaction

  //
  // Send the data to the rollup profile
  //
  _gaq.push(['rollupTracker._addTrans',
    '{ORDER ID}',   // order ID - required
    '{AFFILIATE}',  // affiliation or store name
    '{TOTAL}',      // total - required
    '{TAX}',        // tax
    '{SHIPPING}',   // shipping
    '{CITY}',       // city
    '{STATE}',      // state or province
    '{COUNTRY}'     // country
  ]);
  _gaq.push(['rollupTracker._addItem',
    '{ORDER ID}',       // order ID-needed to associate item with transaction
    '{SKU}',            // SKU/code - required
    '{PROD NAME}',      // product name
```

```
            '{PROD CATEGORY}', // category or variation
            '{UNIT PRICE}',    // unit price - required
            '{QUANTITY}'       // quantity - required
        ]);
        _gaq.push(['rollupTracker._trackTrans']);
        //submits transaction to the Analytics servers
    </script>
```

Not only must you duplicate the transaction code, you must also duplicate the event tracking code and the custom variable code. The reason is that the data must be sent to every distinct profile ID. You can now see how this can become very complicated very quickly.

There is an alternative to this implementation. It is possible to use the Advanced Segment feature to segment traffic to different domains in real time. Figure 10-28 shows an advanced custom segment based on the hostname field.

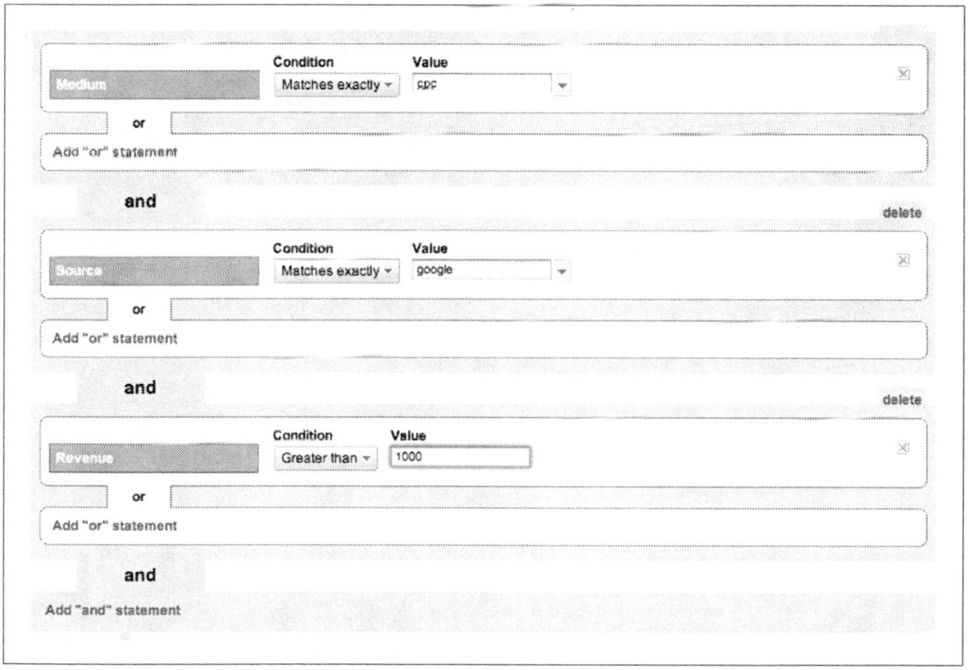

Figure 10-28. Using an advanced custom segment to segment traffic to different sites

However, advanced segmentation uses sampling if you try to segment too much data. Plus, if you need to control access to the data, you must do so using profiles and filters. If you have only one profile and ask users to segment the data using an advanced custom segment, users will still see all data.

Enterprise Implementation Considerations

There has been much debate as to whether Google Analytics is an enterprise-class web analytics tool. The simple fact is that if Google Analytics meets your reporting and analysis needs, it is a viable solution for your organization. I've worked with many organizations that would traditionally be classified as enterprise; they are global organizations with hundreds of websites and many different types of analytics users.

When implementing Google Analytics in these types of organizations, many unique issues can arise. It can take some work to design a solution that is technically viable and meets the overall business needs of the organization. If you're dealing with an enterprise implementation, keep an eye out for these issues.

Issue #1: Roll-Up Reporting

Large organizations tend to have more sites, and more sites mean more data. Collecting the data in a business-centric fashion that allows room for growth and appropriate access for users takes time and planning.

During an enterprise implementation, we usually create a series of accounts and profiles that collect and segment the data based on business logic and access needs. We create a data hierarchy that provides high-level aggregate tracking across the entire online experience (i.e., roll-up reporting) and detailed tracking for each individual property (i.e., website).

Let's consider a totally fictitious scenario: implementing Google Analytics for Major League Baseball (MLB). Obviously, the implementation would begin with documenting the business needs. To simplify our example, we will make some general assumptions:

- MLB needs aggregate data across all team websites as well as individual team tracking.
- Each team has its own site located on a subdomain of *www.mlb.com*.
- Teams should have access to their own data, but not the data of other teams.
- Teams should not see aggregate data for the entire MLB network of sites.
- There is an MLB store and different microsites dedicated to events like the All-Star Games and the World Series.

While the exact implementation will depend on the client's specific needs, it probably involves collecting all the data in a single profile for roll-up reporting, and then creating profiles for each team and microsite for detailed reporting. The following code is the standard page tag that includes the creation of multiple tracking objects (shown in bold):

```
<script type="text/javascript">

  var _gaq = _gaq || [];
  _gaq.push(['teamTracker._setAccount', 'UA-XXXXXX-Y']);
  _gaq.push(['teamTracker._trackPageview']);
  _gaq.push(['rollupTracker._setAccount', 'UA-XXXXXX-2']);
  _gaq.push(['rollupTracker._trackPageview']);

  (function() {
    var ga = document.createElement('script'); ga.type = 'text/javascript';
    ga.async = true;
    ga.src = ('https:' == document.location.protocol ? 'https://ssl' :
    'http://www') + '.google-analytics.com/ga.js';
    var s = document.getElementsByTagName('script')[0];
    s.parentNode.insertBefore(ga, s);
  })();

</script>
```

Issue #2: Unique Visitors

Tracking lots of domains usually leads to an issue with unique visitor tracking. Google Analytics uses a first-party cookie to identify each visitor. This means if a visitor visits three different domains, he will receive three different cookies and appear as three different unique visitors.

Now, Google Analytics has a cross-domain tracking feature to track unique visitors across multiple domains, but what happens if an enterprise wants to know the unique visitor count across 50 web properties? Installing cross-domain tracking on that scale is a huge task (see Chapter 10 for more information). In fact, it's a pain in the ass.

Many of the clients that I've worked with have compromised and ignored unique visitor tracking for the sake of simplifying the implementation.

You may be different. Unique visitors may be the one critical metric that you can't live without. Could you use Google Analytics? Maybe, but you should carefully weigh the implementation needs versus your analysis needs.

Issue #3: Page Tagging

When I first started working with Google Analytics, I never thought that tagging pages would be an issue, but it is. It's not so much a technical issue as it is an organizational issue. Big companies can have so many sites with so many nooks and crannies. It can take a lot of work to identify every site, find an owner, and place the tags in the appropriate place.

There are a few tools that can help simplify the page tagging processes. A tool called TagMan (*http://troni.me/TagMan*) can greatly simplify the tagging process by creating a universal "tag container" for your website. You place this container on every page and place the Google Analytics tag within the container. If you ever need to update the Google Analytics page tag, you don't need to update the code on your pages, you can simply update the tag residing in the TagMan container. You can do this via a nice web interface.

It is also a wise idea to monitor your page tags using some type of automated checking process. There are numerous tools that will crawl your site and ensure the Google Analytics tracking code has been added to the pages. It's not uncommon for the tracking code to get erased during a code update.

And let's not forget non-HTML pages. Tracking non-HTML content with Google Analytics can be a huge challenge. You can't slap a JavaScript tag on a non-HTML file. When we work with large organizations, we usually help them develop an automated click-tracking script. This takes more time and more effort and doesn't always work (usually due to page rendering delays).

Issue #4: Hosting External JavaScript

Some organizations have a policy of not referencing external components in their web pages. These policies are usually based on performance standards or privacy issues. Regardless, it is possible that some internal policy forbids hosting the *ga.js* file on Google's servers.

As mentioned in Chapter 3, it is possible to host the *ga.js* file on your own network. The biggest challenge is ensuring the code is up to date with the version that Google hosts. Refer to Chapter 3 for more information on how to mitigate this issue.

Issue #5: URL Structure

This is probably one of the most difficult challenges we face when working with large sites that have hundreds of thousands of pages. Google Analytics will only track 50,000 unique URLs per day. While this is completely adequate for most sites, enterprise sites can exceed this limit, especially if the site is content-based (think about some of today's largest community sites—they have forums, blogs, and tons of user-generated content).

What happens when you fill Google Analytics with 50,000 unique URLs in a day? You start to see "(other)" in your content reports and you can no longer identify which pages visitors are viewing on your site.

To resolve this issue, we usually need to create some type of bucketing strategy to roll-up pageview data into different content categories. You can normally do this by creating a virtual taxonomy for pageview data. This can be challenging because it requires programming resources to manipulate the GATC on every page. Rather than collecting the standard request URI, you must generate a custom URI.

Another way to mitigate this issue is by categorizing content using custom variables. You can use page-level custom variables to categorize content. For example, we can use custom variables to categorize every page on every MLB website. Then, using the roll-up profiles, we would see the aggregate for all pages of the same type, regardless of the site on which they appeared. The code would look something like this:

```
<script type="text/javascript">

  var _gaq = _gaq || [];
  _gaq.push(['teamTracker._setAccount', 'UA-XXXXXX-Y']);
  _gaq.push(['teamTracker._setCustomVar',1,'PageCat','Page Category Value',3]);
  _gaq.push(['teamTracker._trackPageview']);
  _gaq.push(['rollupTracker._setAccount', 'UA-XXXXXX-2']);
  _gaq.push(['rollupTracker._setCustomVar',1,'PageCat','Page Category Value',3]);
  _gaq.push(['rollupTracker._trackPageview']);

  (function() {
    var ga = document.createElement('script'); ga.type = 'text/javascript';
    ga.async = true;
    ga.src = ('https:' == document.location.protocol ? 'https://ssl' :
    'http://www') + '.google-analytics.com/ga.js';
    var s = document.getElementsByTagName('script')[0];
    s.parentNode.insertBefore(ga, s);
  })();

</script>
```

Issue #6: Campaign Tracking

This is a problem for everyone, not just enterprises! I find very few clients who are diligent about tracking their marketing campaigns using link tagging. As a general rule of thumb, the bigger the client the more challenging it is to track all online campaigns. Why?

Big organizations have different people running different campaigns. Many times they're using one or more agencies to help run their campaigns. Getting everyone to use a cohesive link tagging strategy is a lot of work due to the sheer number of people involved. This is more of a training/process issue than a technical issue. Tagging links for an enterprise requires that every marketing team be on the same page. Some organizations build custom link tagging tools that promote a consistent link tagging strategy, while others build link tagging into the their marketing platform.

Issue #7: Data Integration

Many large organizations need to integrate Google Analytics data with other data sources. For example, most organizations want to merge Google Analytics data with customer relationship management (CRM) data (see Chapter 12). This can help provide more insight into how customers and potential customers interact with the website.

Luckily, this is not a show-stopper issue. Using the Google Analytics API, enterprises can merge Google Analytics data with CRM data and other sources. The biggest challenge is mitigating potential interference with the Google Analytics terms of service, which forbid collecting any personally identifiable information in Google Analytics.

However, the terms of service do not clearly state what personally identifiable information is. Most people, myself included, agree that personally identifiable information includes things like name, email address, and IP address. It does not include transaction IDs or membership IDs.

Issue #8: E-Commerce Data

There are two challenges with tracking e-commerce data at the enterprise level. This first is collecting the data. If you use a roll-up collection strategy, as is the case with our MLB example, e-commerce data must be sent to multiple accounts or profiles. This means the e-commerce code must be replicated multiple times on a page to send the data to the appropriate profiles. Here's the code for our MLB example:

```
<script type="text/javascript">
  var _gaq = _gaq || [];
  _gaq.push(['teamTracker._setAccount', 'UA-XXXXXX-Y']);
  _gaq.push(['teamTracker._trackPageview']);
  _gaq.push(['rollupTracker._setAccount', 'UA-XXXXXX-2']);
  _gaq.push(['rollupTracker._trackPageview']);
```

```
_gaq.push(['teamTracker._addTrans',
    '{ORDER ID}',   // order ID - required
    '{AFFILIATE}', // affiliation or store name
    '{TOTAL}',      // total - required
    '{TAX}',        // tax
    '{SHIPPING}',  // shipping
    '{CITY}',       // city
    '{STATE}',      // state or province
    '{COUNTRY}'     // country
]);
_gaq.push(['teamTracker ._addItem',
    '{ORDER ID}',       // order ID - needed to associate item with transaction
    '{SKU}',            // SKU/code - required
    '{PROD NAME}',      // product name
    '{PROD CATEGORY}', // category or variation
    '{UNIT PRICE}',     // unit price - required
    '{QUANTITY}'        // quantity - required
]);
_gaq.push(['teamTracker._trackTrans']); //submits transaction to
 the Analytics servers

_gaq.push(['rollupTracker._addTrans',
    '{ORDER ID}',   // order ID - required
    '{AFFILIATE}', // affiliation or store name
    '{TOTAL}',      // total - required
    '{TAX}',        // tax
    '{SHIPPING}',  // shipping
    '{CITY}',       // city
    '{STATE}',      // state or province
    '{COUNTRY}'     // country
]);
_gaq.push(['rollupTracker._addItem',
    '{ORDER ID}',       // order ID - needed to associate item with transaction
    '{SKU}',            // SKU/code - required
    '{PROD NAME}',      // product name
    '{PROD CATEGORY}', // category or variation
    '{UNIT PRICE}',     // unit price - required
    '{QUANTITY}'        // quantity - required
]);
_gaq.push(['rollupTracker._trackTrans']);
//submits transaction to the Analytics servers
</script>
```

Another common issue when tracking e-commerce at the enterprise level is multicurrency tracking. Websites that sell products in multiple geographic areas usually allow visitors to buy in their local currency.

The problems arise when local departments want to see revenue in a local currency, but corporate leadership wants to see total revenue in a common currency. The solution is to dynamically convert the transaction currencies into the necessary currency based on real-time values. Basically, you need to change the server-side code to convert the currency before creating the e-commerce page tag. The actual page tag will look the same as the above code sample, but all monetary values passed to the `teamTracker` will be different than the values passed to the `rollupTracker`.

Issue #9: AdWords Cost Data

It is not uncommon for larger organizations to use multiple agencies to manage their paid search. As a result, they may have many, many AdWords accounts. Normally, Google Analytics is limited to linking one AdWords account to one Analytics account.

This causes problems when an enterprise wants to see total AdWords expenditure across all AdWords accounts. In this scenario, Google can link multiple AdWords accounts to a single Analytics account. Once done, you can control which AdWords data appears in specific profiles. This change is made in the Profile Settings. You can literally turn on and offer certain cost data using the checkboxes shown in Figure 11-1.

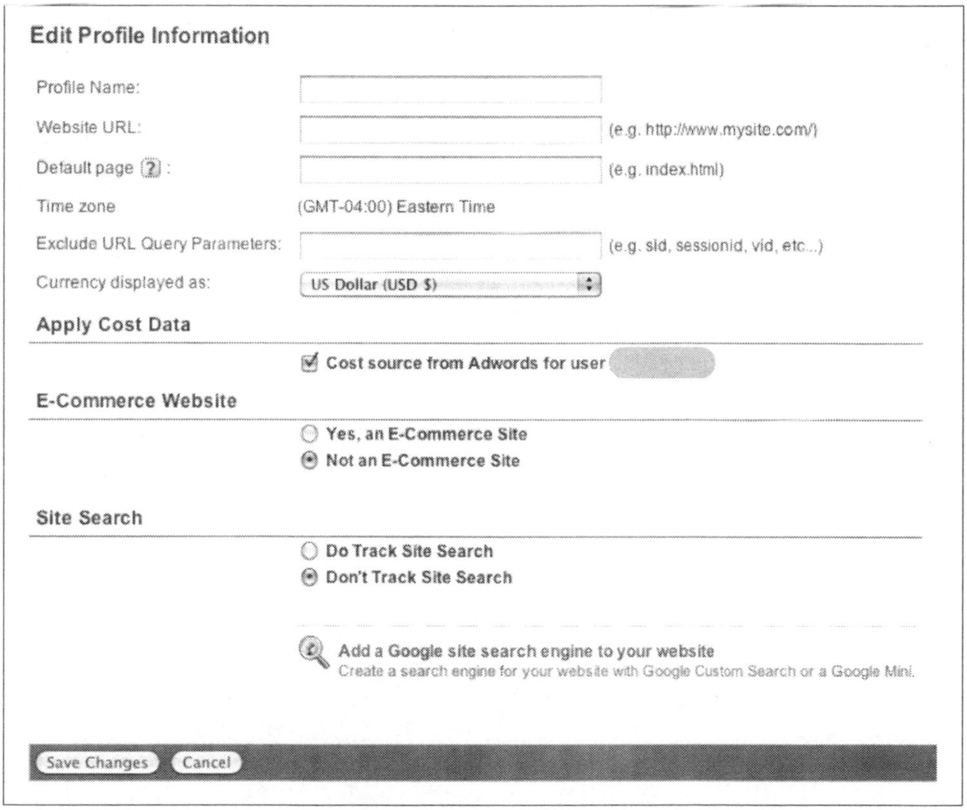

Figure 11-1. Use the checkboxes to apply cost data from different AdWords accounts

CRM Integration

You can use the data stored in the Google Analytics tracking cookies in other applications. After all, the cookies are standard first-party cookies that can you can access using JavaScript or server-side application code. One popular way to use Google Analytics cookie data is with a Customer Relationship Management (CRM) system.

What kind of data can we get from the Google Analytics cookies? Marketing data, custom variable data, and visit history data.

Google Analytics–CRM integration involves extracting the cookie data and adding it to a lead generation form. When the visitor submits the form, the Google Analytics cookie data (which is marketing data, custom segment data, and visit history data) is connected to other information that the individual provides (usually her name and other contact information). Knowing the marketing message that an individual responds to is a valuable piece of information for a sales team.

Direct CRM integration depends on the CRM platform. Some systems allow you to pull form fields directly into the application, and some systems may have a specific Google Analytics plug-in. Check with your CRM provider for information about your specific system.

The technique described next has many different applications and should serve as a template for your implementation.

As I've discussed before, Google Analytics stores all visitor information in cookies. For example, marketing information is stored in the __utmz cookie. You can extract and manipulate the data using very simple JavaScript. The basic process to extract and use the data is as follows:

1. Extract visitor data using JavaScript tracking cookies.
2. Manipulate data as needed using JavaScript code.
3. Place data in hidden form fields.
4. Process data using server-side code.

When the visitor submits the form, the data is passed back to the server, where your CRM application or server-side code can manipulate it.

To simplify step 1, extracting the data from the tracking cookies, I use a function that exists in the *urchin.js* file. Remember, the *urchin.js* file is the old tracking code. However, there's one function, _uGC(), that is so useful it's worth copying it out of *urchin.js* and placing it into the code.

_uGC() takes three arguments:

- A string to search (target string)
- A start pattern
- An end pattern

Here's how the function actually works. It searches the target string for the start pattern. Once it finds the start pattern, it returns all characters between the start pattern and the end pattern. The returned value can be stored in a variable for use in your code. Remember, cookies are just strings of data.

The sample HTML below emulates this process; it extracts campaign information from the __utmz cookie and adds it to hidden form elements. I've also added some code that extracts the custom variable value, stored in the __utmv cookie, and adds it to the hidden form. Google provides a simple method, named _getVisitorCustomVar(), that you can use to extract a visitor-level custom variable. Because there can be up to five visitor-level custom variables, I created a simple loop that looks for a value in each slot. The code also extracts the visit count, found in the __utma cookie. All of this information helps us understand the visitor better.

When the visitor submits the form, the values in the hidden elements are transmitted back to the server:

```
<html>

<head>

<script type='text/javascript'>
_gaq.push(['_setAccount', 'UA-1-1']);
_gaq.push(['_trackPageview']);
```

```
//
// This is a function that I "borrowed" from the urchin.js file.
// It parses a string and returns a value. I used it to get
// data from the __utmz cookie
//
function _uGC(l,n,s) {
 if (!l || l=="" || !n || n=="" || !s || s=="") return "-";
 var i,i2,i3,c="-";
 i=l.indexOf(n);
 i3=n.indexOf("=")+1;
 if (i > -1) {
  i2=l.indexOf(s,i); if (i2 < 0) { i2=l.length; }
  c=l.substring((i+i3),i2);
 }
 return c;
}


//
// Get the __utmz cookie value. This is the cookies that
// stores all campaign information.
//
var z = _uGC(document.cookie, '__utmz=', ';');
//
// The cookie has a number of name-value pairs.
// Each identifies an aspect of the campaign.
//
// utmcsr  = campaign source
// utmcmd  = campaign medium
// utmctr  = campaign term (keyword)
// utmcct  = campaign content
// utmccn  = campaign name
// utmgclid = unique identifier used when AdWords auto-tagging is enabled
//
// This is very basic code. It separates the campaign-tracking cookie
// and populates a variable with each piece of campaign info.
//
var source   = _uGC(z, 'utmcsr=', '|');
var medium   = _uGC(z, 'utmcmd=', '|');
var term     = _uGC(z, 'utmctr=', '|');
var content  = _uGC(z, 'utmcct=', '|');
var campaign = _uGC(z, 'utmccn=', '|');
var gclid    = _uGC(z, 'utmgclid=', '|');
//
// The gclid is ONLY present when auto tagging has been enabled.
// All other variables, except the term variable, will be '(not set)'.
// Because the gclid is only present for Google AdWords we can
// populate some other variables that would normally
// be left blank.
//
if (gclid !="-") {
     source = 'google';
     medium = 'cpc';
}
```

```
    // Data from the custom variable cookie can also be passed
    // back to your server via a hidden form field
    for (i==1. i < 6, i++) {
        if (pageTracker._getVisitorCustomVar(i)) {
          cvar + i = csegment[1];
        } else {
          cvar + i = '(not set)';
        }

    //
    // One more bonus piece of information.
    // We're going to extract the number of visits that the visitor
    // has generated. It's also stored in a cookie, the __utma cookie
    //
    var a = _uGC(document.cookie, '__utma=', ';');
    var aParts = a.split(".");
    var nVisits = aParts[5];

    function populateHiddenFields(f) {
        f.source.value  = source;
        f.medium.value  = medium;
        f.term.value    = term;
        f.content.value = content;
        f.campaign.value = campaign;
        f.cv1.value = cvar1;
        f.cv2.value = cvar2;
        f.cv3.value = cvar3;
        f.cv4.value = cvar4;
        f.cv5.value = cvar5;

        f.numVisits.value = nVisits;

        alert('source='+f.source.value);
        alert('medium='+f.medium.value);
        alert('term='+f.term.value);
        alert('content='+f.content.value);
        alert('campaign='+f.campaign.value);
        alert('custom variable 1='+f.cv1.value);
        alert('custom variable 2='+f.cv2.value);
        alert('custom variable 3='+f.cv3.value);
        alert('custom variable 4='+f.cv4.value);
        alert('custom variable 5='+f.cv5.value);

        alert('number of visits='+f.numVisits.value);

        return false;
    }
</script>
</head>

<body>

<h3>There is a hidden form that contains values for CRM fields</h3>
```

```
<form method="POST" name='contactform'
    onSubmit="populateHiddenFields(this);">
<input type='hidden' name='source' />
<input type='hidden' name='medium' />
<input type='hidden' name='term' />
<input type='hidden' name='content' />
<input type='hidden' name='campaign' />
<input type='hidden' name='cv1' />
<input type='hidden' name='cv2' />
<input type='hidden' name='cv3' />
<input type='hidden' name='cv4' />
<input type='hidden' name='cv5' />
<input type='hidden' name='numVisits' />
<input type='submit' value='Show GA Info' />
</form>

</body>

</html>
```

Extracting referral information from the Google Analytics tracking cookies does not violate the Google Analytics privacy policy. The information in the __utmz, __utmv, and __utma cookies is not, and should not be, personally identifiable.

Using Regular Expressions to Extend Goals

Many times a website may have a subgoal or a conversion event that is a subset of a larger conversion. For example, I like to track the number of RSS subscribers as a goal on my blog. I also like to know how people are subscribing to the RSS feed (Bloglines, Google Reader, etc.). With a little creativity, I can aggregate all RSS clicks as a goal while still identifying which method visitors use to subscribe. I do this using a virtual pageview and a regular expressions. Remember, the destination URL goal can be a regular expression. This means multiple URLs on a website can match the regular expression defined as a goal.

Here's an example. The following two pages represent an RSS subscription conversion on a blog:

> /blog/outbound/rss/google
> /blog/outbound/rss/rss

We can use a regular expression for the goal URL to track both URLs as a single goal. The regular expression would be as follows:

> /rss/(google/rss)$

Both URLs match the regular expression and count toward the goal tally. To drill down into the data and differentiate which URL generated more goals, use the Goal Verification report. This report, shown in Figure 12-1, segments a goal by the different pages that contribute to it.

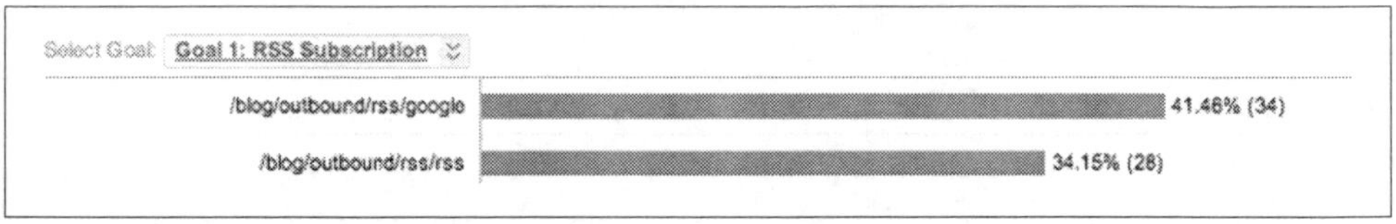

Figure 12-1. The Goal Verification report

Goals for Your Business

Which goals should you configure for your website? That depends on your online business model. Remember, Google Analytics collects business data, so the goals for an e-commerce business may be very different than those for a lead generation business. In general, goals usually involve one of the following:

- Completing an e-commerce transaction
- Submitting a "Contact Us" form
- Subscribing to an email newsletter
- Viewing certain content on a website
- Viewing a minimum number of pages
- Viewing too many pages on a site
- Spending a certain amount of time on the site

Tools and Add-Ons

When Google Analytics announced a standard API for extracting data, it opened the floodgates to third-party developers. The result was many different types of tools that facilitate implementation, reporting, and analysis. The response was so strong that Google created an Analytics App Marketplace to showcase tools built on the Analytics API. You can find the Analytics Application Gallery at *http://troni.me/aLUqBW*. Some of my favorite tools are listed below.

Reporting and Analysis Tools

One of the strong points of Google Analytics is the reporting interface. It's intuitive, easy to use, and facilitates analysis. But sometimes you need a little something extra to get the job done. Below are a few tools that enhance the reporting capabilities of Google Analytics.

Juice Concentrate

Concentrate (*http://troni.me/8XEOXL*), from Juice Analytics, is a keyword tool that categorizes keywords to help you understand the key phrases people use to find your site. Anyone doing CPC or SEO should be using this tool.

Google Analytics Report Enhancer

This Firefox extension was created by Jeremy Aube at ROI Revolution (a Google Analytics Authorized Consultant). His tool tweaks the interface a number of ways to reveal missing dimensions and some simple metrics. For example, it shows the number of conversions rather than the conversion rate. Check out the ROI Revolution blog (*http://troni.me/diGL88*) for instructions.

Keyword Trends in Google Analytics

This is another tool created by the team at Juice Analytics. This Greasemonkey script makes it easy to see what new keywords people are using to find your site. Basically, this is a "what's changed" button for your keyword reports. You can find it at *http://troni.me/bG1MPt*.

Debugging Tools

Here is a list of must-have tools for debugging Google Analytics. All of these tools help you determine what data Google Analytics is storing in the tracking cookies and what information is sent to the Google Analytics servers.

Firebug

Firebug (*http://troni.me/bf8eX2*) is a Firefox extension that provides a wealth of information about a web page. You can view HTML source code, view CSS, debug JavaScript, and monitor server requests. This is a great tool to check the GATC and view the image request.

LiveHTTPHeaders

LiveHTTPHeaders (*http://troni.me/cvBrXe*) is a Firefox plug-in that displays all of the headers sent between a web page and the various servers that contribute the content for it. Using this plug-in, you can validate that a request is made to the Google Analytics server for both the *ga.js* and *utm.gif* files. If you are using Internet Explorer version 6 or 7, you can use HttpWatch (*http://troni.me/aDJI2c*).

Firefox Web Developer

If you're working with web pages, you probably already have this installed. I like the Web Developer (*http://troni.me/cqK6LG*) because it provides quick access to Google Analytics tracking cookies and the HTML source code for a page. Validating that the Google Analytics cookies are set correctly is one of the first things you should do when debugging a Google Analytics problem.

Regex Coach

This is a tool for testing your regular expressions. Regex Coach (*http://troni.me/92j3PS*) is a graphical application for Windows and Linux that you can use to experiment with regular expressions interactively. If you have any questions about the validity of your regular expressions, you should test them with the Regex Coach.

Time

The most challenging part of working with Google Analytics is waiting for your changes to take effect. Once you change a filter or profile setting, it may be three hours before the data in Google Analytics is affected. Debugging problems in Google Analytics takes time, so be patient. The more you can do to understand the implications of a change prior to making the modification, the better. Manage expectations accordingly.

Google Analytics Compliance with WAA Standards

Table A-1 includes a list of all standards defined in the Web Analytics Association (WAA) metrics definitions document and Google Analytics compliance with each definition. Google Analytics is compliant with 19 of the 26 metrics. Most of the noncompliance is due to the fact that Google Analytics does not offer all the metrics that the WAA defines. You can learn more about the WAA standards on the WAA website, *http://troni.me/ch5G4A*.

Table A-1. Google Analytics compliance with WAA standards

Term	Compliant	WAA definition	Google Analytics definition
Page	Yes	A page is an analyst-definable unit of content.	Same as WAA.
Page view	Yes	The number of times a page (an analyst-definable unit of content) was viewed.	Same as WAA. Google Analytics refers to this metric as the *pageview*. A pageview is created each time the `_trackPageview()` method is executed. Any value passed to the `_trackPageview()` method will appear in the Content reports, thus making a page analyst-definable.
Visits/sessions	Yes	A visit is an interaction an individual carries out on a website consisting of one or more requests for an analyst-definable unit of content (for example, "page view"). If an individual has not taken another action (typically additional page views) on the site within a specified time period, the visit session will terminate.	Same as WAA. By default, a visit will terminate after 30 minutes of inactivity by the visitor. You can configure the inactivity timeout by altering the Google Analytics tracking code.

Term	Compliant	WAA definition	Google Analytics definition
Unique visitors	Yes	The number of inferred individual people (filtered for spiders and robots) within a designated reporting time-frame, with activity consisting of one or more visits to a site. Each individual is counted only once in the unique visitor measure for the reporting period.	Same as WAA . In Google Analytics, a visitor is defined using a unique numeric identifier stored in the Google Analytics tracking cookies. This value is set at the time of the visitor's first visit. Each visitor is counted only once in the unique visitor metric, regardless of how many times he returns to the site during the reporting period.
New visitor	Yes	The number of unique visitors with activity, including a first-ever visit to a site during a reporting period.	Same as WAA. While Google Analytics shares the same definition for a new visitor, it does not count the number of new, unique people (visitors) who visited the site during the reporting period. Google Analytics counts the number of *visits* generated by new people. Google Analytics calculates the number of New visitors by identifying the number of new unique visitor IDs created during the reporting period. It is possible to measure the number of new visitors using a profile and include filter.
Repeat visitor	No	The number of unique visitors with activity consisting of two or more visits to a site during a reporting period.	By default, this metric does not exist in Google Analytics. You can create this metric with an elaborate mix of filters and custom reports.
Return visitor	Yes	The number of unique visitors with activity consisting of a visit to a site during a reporting period and where the unique visitor also visited the site prior to the reporting period.	Same as WAA. While Google Analytics shares the same definition for a return visitor, it does not count the number of returning unique people (visitors) who have visited the site during the reporting period. Google Analytics counts the number of visits generated. Google Analytics defines a return visitor as any visitor whose unique identifier cookie was set prior to the reporting period.
Entry page	Yes	The first page of a visit.	Same as WAA.
Landing page	Yes	A page intended to identify the beginning of the user experience resulting from a defined marketing effort.	Same as WAA.

Term	Compliant	WAA definition	Google Analytics definition
Exit page	Yes	The last page on a site accessed during a visit, signifying the end of a visit/session.	Same as WAA.
Visit duration	Yes	The length of time in a session. Calculation is typically the timestamp of the last activity in the session minus the timestamp of the first activity of the session.	Same as WAA. Google Analytics calls this metric "average time on site." It is calculated by dividing the total time spent on the site by the total number of visits.
Referrer	No	The referrer is the page URL that originally generated the request for the current page view or object.	The referrer in Google Analytics is the page URL that originally generated the request for the current visit. This value is then added to all pageviews in that visit. The referrer is identified in Google Analytics as any source whose medium is "referral." Google Analytics also has a field called "referral" which conforms to the WAA's definition of "referrer." However, this field is not displayed in any report—it is available only as a filter field.
Internal referrer	N/A	The internal referrer is a page URL that is internal to the website or a web property within the website as defined by the user.	N/A This metric is not available in Google Analytics.
External referrer	N/A	The external referrer is a page URL for which the traffic is external or outside the website or a web property defined by the user.	N/A This metric is not available in Google Analytics.
Search referrer	N/A	The search referrer is an internal or external referrer for which the URL has been generated by a search function.	N/A This metric is not available in Google Analytics. While Google Analytics tracks both external search phrases and internal search phrases, the term "search referrer" is not used in reporting.
Visit referrer	Yes	The visit referrer is the first referrer in a session, whether internal, external, or null.	Same as WAA. This data is called a "referral" in Google Analytics and can only be the external referrer.
Original referrer	N/A	The original referrer is the first referrer in a visitor's first session, whether internal, external, or null.	N/A This metric is not available in Google Analytics.

Term	Compliant	WAA definition	Google Analytics definition
Clickthrough	Yes	The number of times a visitor clicked a particular link.	Same as WAA. Google Analytics refers to clickthroughs as "clicks". This metric is available only in the AdWords reports.
Clickthrough rate/ratio	Yes	The number of clickthroughs for a specific link divided by the number of times that link was viewed.	Same as WAA. Clickthrough and clickthrough rate are the percentage of impressions that resulted in a click. It is calculated by dividing the number of clicks on an ad by the number of impressions for the ad. This metric is available only in the AdWords reports.
Page views per visit	Yes	The number of page views in a reporting period divided by the number of visits in the same reporting period.	Same as WAA.
Page exit ratio	Yes	The number of exits from a page divided by total number of page views of that page.	Same as WAA. In Google Analytics, this metric is called Exit Rate and is shown in Content reports as "Exit %".
Single-page visits	N/A	Visits that consist of one page regardless of the number of times the page was viewed.	N/A This metric is not available in Google Analytics.
Single page view visits (bounces)	Yes	Visits that consist of one page view.	Same as WAA. Bounces can be modified by other Google Analytics features, specifically event tracking. When event tracking is used, the Google Analytics tracking code will request the invisible *.gif* from the Google Analytics server. Google Analytics will interpret this *.gif* request as a visitor action and will conclude the visitor is engaged with the web page and will not count it as a bounce. For example, if a visitor lands on a page, views a video that is tracked using event tracking, and then leaves the site from the original landing page, it will not be counted as a bounce.

Term	Compliant	WAA definition	Google Analytics definition
			The same is true for custom segmentation. If a visitor is placed in a custom segment on a landing page and does not view any other pages, it will not be counted as a bounce.
Bounce rate	Yes	Single page view visits divided by entry pages.	Same as WAA.
Event	Yes	Any logged or recorded action that has a specific date and time assigned to it by either the browser or server.	Same as WAA. There are multiple attributes to an event in Google Analytics. These are objects, actions, and labels. Event tracking is a Google Analytics beta feature and may not be enabled for your account. You can read more about event tracking in Chapter 10.
Conversion	Yes	A visitor completing a target action.	Same as WAA. In addition to conversions, Google Analytics will also calculate the conversion rate. The conversion rate is the total number of visits resulting in a desired action divided by the total number of visits. A conversion will only be recorded once per visit. Visitors cannot convert more than one time per visit. You can read more about goals in the post All About Google Analytics Goals (*http://www.epikone.com/blog/2007/07/07/google-analytics-goals/*).

Regular Expressions

A *regular expression* (sometimes referred to as a regex) contains a mix of regular characters (like letters and numbers) and special characters that form a pattern. The pattern is applied to a piece of data and, if the pattern matches, the regular expression returns a positive result.

Many regular expressions include regular alphanumeric characters. For example, you may have a list of keywords, and you need to identify those keywords that contain "goo." These three characters are a valid regular expression. Google Analytics will apply "goo" to the target data—in this case, the keywords. If "goo" matches any part of the data, the regex will return a positive result. Table B-1 shows some simple patterns and gives examples of data that match.

Table B-1. Regular expressions that contain only alphanumeric characters

Pattern	Description	Example matches
go	Match the characters **go**	**go**ogle, **go**, merry-**go**-round, **go**lf
bos	Match the characters **bos**	**bos**s, **bos**ton, my **bos**s, em**bos**s

As illustrated in Table B-1, a regular expression does not need to be a complicated mix of special characters. However, it's the special characters that make regular expressions powerful and flexible.

There are four basic types of special characters in regular expressions: wildcards, quantifiers, operators, and anchors.

Google Analytics uses Perl Compatible Regular Expressions (PCREs). Any special characters that are specific to PCREs will work in Google Analytics.

Wildcards

Wildcards are used to indicate what type of characters the regular expression should match. When you type the letter "g," the regular expression looks for the letter "g." But what if you need to match any character, not just a specific letter? This is where wildcards come in. The most common wildcards are shown in Table B-2.

Table B-2. Basic regular expression wildcards

Pattern	Description	Example	Example matches
.	Match any character	a.c	abc, aec, adc, a3c
[ ]	Match all characters, plus one item in the list of characters within the brackets	a[bB]c	abc, aBc
[^]	Match one item *not* in the list of characters in the brackets	a[^bB]c	adc, a3c

Quantifiers

Quantifiers (shown in Table B-3) indicate how many times a character can be matched. Wildcards describe what type of character to match, and the quantifier describes how many times to match it. Quantifiers are applied to the character *directly* preceding it. So, you can apply a quantifier to a wildcard or to a standard alphanumeric character.

Table B-3. Basic regular expression quantifiers

Pattern	Description	Example	Example matches
*	Match zero or more of the preceding character	ab*c	ac, abc, abbc, abbbbc
+	Match one or more of the preceding character	ab+c	abc, abbc, abbbc
?	Match zero or one of the preceding character	ab?c	ac, abc

Operators

Operators (listed in Table B-4) perform some type of logic within the regular expression.

The most common operator is the escape character (\). When used in a regular expression, the escape character transforms a special character into a regular character. For example, the question mark (?) is a special character in regular expressions. However, if you place the escape character before the question mark, as follows, the question mark becomes a literal question mark:

    \?

Rather than trying to interpret the question mark as a special character, the regular expression will interpret it as an actual question mark.

Table B-4. Common regular expression operators

Pattern	Description	Example	Example matches
\	Escape any pattern. The character after the escape symbol will be interpreted literally.	a\.c	a.c, website\.com, index\.php
|	OR operator. Match one item or another.	abc|def	abc, def
()	Group characters into a pattern or capture the characters in the parentheses.	(abc|123)	abc or 123, and will return whichever is matched

The pipe character (|) is the logical OR operator, which literally means, "match this OR match that." This is very powerful, because you can use it to create lists of things to match. For example, you can use the following expression to match a list of keywords:

    justin|cutroni|google

The final operator is the parentheses. This operator has two uses. First, you can use it to group expressions and then apply a regular expression operator (for example, a quantifier) to the entire group. For example, the expression (abc)+ means match "abc" one or more times.

You can also use parentheses to retain part of the data when using advanced filters. Placing an expression in parentheses, like (a.b), will force Google Analytics to retain the value that the pattern a.b matches. This could be "aab", "abb", "a2b", etc.

Anchors

Anchors (listed in Table B-5) describe where the regular expression should be applied to the data being evaluated. When you use an anchor, the value that the regex is applied to must begin (or end) with the appropriate pattern. Essentially, they mean "match at the beginning or match at the end."

Table B-5. Regular expression anchors

Pattern	Description	Example	Example matches
^	Match at the beginning of the data	^abc	abc, abcdef, abc123
$	Match at the end of the data	abc$	abc, dfghabc, 12jdkjfabc

 LunaMetrics, a web analytics consulting company in Pittsburgh, has a wonderful regular expressions tutorial. I highly recommend it. You can find it at *http://troni.me/9o40hD*.

Index

Symbols

\# (hash/pound symbol) JavaScript insertion, 103
$ (dollar sign), regex anchor, 189
& (ampersand), parameter separator, 94
( ) regex grouping operator, 189
* (asterisk), regex quantifier, 188
+ (plus), regex quantifier, 188
. (period), regex wildcard, 188
? (question mark), regex quantifier, 188
[ ] (brackets), regex wildcard, 188
[^] (brackets with caret), regex wildcard, 188
\ (backslash) regex escape operator, 189
^ (caret), regex anchor, 189
| (pipe) regex OR operator, 189

A

A/B testing, 66, 92
access, 41, 82
accounting and e-commerce tracking, 123
accounts, Analytics, 18
  (see also AdWords)
  (see also profiles)
  access levels to, 41
  account number, 18, 21, 34–35
  creating, 35–39
  default page, 48
  e-commerce feature, 77
  excluding URL query parameters, 49–52
  Google account vs. Google Analytics account, 33
  profiles nontransferable between, 39
  time zone, 48
Action report, 139, 143

add-ons and tools, 177–179
_addItem() method, 125
_addTrans() method, 125
administrator access level, 41
advanced profile filters, 66
Advanced Segmentation feature, 5, 152, 153, 161
AdWords, Google
  autotagging, 30, 93, 96
  clickthrough rate/ratio, 184
  cost data, 36, 40, 58, 169
  creating an Analytics account through, 35, 48
  defined, 5
  linking to Analytics account, 96
  report, 40
  unlinking from Analytics, 96
Affiliate Value, 128
Ajax, 149
All Traffic Sources report, 128, 134
ampersand (&), parameter separator, 94
Analytics, Google
  access levels, 41
  in the analytics ecosystem, 7
  code configuration tool, 113
  compliance with WAA standards, 181–185
  data collection overview, 13–16
  data processing overview, 15
  data-sharing options, 37
  debugging tools, 178
  keeping a configuration change log for, 87
  overview, 4–7
  per-day unique URL tracking limit, 166
  per-visit GTAC request limit, 142
  privacy policy, 52, 167, 175

We'd like to hear your suggestions for improving our indexes. Send email to *index@oreilly.com*.

Excel, Microsoft Office, 68
Exclude URL Query Parameters field, 50
Extract field, 66

F

Field A/B, 66
Field A/B Required, 67
fields, 16
filters
    applying to campaign profiles, 82
    attaching hostname to request URI, 116,
       121
    custom, 59
    custom variables and profile, 153
    and e-commerce, 128, 158
    and events, 158
    to exclude outbound clicks, 28
    fields, 60
    patterns, 61
    predefined, 59, 70
    recommended for master data profile, 82–
       87
    and site search data, 56, 57
    for subdomain-specific profiles, 119
    three components of, 59–61
    types, 61
Firefox, Mozilla
    asynchronous loading support, 19
    Firebug extension, 178
    LiveHTTPHeaders plug-in, 178
    Report Enhancer extension, 177
    Web Developer, 178
first-click attribution, 105
first-party cookies, 30
Flash, 106, 149
forms, 129–134, 149, 171
4Q, 2
frames and iFrames, 121–123
Funnel Visualization report, 78, 82
funnels
    defined, 78
    Required field, 79
    setting up, 78–80
    visit timeout limit, 102

G

ga.js file, 14, 18, 126
    change log, 20
    hosting locally, 19, 166
    increasing number slots with, 146
ga.php file, 21
_gaq queue, 18, 115, 142
GATC (see tracking code (GATC))
gclid, 96, 173
geographic location data, 126
_getLinkerUrl() method, 122
_getVisitorCustomVar() method, 172
.gif request, 184
goal page, 75
Goal URL field, 76
Goal Value field, 77
Goal Verification report, 176
goals
    additional settings for, 76
    defined, 4, 176, 185
    for email, 102
    extending with regular expressions, 175
    negative, 75
    pageview, 74
    report tab, 5, 109
    Time on Site, 73
    URL destination, 75
Google Analytics Tracking Code (see tracking
    code (GATC))
Greasemonkey, 178

H

hash/pound symbol (#) JavaScript insertion,
    103
head matches, 77
historical data, 16, 81
Hostname filter field, 60, 128
Hostnames report, 85

I

iFrames, 122
implementation plan, creating an, 9–12
include/exclude filters, 61
inclusion, 61
index, custom variable, 146–149
inflated revenue, 129
internal campaigns, tracking, 105–110
internal traffic, excluding, 82
IP addresses, 84, 126

creating additional, 39–41
e-commerce, 52
filters to segment data in, 57, 82
initial creation of, 38
multiple for single website, 34, 43
naming conventions for, 44
nontransferability between accounts, 39
overview, 43–53
and roll-up reporting, 157
for subdomains, 119, 157
website URL value, 46–48

Q

qualitative data, 2
quantifiers, regex, 188
quantitative data, 2
query (query-string) parameters
gclid, 96
ici, 109
and link tagging, 89–92
no_override, 102, 104
stripping, 107
URL, 49–52
utm, 22, 30, 100, 114
Query Parameter field, 55, 107
question mark (?), regex quantifier, 188

R

raw data profile, 81
real-time segmentation, 161
receipt pages, 123, 128
referral segments, 89
referral traffic, 92, 93, 104
referrer-tracking cookie, 29
referrers, 183
Regex Coach tool, 178
regular expressions (regex), 61, 77, 175, 187–189
Report Enhancer Firefox extension, 177
reports, 16
(see also Top Content report)
Action, 139, 143
AdWords, 40
All Traffic Sources, 128, 134
Campaign, 94
Category, 142
Content, 181, 184
Custom Report Sharing feature, 110

Custom Reporting interface, 6
Custom Variable, 150, 152
e-commerce, 126
E-Commerce Transactions, 133
Events, 142
Funnel Visualization, 78, 82
Goal Verification, 176
Hostnames, 85
Label, 143
Map Overlay, 4
Product Overview and Product Categories, 128, 133
Search Term Refinement, 57
Search Terms, 53, 108
Site Overlay, 47, 118
Site Search, 57
Start Pages, 109
third-party tools/add-ons to enhance, 177
Traffic Sources, 5, 92
Usage, 108
User Defined, 68
Request URI field, 24, 60, 67, 77, 85, 116
revenue, inflated, 129
ROI calculations, 77
roll-up reporting, 156–161
enterprise-implementation issues, 163
RSS
clicks, 175
subscribers, 175

S

scope, variable, 146, 150
search and replace filters, 63
Search Category Reporting feature, 55
search engine traffic, 104
Search Term Refinement feature, 110
Search Term Refinement report, 57
Search Terms report, 53, 108
SearchRev, 99
segmentation
Advanced Segment feature, 161
campaign example, 94
coupon usage example, 155
custom cookie, 149
Custom Segmentation feature, 145, 185
default referral, 89
using filters/profiles for, 61, 82–87
of goal by different pages example, 175

About the Author

Justin Cutroni is a web analytics expert and Google Analytics Certified Partner. Justin commonly interacts with senior level management to drive the strategic use of web data and collaborates with marketing and IT teams to develop implementation plans and processes needed to generate actionable data and business insights. An active participant in the web analytics community, Justin speaks at various industry events with a strong passion for sharing knowledge and advancing the analytics industry.

Justin is authorized by Google to teach Google Analytics Seminars for Success and has conducted numerous training events in the US and Europe.

Colophon

The animal on the cover of *Google Analytics* is the African sacred ibis (*Threskiornis aethiopicus*). This bird was revered in ancient Egypt as a symbol of the god Thoth, who was usually portrayed with the head of an ibis. It was common for the birds to be ritually mummified and buried with high officials as representations of wisdom—however, killing them for secular reasons was punishable by death. The word "ibis" is Greek, but itself derived from the ancient Egyptian "hîb."

Though worshipped there in the past, the sacred ibis no longer ranges through Egypt. In that country, its marshland habitat has been largely destroyed by the spread of civilization. The birds still thrive in sub-Saharan Africa and parts of Iraq. They have also been introduced into France, Italy, and Spain, perhaps to the detriment of local species like terns and egrets: the ibises prey upon them and usurp their nesting grounds. The sacred ibis is highly social and lives in large colonies not only for nesting season, but also for regular activities like feeding and sleeping, making it rather formidable competition.

Sacred ibises are large long-legged birds (around 25–29 inches tall) with white plumage and black tail feathers. An ibis's head and neck are bald, with black scaly skin. All ibis species have slender downturned beaks, with which they forage for food in shallow water, mud, and occasionally dry land. Their diet consists primarily of small aquatic insects and amphibians, but they will also eat smaller birds, reptiles, and mammals.

Folklore has it that the ibis is the last wild animal to take shelter before a hurricane, and also the first to appear afterward, showing that the storm has passed. Presumably, the bird has an innate instinct for predicting the timing of bad weather.

The cover image is from *Cassell's Natural History*. The cover font is Adobe ITC Garamond. The text font is Linotype Birka; the heading font is Adobe Myriad Condensed; and the code font is LucasFont's TheSansMonoCondensed.

CPSIA information can be obtained at www.ICGtesting.com
Printed in the USA
240580LV00005B/1/P